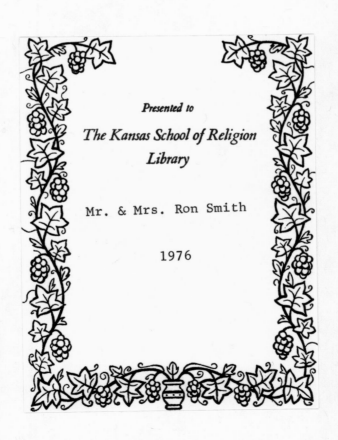

# WOMEN IN JUDAISM

## The Status of Women in Formative Judaism

by

## Leonard Swidler

## The Scarecrow Press, Inc.
## Metuchen, N.J.      1976

Library of Congress Cataloging in Publication Data

Swidler, Leonard J
    Women in Judaism.

    Includes index.
    1.   Women in Judaism.   I.   Title.
BM729. W6S9         296         75-46561
ISBN 0-8108-0904-4

"He who has no wife dwells without good, without help, without joy, without blessing, and without atonement."
--Genesis Rabbah 18, 2


A woman is "a pitcher full of filth with its mouth full of blood, yet all run after her."
--Talmud, b. Shabbath 152a


"The difference in the relations of men and women to each other makes a constant difference between the Rabbis and ourselves. It is always cropping up. Modern apologists tend to ignore or evade it. They quote a few sentences such as 'Who is rich? He who has a good wife'; or they tell of a few exceptional women such as Beruria. It is quite true that wife and mother played a very important part in Rabbinic life; it is true the Rabbis were almost always monogamists; it is true that they honoured their mothers profoundly, and usually honoured and cared for their wives. But that is only one side of the story.... Women were, on the whole, regarded as inferior to men in mind, in function and in status."
C. G. Montefiore, A Rabbinic Anthology (Philadelphia, 1960), pp. xviii-xix

CONTENTS

v

# CHAPTER I

## PURPOSE AND SETTING

### 1. RATIONALE OF THE STUDY

This study attempts to answer the question: What was the status of women in the period of formative Judaism; that is, where did women stand in the social scale in comparison to others, namely, men? Were they thought of as having the same rights and responsibilities as men, and if not, how, and why, were they different, and with what results? By formative Judaism is meant the time span from about the second century before the Common Era (B. C. E.) to the fifth century of the Common Era (C. E.), and the geographical area first of all in Palestine and secondly in Babylonia. This was the time and locus of the formation of what emerged as mainline Judaism. Of the various Jewish "sects" teeming in the first decades of the Common Era, such as Pharisees, Sadducees, Essenes, Zealots, and Christians, only the first and the last persisted in an organized fashion, coming down to us as Judaism and Christianity. I hope also to study the status of women in formative Christianity, but that will be a subsequent volume, which of course could not be attempted until this study was completed.

The reason for undertaking such a study is not unlike the motive of the teller of the story of Adam and Eve; namely, how can we explain the contemporary relationships between men and women? Our attempt to answer the question, instead of using mythic means, will use the historical-critical method. Naturally all serious history attempts to be as "objective" as possible, i. e., to "tell it like it was" ("wie es eigentlich gewesen"), as much as that is possible within inevitable human limitations. Like most historiography, this study is prompted by a question that is important in contemporary life; in this case, the place of women in human society and their relationship to men. Surely this is a fundamental question and one worthy of being put to our past. Any attempt at responsible history will seek to avoid tenden-

1

tiousness and hold the conclusions to what the evidence will
bear. Concerning the present subject, on the one hand the
positive evaluations of women in formative Judaism will have
to be sought out and recorded. But, given the subject matter, it will be particularly important to guard against the
sort of apologetic that became especially prevalent since the
Enlightenment and the rise of the subsequent feminist movements: the tendency to claim that Judaism, and Christianity,
have really valued women very highly and even made them
"equal" to men, a claim that an earlier day would have rejected. Josephus stated quite clearly that "The woman, says
the Law, is in all things inferior to the man,"[1] and his contemporary, Paul of Tarsus, echoed the same idea: "Let a
woman learn in silence with all submissiveness. I permit
no woman to teach or to have authority over men; she is to
keep silent."[2]

A second tactic which embarrassed modern Jewish,
and Christian, scholars have adopted has been to grant,
grudgingly, that women were treated "differently" from men,
but to insist either that this did not mean that they were
thereby any less valued, or that in any case it was "better"
that they be thus "differently" treated. Of course, treating
two groups of human beings differently does not automatically
mean in logic that one group is valued more or less than the
other, but empirically, when groups of mature human adults
with millions upon millions of members and a highly system-
atized social differentiation of major proportions are in question, then there is more than ample prima facie evidence
that a higher and lower valuation of the groups is involved.
To argue oppositely merely on the grounds of logic or some
references to structurally superficial evidence, without a
thorough analysis of the structure of the society involved,
and its presuppositions and inevitable results, is to argue
speciously. This was the sort of argumentation that stated
in America that it was a good thing for Black slaves to be
treated "differently," that they were in fact happier so, and
referred to some statements and actions of "happy" Black
slaves and the paternal attitude of some benign slave holders.
The same approach led to the second line of defense after
the abolishment of slavery; namely, that Blacks were to have
"different" schools, etc. from Whites, but of course they
would be equal! The United States Supreme Court finally dismissed that line of argument as the rationalization of the
White group in power oppressing the Black group not in power. Such a manner of arguing was not honest; it did not
seek to describe reality "wie es eigentlich gewesen." To

so argue in the matter of the status of women would be similarly dishonest.

At the same time this study cannot be an attempt to argue that the past under scrutiny necessarily could, or should, have been different than it was, or that the values of contemporary society are necessarily better than those of the past. Rather, as initially stated, it can only be an attempt to answer as accurately as possible on the basis of evidence, the question proposed by the author--which naturally is prompted by a contemporary concern. As an historical study, this work can only stand or fall, in whole or in part, on the basis of the gathering and analysis of, and argumentation from, the evidence available. However, distinct from that study, but based on it, the author, not so much as historian but as a concerned human scholar, who is also committed to religion, institutional and otherwise, should also be able to offer an evaluation, indicating something of the study's significance for contemporary society. That I expect to do in a concluding chapter.

The main documentary sources for this study are the following: the later books of the Hebrew Bible (mainly the Wisdom literature); the apocrypha, that is, the additional books found in the Jewish translation of the Scriptures into Greek (the Septuagint); the pseudepigrapha, i. e. , Jewish writings around the beginning of the Common Era which were not taken into the scriptural canon; the Dead Sea scrolls; the works of Josephus, a Jewish historian of the first century C. E. ; the writings of Philo, the great first century C. E. Jewish philosopher and religious thinker; and the rabbinic writings. These latter include primarily the Mishnah, a collection of the sayings, discussions and decisions of early rabbis, called Tannaim, on how to live according to the Torah (codified around 200 C. E. ); the Babylonian Talmud, commentary of later rabbis, called Amoraim, on the Mishnah (codified in Babylonia in the fifth century C. E. ); to a lesser extent the smaller Palestinian Talmud (codified in the fourth century C. E. in Palestine), the Tosephta, Mechilta, Sifre, and Sifra Scripture commentaries (mostly all additional materials from the Tannaim), and the early midrash--i. e. , rabbinic stories, etc. illustrating the Torah--mainly the Genesis Rabbah (codified in the fourth century C. E. ).

2.  STATUS OF WOMEN IN THE ANCIENT FERTILE
    CRESCENT AND THE GRECO-ROMAN WORLD

To understand any human event it must be seen in its
historical context, for every human event is the product of
the interplay of the forces of the past and the responses of
the forces of the present.  We can no more understand a human event outside of its historical context than we can grasp
the concept of the sound of a single hand clapping--Zen Bud-
dhism notwithstanding.  The importance of the historical context is even further heightened when the human event being
investigated is a person's, or a society's, attitude concerning
the status of the most broadly distributed class of persons in
a society, namely, the status of women in society.  Hence,
to approach properly the subject of this investigation--the
status of women in formative Judaism--it is essential to seek
to learn the attitude toward women prevalent in the surrounding milieux as this Jewish society developed.

a.   Ancient Fertile Crescent

By way of remote background it should be noted that
the status of women in the ancient Near Eastern world was
generally that of an inferior. [3]  Of the perhaps most ancient
of those civilizations, the Sumerian, it has been said that it
was male-dominated:  men ran the government, managed the
economy, administered the courts and schools, manipulated
the theology and ritual, and therefore women generally were
treated as second-class citizens without power, prestige, or
status. [4]  However, as the eminent Sumerologist Samuel Noah
Kramer has pointed out, there are some indications that this
was predominantly true only of later Sumerian society, i. e.,
from about 2000 B. C. E. on.  In the earlier period the Sumerian woman may well have been man's equal socially and eco-
nomically, at least among the ruling class.  Further, in the
area of religion, the female deity was worshipped from earliest times to the very end of Sumer's existence.  In spite of
some manipulative favoritism on the part of the male theologians, God in Sumer never became all-male.

Among other things, Kramer points out that polyandry
apparently existed in Sumer previous to 2400 B. C. E., for
one of the Urukagina "reform" documents of that period reads:
"The women of former days used to take two husbands, (but)
the women of today (if they attempted this) were stoned with
stones (upon which was inscribed their evil) intent. " Kramer

pointed out that, judging from this rather strident boast, some women in pre-Urukagina days practiced polyandry, and got away with it--which hardly smacks of a male-dominated society. In this early period of the twenty-fourth century some women also owned and controlled vast amounts of property, enjoyed some laws which in effect enjoined something like equal pay for equal work, and were able to hold top rank among the literati of the land, and be spiritual leaders of paramount importance. [5]

By the year 2000 B. C. E., and onward, the role of women deteriorated considerably and on the whole the male ruled. For example, marriage was then theoretically monogamous, but the husband was permitted one or more concubines, while the wife had to remain faithful to her one and only spouse. [6] Continuing in this trend, the Babylonian Code of Hammurabi (1728-1636 B. C. E.) and similar laws legislated, for example, that men were free to repudiate their wives for any or no reason, [7] though the woman was able to divorce the husband only for very serious cause; [8] indeed, even if in such a case a wife were "a gadabout," her life was forfeit: "If she was not careful, but was a gadabout, thus neglecting her house (and) humiliating her husband, they shall throw that woman into the water. "[9] Polygyny was accepted, but not polyandry; hence adultery was solely a crime against the husband. [10] However, it should be noted that the oriental woman enjoyed, on the other hand, a very large legal capacity. In the presence of the man (father or husband) the oriental woman was silent and passive; but if the man disappeared--and not only by death or by absence in the technical sense, but even by a temporary absence--the woman became a fully capable person. [11]

Such general disability of women was not uniformly the case in the other massively important cultural milieu in the ancient fertile crescent, including Palestine, i. e., in Egypt. In fact, during half the history of ancient Egypt, the age of the pyramids (2778 B. C. E. and following) to the end of the Hellenistic period (30 B. C. E.), women enjoyed a high status. For example, during the third, fourth, and into the fifty dynasties (2778-2423 B. C. E.), when the highest level of culture of the Old Kingdom was reached, daughters had the same inheritance rights as sons, marriages were strictly monogamous (with the exception of royalty) and tended to be love matches; in fact, it can be said that in the Old Kingdom the wife was the equal of the husband in rights, although her place in society was not identical with that of her husband. [12]

With the decline of the Old Kingdom (2270 B. C. E.), centralized control also waned and feudalism arose, which
brought in its wake the decline of individual rights and the
rise of corporate rights in private law; this meant that
women lost their equality of rights and were subordinated to
men, usually fathers or husbands. At any rate, this was
true among the nobility (where polygyny then also became
widespread) and on the land; in the cities, commerce continued to be based on individualism in private law (i. e. , urban property remained free and alienable), and the equality
of the sexes persisted as under the classic law of the Old
Kingdom. In the cities the woman had an independent legal
personality. [13]

        The situation was reversed again during the New Em-
pire (1580-1085 B. C. E. --18th, 19th, and 20th dynasties) and
women again generally enjoyed equality of status, particularly
during the 18th dynasty (1580-1341 B. C. E. ). Centralization
was restored in the monarchy and individualism triumphed
in private law, and consequently during the 18th dynasty
women recovered their entire independence and their own
legal personalities. They again took up the social role they
had had, at the side of their husbands, in the Old Kingdom. [14]
(It was during this period that the Hebrew people traditionally are said to have lived in and left Egypt. ) Once again in
1085 B. C. E. the Egyptian empire disintegrated into a feudal
pattern, with its stress on corporate rights in private law
and the consequent subordination of women to men.

        With the beginning of the 26th dynasty (663-525
B. C. E. ) and its centralized monarchy a definitive change in
favor of equality for women in ancient Egypt took place.
Women possessed a situation of legal independence and from
then on disposed of themselves freely. Absolute equality of
spouses was established in marriage. Strictly monogamous,
the conjugal union was based on the mutual consent of the
partners and imposed on the spouses identical obligations:
the infidelity of the husband as well as that of the wife permitted the injured spouse to obtain a divorce at her or his
own profit. [15] Thus, as Jacques Pirenne put it, "we have
arrived at the epoch of total legal emancipation of the woman. That absolute legal equality between the woman and
the man continued to the arrival of the Ptolemies in
Egypt. "[16]

        Pirenne provides a very precise overview of the his-
tory of the status of women in ancient Egypt from the

beginning, excluding the Hellenistic and Roman periods.
Women in ancient Egypt were considered legally the equal
of men in the epochs of individualism.  They were, on the
contrary, treated as minors and placed under tutelage in
feudal-seignorial epochs, during the course of which those
social groups founded on the solidarity of authority and
hierarchy were restored.   Pirenne argued that although that
conclusion could, in varying degrees, well be extended and
adapted to all civilizations, none, at least in antiquity, ac-
corded to women an independence equal to that which they
knew in Egypt.  Greek civilization itself, which one nevertheless generally admits was the most individualistic in
antiquity, was far from granting women the independence
which they knew in Egypt during the periods of its apogee.

> There is there a very important element which
> perhaps ought to stimulate historians of law as
> well as moralists to study, in comparison with
> Greek individualism, Egyptian individualism which,
> before our period, alone issued in the complete
> legal emancipation of the woman. [17]

**b.   The Greek World**

Let us now turn our attention to those cultural forces,
Hellenism and Romanism, which largely formed the immediate context within which so much of formative Judaism developed.

Some scholars argue that the almost omnipresent
patriarchy perceived from the beginning of humanity's written records was preceded by a very long, beneficent period
of matriarchy. [18]   This thesis, which is lent at least some
support by the findings of the Sumerologist Kramer (discussed above) and the Etruscanologist Heurgon (discussed below), is, however, disputed.  In any case, as a very careful historian, Vern L. Bullough, noted in general scholars
have argued that women in the Homeric poems, which probably were put into final form in the ninth century B. C. E. ,
had a higher position and were better regarded than later in
Greek society.   However, by the time of Hesiod in the
eighth century B. C. E. , male dominance was no longer in
doubt, and in Athens in the fifth and fourth centuries B. C. E. ,
the "golden age" of Pericles, the status of women seemed
to have reached some kind of nadir in Western history. [19]

In this period of "classical" Greece there was also
a large difference between the status of women in Athens
and in Sparta. Of the two largest Greek city states, Sparta
provided women with by far the greater freedom, i. e. ,
scope for human development, and equality with men. In
Sparta women wore clothes which did not restrict their
movement (e. g. , their robes were open on the side),[20] and
took part in sports (e. g. , see the Vatican girl racer, a
statue originally from the time of the Persian wars), in
politics,[21] and in the owning and running of businesses and
farms; in fact, women owned almost forty per cent of all
the real estate of Sparta,[22] which in itself also tended to
increase and sustain the high estimation of women in Sparta.

Though Athens was only a short distance away from
Sparta and though the two spoke basically the same language, the styles of life of the two city states were dramatically different--and so was the status of women in each.
In Athens women did not participate in politics; in fact they
were largely shut out of social life as well. Among the
works attributed to Demosthenes we find the statement of
one fourth-century Athenian: "We have hetaerae for our
pleasure (hedone), concubines for the daily needs of the
body (therapeia), and wives so we may have legitimate children and a faithful steward of our houses."[23] Only the
hetaerae ("companions") were educated and entered into male
society. They were like courtesans who were to provide
men with interesting conversation and entertainment as well
as venereal pleasure--in short, social intercourse and sexual
intercourse. Marriage was usually monogamous in that there
was only one legitimate wife at a time. However, she normally did not mix with the husband's male friends, but was
largely the bearer and rearer of legitimate offspring and the
administrator of the household--to which she was largely
confined. In Athens the wife "lived entirely or almost entirely as in a harem."[24]

Leipoldt has some very enlightening remarks about
how Athens developed the harem-like condition for its wom-
en:

> Athens, especially through its export business and
> commerce, became a rich city. There were men
> who no longer worked (the rabbis have a very in-
> structive definition: a settlement is to be desig-
> nated a city when there are to be found in it at
> least ten men who do not pursue a profession--

> Megilla 1,3), and all necessity for the women to
> work outside the home disappears--why else have
> slaves? Whoever has such trains them to take
> over all toilsome work (<u>ponos</u>). Some wives will
> at first find that pleasant and a reason to carry
> their heads higher. But now there awakens the
> feeling among the men that the women are their
> personal possessions, useless, but ornamental
> pieces, which one can best preserve by keeping
> them at home (the notion of envy probably says
> too little here). Thus is the path to the harem
> entered upon. 25

An important point that is alluded to here is that
within the same culture women tend to be more restricted
in cities than in villages or in rural areas (distinct of
course from the lot of women of the landed nobility in a
feudal society, as in Egypt, where even women in cities
tended to retain a certain legal liberty, as noted above).
The present writer experienced this personally within the
Arab Muslim culture in the fall of 1972 when visiting the
Muslim city of Hebron (south of Jerusalem) and a number
of Muslim villages nearby. In the villages the women always wore a head covering, but never veiled their faces;
in Hebron, however, many of the women in the streets went
about with face veils. Something of the same thing occurred
in the movement of populations to urban areas in nineteenth
and twentieth century America; pioneer and rural women had
a whole range of indispensable roles to play in their families and societies, including a key economic one, and consequently led a human life relatively as full as their husbands'. But when it was no longer necessary to share in
the fighting of Indians, or in working to help provide food,
clothing, and other necessities, they tended to become the
"ornamental pieces" mentioned above; the wives of most
professional men did not take a job, and so there later developed the mysterious malaise among suburban women which
Betty Friedan called the "feminine mystique."

Thus, economical and technological progress gradually released more and more women from hard physical
labor into being "ornamental pieces," but this same progress also tended to equalize men and women in that the
male's physical strength became less and less important--a
tiny woman with a machine-gun was as deadly as any mus-
cular male with the same. More and more in a technologi-
cally advancing society, knowledge and experience became

the important things--and women could gain these as well
as men.   Hence, although women are at first lowered in
importance vis-à-vis men as a civilization "advances," if
this advance continues sufficiently it bears within it the
seeds of a growing movement of women's liberation.   This
can, of course, be seen in the development of the feminist
and women's liberation movements of nineteenth and twentieth century America and Europe.   But the same thing also
happened in the Hellenistic and Roman world, as we shall
see in somewhat more detail later.

The phenomenon of ancient women--and modern wom-
en--becoming "ornamental pieces" was carefully analyzed by
the twentieth-century sociologist Thorsten Veblen, who in
the process coined the concepts "conspicuous leisure" and
"conspicuous consumption. "   When men earned more than
they really could use they would tend to use their superfluous wealth in a public way that would call attention to it--
like lighting a cigar with a ten-dollar bill.   The wives of
these men, of course, became veritable clothes models, for
by the extravagance of a woman's attire people could see
something of her man's wealth--vicarious conspicuous consumption.   Likewise, the women of wealthy men, or men
who had pretentions of wealth, usually did not work, again
to show publicly that the husband had so much money that
the wife need not work--vicarious conspicuous leisure.
Thus, the woman contributed little to the family or society,
became just an ornamental piece, a conspicuous consumer
of commodities for the sake of showing the husband's wealth.
As wealth massively increased in Athens it was no wonder
that such women had no significant part in the world of de-
cision-making, that men came to think of them as their pos-
sessions which they needed to protect from thieves--in a restricted, harem-like existence. [26]

Shortly after the time of the great philosophers of
classical Greece--that is, from the end of the fourth century
B. C. E.  on--an extraordinary change in the general societal
feeling took place, at first in Greece and then elsewhere in
the Hellenistic world; a sensitivity developed for other persons, particularly the previously overlooked, and for animate
and inanimate reality all around.   It was a cultural phenomenon something like the Romantic Movement which burst
upon the Western world at the beginning of the nineteenth
century.   This change, which continued to develop with the
passage of time and spread throughout the Mediterranean and
Near East through Hellenistic military and cultural

expansion, was expressed in many ways, including painting, poetry, the emotions, and concern for animals, slaves, children--and women.

An appreciation of landscapes is usually something that children do not possess; it comes only with the development of more intense human emotions. Just as such an appreciation was often reflected in the paintings of the Romantics and afterward, so too in Hellenistic and Roman paintings the beauty of the countryside was higlighted--which was not done in earlier Greek art--for example, in extraordinary wall paintings in Pompeii. [27] This more highly developed emotion and sensitivity was also reflected in the much more frequent reports of expressions of joy or sorrow and of crying than was earlier the case. [28]

There was also an increase in fondness for animals. For example, those in the Greek world who did not possess a dog were thought poor, [29] and yet domestic dogs were almost unknown in the East in pre-Hellenistic times; they were introduced through Greek influence, as can partly be seen in the stories of Tobit and the Syrophoenician woman whose daughter Jesus healed. [30] This Hellenistic fondness for animals was also expressed in poems dedicated to pets that had died. It is perhaps significant that it was a woman, Anyte of Tegea in Arcadia (around 300 B. C. E.), who firmly set the custom in Greek culture. Couplets by her, some in the form of grave inscriptions, exist on a hunting dog, a locust, a dolphin, a war-horse, and a rooster. Leipoldt says of her work: "These are really works of art: brief texts in chosen language, without exaggeration, full of genuine love for the animals; and each of the little poems is differently constructed. "[31] Another scholar has gathered together over fifty such examples from antiquity, [32] including the Latin: Catullus' poem on the dead sparrow of his daughter is perhaps the best known example.

Even more important is the fact that this new sensitivity was also extended to "inferior" human beings. Slaves were more often viewed as other humans with various talents, feelings, etc., and were consequently more humanly appreciated; e. g., they often were given grave stones. Children received a greater appreciation, especially small children. [33] (Again one is reminded of similar developments in early nineteenth-century Europe under the leadership of children's education pioneers like Pestalozzi.) This "discovery" of children can be seen in the Greek plastic arts:

in the earlier period children were obviously not thought important enough to observe carefully; only after the time of
Alexander the Great were the sculpted figures of children
properly proportioned.   The figure of Eros on the east
frieze of the Parthenon and on vase paintings is that of a
half adult; later it becomes a real infant.

      The question naturally arises:  Why the development
of this new sensitivity toward the end of the fourth century
B. C. E. ?   The causes of such a complex historical development can only be proportionately complex, but a few
"causes" do lie close to the surface.   The new sensitivity
became apparent a generation after Alexander exploded the
Greek world of city states into the vast imperial world of
Hellenism.   Energies that most Greek citizens had formerly
devoted to politics could now be turned to themselves, persons, and things around them, all of which they had not had
much time or energy to really observe or appreciate before.
Also, most humans cannot live merely as a single unit in a
massive impersonal organization; they must also have satis-
fying personal relations; they must live in a personal community, or communities.   That was possible as a citizen
in a city-state such as Athens or Corinth, but not in an
empire.   Hence, not only was there now time and energy
available to devote to new relations, but there was also a
need to find a more human community (witness the incredible
popularity of the mystery religions at this time; indeed, the
massive spread first of Judaism--perhaps ten per cent of
the population of the Roman empire at the beginning of the
Common Era!--and then of Christianity are still further evidence).   Whatever other "causes" of this historical event
are put forth, these two will at least have to be reckoned
in.

      In ancient Greek society, as in many others, women
were often categorized with the other "inferior" beings,
slaves and children--usually to place some restrictions on
them.   Quite naturally, the development of the new sensitivity which raised the status of slaves and children also led
to the raising of the status of women.   In fact one can
speak of a gradually developing women's liberation movement
in Hellenism.   It did not move as rapidly or as dramatically
as the one in the nineteenth century of Western civilization,
but it was clearly there and made enormous advances from
the time of Alexander to Constantine.   In fact, already in
the fifth century, in Periclean Athens, there were at least
the beginnings of a movement, particularly in the areas of

philosophy and politics, as is attested to by the plays satir-
izing gynocracy and, just a little later, by Aristophanes'
play on the first "Women's Strike for Peace," Lysistrata. [34]
In speaking of a Greek women's liberation, however, it is
well to keep in mind what was succinctly stated by Klaus
Thraede: "One does well, when concerned with the development of a freer situation [for women], which nevertheless
did take place in Hellenistic times, to distinguish between
Asia Minor and Athens and Sparta as well as between city
and land."[35]   One might add to this the need at times to
distinguish between early and late Hellenism and, perhaps
more importantly, between social classes.   Likewise, one
must keep in mind the advanced state of the liberation of
women in Etruria, as well as Egypt, which persisted in
the Hellenistic period[36] and also doubtless spread these
ideas throughout the ancient world through the medium of
Hellenistic culture.

In terms of "causes" of the spread of this women's
liberation movement in the Hellenistic world, one must cal-
culate, in addition to what has been discussed above about
the new sensitivity and about Egypt, the important influence
of the queens, princesses, and other royal women of Hellenistic courts. [37]   The court of Philip II was not marked by
great elegance and refinement, but to it belonged Olympias,
and where such an imperious and self-willed woman reigned,
her sex must have enjoyed a freedom and consideration not
possible in Athens.   It was, however, on the model of the
Macedonian court that the officers of Alexander ordered
their households, and when Eastern customs were considered, they were the customs of the Persian and Egyptian
monarchies, where the queen and the queen-mother were always potent personages.   Hence they could but strengthen
Macedonian tendencies to accord women social and political
importance.   "The influence of a court is always far-reach-
ing, and in this case it accelerated a movement, of which
the Greek courtesans had been hitherto the leaders, for the
emancipation of women."[38]

William Ferguson added a further insight into the
spread of Hellenistic women's liberation when he described
how an Athenian girl installed in a new home in Elephantine
or in Antioch was dependent upon her own resources to a
much greater degree than one who remained at home surrounded by her kinsmen and within easy reach of her natural
guardian.   She had to be given freedom of access to the
courts and personal right to hold property, without which she

would have been entirely at the mercy of her husband.  In
other words, her parents were bound to see that privileges
were guaranteed to her in the marriage contract which they
would not think of demanding for their daughters who married their neighbors' sons.  The instability of life, the enormous increase of opportunity to move from one place to
another, made new safeguards for the wife and mother ad-
visable.  The consequence was that everywhere in the Hellenistic world the old rules of society were being abandoned,
and new ones, dealing with woman's liberties, were being
formed to take their place.

There had been no such occasion for the creation of
a new social regime since the seventh century B. C. E.   In
Athens, as for that matter in the cities of old Greece generally, these causes of social change were not directly op-
erative.  A royal family did not exist there; the city was
not dependent for its prosperity upon its attractiveness to
immigrants; there was no new contact with foreign races.
Hence it is the influence of the hetaerae upon the structure
of Athenian society, and the reaction of the new world upon
the old, that must be considered and, if possible, measured
at this point--"... the emancipation of women made slow, if
any, progress in Athens.  It was, in fact, an unfriendly
territory for the social innovations of Hellenism."[39]

The above mentioned "cautions" having been noted,
a rather impressive list of indications of a gradually developing women's liberation movement in the Hellenistic
world can be put forward.  Even the form of address to a
woman that grew up in this period is an indication of her increase in status:  as it became customary in late Greek
times to address men as "Lord" (kyrie), it became equally
customary to address women as "Lady" (kyria); the custom
spilt out of the Greek language area into Latin as well,
where men and women tended more and more to be addressed as dominus and domina. [40]

To this one can add the fact that in growing contrast
to the earlier frequent social restriction of the Greek married woman, in Hellenistic times the wife was quite likely
to turn up at social gatherings, at symposia;[41] and women
went on long journeys. [42]  Whereas earlier it was customary
for Spartan women to participate in sports, including the
Olympics, women's involvement in this area advanced in late
Hellenistic times to the point where there were women professional athletes, as, for example, the three daughters--

Tryphosa, Hedea, and Dionysia--of Hermesianax of Tralles, who engaged in foot and chariot races in the years 47 to 41 B. C. E. [43]  Many women pursued music as a profession, [44] but not many became actresses or dancers (at least not "socially acceptable" women), [45] although we hear of women who traveled about Greece giving recitations, such as Aristodana of Smyrna who was accompanied by her brother as a manager. [46]  Asia Minor was known for its women physicians, [47] though according to Pliny the Elder much of the information about these women physicians was deliberately suppressed. [48]  On the level of skilled artisans, women often pursued a craft similar to their husbands', e. g. , a woman goldsmith and a man armorer. [49]

The position of women within marriage is, of course, an important key to the status of women in society in general.  We have noted something of the atypical freedom and equality Spartan women enjoyed in classical times, and something of the extremely limited position of other Greek married women (being shut out of politics and social life and having to run competition with the hetaerae and the concubines--that is, mostly slave women who were always totally at the disposal of the husband, sexually and otherwise). [50] The Greek wife of classical time did nevertheless retain her right over her dowry, even if a divorce occurred; and she as well as the husband could initiate a divorce--quite a different situation than existed in the Jewish world, where only the husband could initiate a divorce; but that will be discussed in detail later.

In the Hellenistic period the status of women in marriage advanced quite dramatically, allowing, of course, for wide variation according to the location and the dominant local legal tradition.  Marriage was monogamous in classical Greek times and it continued to be so in an even more intense fashion in the Hellenistic period, e. g. , the restriction on concubines--as reflected in a late fourth century (311 B. C. E. ) marriage contract, presumably drawn up according to the Greek law dominant on the island of Cos (off the coast of Asia Minor).  Part of it runs as follows:

> Contract of marriage of Heracleides and Demetria. Heracleides takes for his legitimate wife Demetria of Cos.  He receives her from her father Leptine of Cos and from her mother Philotis.  He is free. She is free. . . .  It is not permitted to Heracleides to take another woman, for that would be an injury

to Demetria, nor may he have children by another
woman, nor do anything injurious to Demetria under any pretext.   If Heracleides be found performing any such deed, Demetria shall denounce him
before three men they will both choose.   Heracleides will return to Demetria the dowry of 1000
drachmas, which she contributed, and he will pay
an additional 1000 drachmas in Alexandrian silver
as an additional fine. [51]

Here the husband is not only committed to monogamy
and to marital fidelity (as is the wife, elsewhere in the contract) but is even subject to a double penalty if he violates
that commitment.   The contract also clearly assumes an
equal right for both spouses to initiate a divorce on the
grounds of infidelity.   (It is also interesting that the bride
is given away by the mother as well as the father.)   It
should be noted that this advance in the status of the married woman took place at a time and place where the forces
at work were probably Greek.   The later Egyptian influence
could only further raise the status of women, which can be
seen in, among other things, the fact that in Hellenistic
Egypt the wife, as well as the husband, could initiate a divorce when and as she wished. [52]

Klaus Thraede speaks of Hellenism's linking of the
goal of women's liberation with equality in marriage:   "In a
more progressive civilization equal rights for both women
and men is a condition for married harmony (the Stoics
formulate it the same way also).   Hellenism discovered that
because the value and individuality of the woman is fulfilled
in marriage, monogamy is required."[53]

Women in Hellenistic times also exercised extensive
rights in the economic sphere.   A woman could inherit a
personal patrimony--equally along with sons!--buy, own, and
sell property and goods, and will them to others. [54]   Indeed,
in Hellenistic times there were wealthy Greek women, some
of whom were greatly honored for their philanthropy. [55]
Thraede sums the matter up when he says:

The emancipation of the woman in private law was
decisive for the development which began already
in the classical period:  the equalization in inheritance and property rights as well as the de
facto independence in marriage and divorce. [56]

In classical Greek times a woman usually could undertake a public act--i. e. , one involving property or marriage--only with the cooperation or approval of a kyrios (lord), who usually was the father, then the husband. This institution, reflective of ancient familial solidarity, continued into Hellenistic times. [57]  The custom, however, was resisted in Hellenistic Egypt, and was eventually eliminated. [58]  For some time then, the Hellenistic woman exercised her quite large public capacity with a kyrios under Greek law and without a kyrios under Egyptian law. However, even outside Egypt the institution of the kyrios declined to a mere formality[59] and finally was eliminated in Roman times, i. e. , after the Antonine constitution of 212 C. E. [60]  Nevertheless, even in the third century B. C. E. many women initiated a wide range of legal actions, civil, penal, and administrative-- without a kyrios. [61]  Not only Egyptian women did so, but even Greek. "This capacity is without a doubt an innovation in regard to women living under Greek law when compared to the institutions of classical times. "[62]  It is also an "innovation" when compared to the situation in contemporary Judaism, where women were not able even to bear legal witness. [63]

From one perspective the dramatic difference in the status of women in classical Athenian society and Hellenistic society reflects the difference in the societal structures: the former was patriarchally collective and the latter was individualistic. Parenthetically, it should be noted that Jewish society was built only on the patriarchal collective model: "Talmudic family structure is based upon the biblical patriarchal system, which for its part is the continuation of the custom of the tribal age. Preference is given to males, within the family as well as in society. A person's status is determined by his descent and for this purpose the paternal rather than the maternal relationship is decisive. "[64] On the other hand, Hellenistic law of persons and family assumed a definitely individualistic shape. [65]  Furthermore, behind the legal, though not necessarily social independence of women, there was the fundamental fact that a new type of family, which rested entirely on blood relationship, had replaced the classical oikos. This new family was based purely on personal ties and, consequently, there was no patriarchal family organization at all. Various restrictive practices atrophied in a gradual change of custom that was inherent in the logic of a social development which did away with the concept of a family in which women were subject to the head of the "house. " "The husband had no conjugal power over his wife. "[66]

In an advanced civilization the key to advanced status
is education; by itself it will not accomplish everything, but
without it usually little will be possible.  Whereas in classical Athens usually only the hetaerae had any kind of an
education, education for young girls became ever broader
and more widespread throughout the Hellenistic period, and
one result was that more and more wives as well as husbands were educated. [67]  In fact, in Hellenistic Egypt there
were more women who could sign their names than men, [68]
"and thus Hellenistic literature, particularly the novel, was
written for a feminine public. "[69]  Another result of the
broader Hellenistic education of women was the appearance
of a flood of Hellenistic women poets. [70]

It is perhaps most of all in that discipline of the
spirit for which the Greeks are most renowned, philosophy,
that one can see the striving for women's liberation.  We
hear from an ancient biographer of Pythagoras that already
in the seventh century B. C. E. there were many women students of Pythagoras. [71]  The comedy writer Alexis even
wrote a piece entitled "The Women Pythagorians" (Pytha-
goridzousa). [72]  The comment on the "woman question" by
one of the women philosophers of the Pythagorean school,
Theano, who was either the wife or daughter of Pythagoras,
is still extant.  Within the context of the primitive assump-
tion that sexual intercourse makes a person "unclean," she
was asked: "In how many days after intercourse with a man
will a woman be clean?"  Her reply: "If it is her own husband, she is immediately clean; if it is with a stranger,
never. "[73]  Continuing this tradition, the sophists and Socra-
tes (470-399 B. C. E.) raised criticisms of the subordinate
position of women in society. [74]

In his writing about the ideal state Plato (427-347
B. C. E.) made a rather extraordinary breakthrough concerning the status of women; he argued in favor of equality for
women with men--indeed, equality was in the nature of
things.  He wrote:

> Are we of the opinion that the female watchdogs
> must perform their guard duty just as the male
> watchdogs?  Do they have to go on the hunt and
> do everything with the rest?  Or do the female
> dogs remain at home, incapable because they must
> bring offspring into the world and nourish them,
> whereas the male dogs do all the work and take
> care of everything involved in shepherding?

> Everything must be done together! Only we as-
> sign lighter tasks to the former and heavier ones
> to the latter. Is it possible, however, to assign
> to any beings the same kind of tasks if the same
> education and training are not available to all
> alike? Impossible. Therefore, if we wish to
> engage the women in the same work as the men,
> they must also be allowed to learn the same
> things. The men receive intellectual and physical
> education. Thus, the women must also learn and
> appropriately employ these two disciplines and the
> art of warfare.... They must take part in war
> and everything involved in guard duty.[75]

However, although educated women thus were seen by Plato
as equally a boon for the state as men, he nevertheless
wished to curtail the development of too much freedom for
women by legally limiting their lifestyles.[76] (It should also
be noted that we do know of at least two women philosophical
disciples of Plato.)[77]

Like his teacher Plato, Aristotle (384-322 B. C. E.)
also paid lip service to the desirability of the freedom of
women in a democracy,[78] but at the same time he argued
that too much freedom for women was a political evil[79] and
that women should take a subordinate position.[80] However,
we know that one of Aristotle's followers, Theophrastus
(d. 287 B. C. E.), had both a woman disciple, Pamphile
(some of whose writing is extant), and a woman opponent,
unfortunately anonymous. Thereafter to some extent the
Cynics also spoke out in favor of equal rights for women,
and women played a prominent role in the school of Epicurus
(343-270 B. C. E.), not only as disciples but even as favorite
teachers.[81]

The philosophical school which did most to promote
the improved status of women was that of the Stoics. These
grassroots philosophers stressed the worth of the individual
woman, the need for her education (consequently there were
many women followers of Stoicism), strict monogamy and a
notion of marriage as a spiritual community of two equals.[82]
"In the woman question the Stoics of later times are much
more influential because they concern themselves above all
with the proper living of everyday life."[83] The Roman
knight C. Musonius Rufus, a contemporary of the apostle
Paul, discusses at length whether women should also pursue
philosophy and whether daughters should be brought up the

same as sons; he answers yes to both questions.   The dependence on Plato's Republic is everywhere apparent in the
essay.   Even the male and female dogs are reported on in
similar fashion.   What is decisive is that both sexes have
the same relationship to virtue and must be correspondingly
educated.   Indeed, both receive the same spiritual capabili-
ties (the same logos) from the gods.   Furthermore, it is
specifically the profession of housewife that the woman can
correctly fulfill only when she is a philsopher.   These
thoughts of Musonius have a great significance for intellectual
history, for they influence later thinkers, as can be seen,
for example, in Plutarch and Clement of Alexander.   In fact,
we know of a third century C. E. Syrian princess with the
Arabian name of Zenobia who lived according to the precepts
of Musonius. 84

What makes the teachings of the Stoics especially important in the spread of the liberation of women in the centuries just before and after the beginning of the Common
Era is not only that they keenly stressed woman's personal
value and equality with men, but also that they were so
widely spread abroad even on the grass-roots level.   Many
educated people were counted among the adherents of Stoicism, but so too were many others who had never heard a
professional Stoic teacher, for many of their ideas and sayings became standard elements of traditional education.
However, there were many Stoic popular speakers who went
about like circuit preachers, speaking in homely language
about their ideas of life.   They thus penetrated all classes,
even that of the slaves. 85   "But all this was not only the
result of stoical stumping; the masses were especially pre-
pared to receive the teachings of the Stoa because they
helped the oppressed to preserve at least the feeling of inner
freedom. "86

Not every aspect of every teacher, let alone adher-
ent, of Stoicism reached the full height of complete equality
between men and women in its expression, 87 nor, doubtless,
did every professed disciple always practice fully what he
preached.   Still, Stoicism and the other forces discussed
above surely spread ideas of women's liberation far and wide
throughout the Hellenistic world and massively influenced
many people to live by them.

In religion and cult women in classical Greece experienced restrictions that were broad, but by no means absolute.   There were a number of religious activities or

places that they could not enter upon, as, for example, the
very important oracle of Delphi, the cult of Hercules; and
only maidens, not married women, usually could watch the
sacred games at Olympia.   Women were also almost entirely
absent from, or were kept in the background of, state religion activities.   Still, in some cults, such as those of Ar-
temis and Dionysius, women did play a significant role. [88]
The restrictions, however, along with a lesser education,
encouraged the popularity of superstition and magic among
women; their normal human need for religious expression
naturally moved in the direction of the occult when the more
"legitimate" outlets were restricted.   Strabo (63 B. C. E. -24
C. E.), e. g., unknowingly pointed toward this when he com-
plained that women were the originators of superstition
(deisidaimonias archegoi). [89]   The rabbi Hillel (70 B. C. E. -
10 C. E.) also unknowingly pointed to the same outcome of
the religious restriction of women when he said:   "Many
women, much magi. "[90]

It was doubtless the same kind of pressure, plus the
burgeoning liberation of women in the Hellenistic period,
that led to the extraordinary popularity at that time of the
Eastern cults and mystery religions, particularly among
women. [91]   Women not only took part in these religious
cults, but often did so in great numbers and often in leading
and even priestly roles, as, for example, in the Eleusian,
the Dionysian and the Andanian mysteries (indeed, it would
seem it was just such placing of women on a level with men
in religion and cult that provoked a Christian polemic against
the equality of women by Cyril of Alexandria--376-444
C. E.). [92]   The cult of the goddess Isis, which came from
Egypt but spread all over the Hellenistic and Roman world,
was at the beginning of its popularity exclusively a women's
cult, and even after men were admitted it still provided
women with leading religious roles[93] and justly had the reputation of being a vigorous promoter of women's equality and
liberation. [94]   The extraordinary appeal to women of the
Hellenistic world of Judaism (reflected, for example, in
Josephus' remark that almost all of the women of Damascus
embraced Judaism!)[95] and then Christianity (e. g., the first
European convert to Christianity was a woman, Lydia of
Philippi)[96] also must be at least partly traced back to the
same forces of restriction, reaction and liberation discussed
above--the latter was also doubtless responsible for the fact
that the status of women in diaspora Judaism and Pauline
Christianity was higher than it otherwise would have been. [97]

c.   The Roman World

Although it was the Hellenistic cultural world that exercised the greatest outside influence on Palestinian Judaism,
the influence of Rome was also present in its own way, i. e.,
mostly political, legal, and military, from the time of Pom-
pey's conquest in 63 B. C. E.   Hence, it is proper to note
briefly the condition of women among Romans.

Behind the culture of Rome there stood the extraordinarily developed culture of the Etruscans, stretching in
space from Rome up to Pisa, and in time from before the
seventh into the third centuries B. C. E.   Whether one agrees
with Jacques Heurgon or not when he says that "one must
imagine, at the outset, in Italy, as also in Minoan Crete, a
civilization dominated by the importance of Chthonian cults
and by the pre-eminence of women,"[98] it must be granted
that he offers ample documentation that the Etruscan women
"went out" a great deal.   Everywhere women were at the
forefront of the scene, playing a considerable role and never
blushing from shame, as Livy says of one of them, when
exposing themselves to masculine company.   In Etruria it
was a recognized privilege for ladies of the most respectable
kind, and not just for courtesans as in Greece of the contemporary classical period, to take part with men in ban-
quets, where they reclined as the men did.   They attended
dances, concerts, sports events, and even presided, as a
painting in Orvieto shows, perched on a platform, over box-
ing matches, chariot races and acrobatic displays. [99]

Heurgon notes that in addition to the documentary evidence of the high status of women in Etruscan society, there
is also decisive evidence from archaeology, not just in paintings where we see Etruscan women participating with men
in numerous aspects of social life, not only in the epitaphs
where the matronymic often is given a prominent place, "but
in certain evidences, not sufficiently noted before, which are
provided by the contents and the disposition of the tombs."[100]
A large number of the Etruscan tombs clearly set women in
the pre-eminent position:   "It is as if, between 650 and 450,
the Etruscans, or at least those of Caere, had considered
women to be of a superior essence and more and more sus-
ceptible of divinization than men."[101]

All the evidence taken together allows Heurgon to at-
tribute a privileged position to the Etruscan woman, in a society where "we see her mingling with such brilliance in the

business and the pleasures of men, her character torn to
pieces by envious outsiders but invested in her country with
an authority that was almost sovereign; artistic, cultivated,
interested in Hellenic refinements and the bringer of civilization to her home; finally venerated in the tomb as an
emanation of divine power."[102]

However, we do not find in Etruscan society either a
theoretical Mutterrecht or an ideal gynaeocracy, but rather a
stage in a long development, an unstable equilibrium of anta-
gonistic forces in evolution which is given its full significance only if compared with Greece and Rome.     Furthermore, "Etruscan civilization was an archaic civilization.    Its
feminism, strange as it may seem to us, is not so much a
recent conquest as a distant survival threatened by Graeco-
Roman pressures; it recalls in many respects the Crete of
Ariadne and the paintings of Cnossos more than the Athens
of Solon and Pericles."[103]

Women, of course, did not enjoy such a high status
in contemporary Greece, nor did they in early Rome.    But
by the third century B. C. E. Rome moved to improve the
property rights of women.    Somewhat later in the republic,
doubtless due to the influence of Etruscan culture and the
growing pressure of the women's liberation movement in
Hellenism, the condition of women improved to the point
where a woman could in general marry and divorce on her
own initiative and even choose her own name.[104]    In speaking of the improvement of women's legal position in the late
republic, Thraede wrote: "Toward the end of the republican
period the goal was to some extent attained"; he then referred
to the capability of women to bear legal witness.[105]    During
the same period the image of leading women appeared on
coins--for the first time.[106]

The Roman Cornelius Nepos (d. 32 B. C. E.) even felt
that the advanced status of Roman women was something to
boast about (in doing so he perhaps painted the situation of
the Greek women as too uniformly bleak--so as to enhance
the contrast with that of Roman women):

> What Roman would find it annoying to be accom-
> panied by his wife to a banquet?  Or what house-
> wife does not take the first place in her house or
> go about in public?  Quite different in Greece.
> There the wife is not brought to a banquet, except
> when relatives are involved; and she occupies only

the inner part of the house, the so-called <u>Gynai-</u>
<u>konitis</u>, where only close relatives can enter. [107]

The status of women continued to improve dramatically under the empire.  Indeed, the political activity of women
of the senatorial class developed so vigorously that we find
on the walls of Pompeii the names of women running for office, a definite advance over Egyptian and Greek women, who
had few political rights; women were sent on imperial mis-
sions to pro-consuls; the possibility of a woman consul was
even discussed. [108]  Women were everywhere involved in
business and in social life--i. e. , theaters, sport events,
concerts, parties, traveling--with or without their husbands.
They took part in a whole range of athletics, and even bore
arms and went into battle:  "A still more marked sign of the
advanced emancipation is the conquest of the world of pro-
fessions by the women of the empire. "[109]

In family affairs one would have to speak of "a veritable equality of the sexes in daily life. "[110]  The woman's
consent was necessary for marriage;[111] "the woman had no
obligation to obey; the husband had no right to correct her....
legally the husband had no right of power over his wife ...
from the point of view of money, the regime was one of
equality and of separation. "[112]  "The equality of the spouses
was in effect total, whether concerning the full liberty of
divorce in classical law, the limiting causes of that liberty
in the late empire, or the sanctions of an unjustified divorce. "[113]

Republican Rome, acting originally under the influence
of Etruscan culture, took up the impulse of women's liberation from Hellenism and carried it forward to where the empire also made it its own and continued to promote it ever
further throughout the first several centuries of the Common
Era.

In sum:  The status of women in the ancient world of
the fertile crescent after the early Sumerian period was quite
uniformly low except in Egypt, where it was early and often
quite high.  In the classical Greco-Roman world the condition of women was varied, but often quite restricted, with the
clear exception of Etruscan culture.  It nevertheless improved,
particularly during the Hellenistic period, so vigorously and
continually that one must speak of a women's liberation movement which had a massive and manifold liberating impact on
the lot of women--not everywhere and in every class and at

every period equally effective, of course.  This improving
impulse was picked up and carried forward by Rome.  In
fact, I believe we can accept as a general rule the statement of Oepke[114] that "the general rule in this matter is
that the further west we go the greater is the freedom of
woman.  In detail, however, there are the greatest possible
variations," and add to it that in general there is also a
progression in the freedom for women according to time as
well.  Thus, as the women of Rome tended to be freer than
those of Greece, who were more liberated than women of
the oriental world, so also the women of the time of the
Roman empire had greater freedom than those of the time
of the Roman republic, and their sisters in the Hellenistic
world and period were less restricted than those of Greece
at the time of the Athenian empire.  Due account must be
taken, of course, of the unsympathetic vagaries of all human
history, and the fact that in so many ways the liberation of
women was long since preceded in ancient Sumer, in Egypt,
and later also in Etruria.

It is in this context and under this surrounding and
pervading influence of the Greco-Roman (Egyptian) world that
Judaism developed.


3.   ANCIENT HEBREW BACKGROUND

Although it would be very helpful to a study of the
status of women in formative Judaism to first do a thorough
study of the status of women in pre-exilic Hebrew society,
it is, fortunately, not essential.  Nevertheless, it is very
important to highlight at least one significant fact from that
earlier period that will shed a good deal of light on the status of women in the post-exilic, formative period of Judaism:  namely, that there are in the Bible two traditions
about women.[115]

These two traditions about women depict her first--
i. e. , before the Fall--as the equal of man, if indeed not the
perfection of humanity, and secondly--after the Fall--as subject to man; under the curse.  This bifurcation is clearly
seen in the Yahwist story of creation in Genesis 2, which is
the older scriptural tradition.  Contrary to much later, and
often superficial, interpretation of this story, a careful analysis reveals that the Yahwist writer did not think of woman
as lesser because she was created after Adam.  Quite the
contrary.  The pertinent passage reads:

Yahweh God said, 'It is not good that the man
should be alone.  I will make him a helpmate. '
So from the soil Yahweh God fashioned all the wild
beasts and all the birds of heaven.  These he
brought to the man to see what he would call them;
each one was to bear the name the man would give
it.  The man gave names to all the cattle, all the
birds of heaven and all the wild beasts.  But no
helpmate suitable for man was found for him.  So
Yahweh God made the man fall into a deep sleep.
And while he slept, he took one of his ribs and
enclosed it in flesh.  Yahweh God built the rib he
had taken from the man into a woman, and brought
her to the man.  The man exclaimed: 'This at
last is bone from my bones, and flesh from my
flesh!  This is to be called woman, for this was
taken from man. '  This is why a man leaves his
father and mother and joins himself to his wife,
and they become one body.  Now both of them
were naked, the man and his wife, but they felt
no shame in front of each other.  (Genesis 2: 18-
25)

Here, first of all, the creation of woman was set in
contrast to that of the animals, which preceded.  The latter
were to have been understood by, and placed under, the authority of the man--they were not to have been worshipped,
even symbolically, as they were in Canaanite and Egyptian
cults.  But the main point of the text was man's relationship
to woman.  Clearly woman's creation was also essentially
related to man, since his solitude was the occasion for her
creation.  But was she to be seen as simply an afterthought,
a companion slightly higher than the animals?  Such an understanding would hardly square with the tone of the story
wherein Yahweh was depicted as knowing well what he was
doing and as having done everything purposefully.  Yahweh
was not a hesitant potter who tried one thing after another
in hopes of final success; rather, he was the Almighty, whose
actions carried lessons of major importance.  Rather than
seeing woman's creation as the lowest in a series of creation attempts that started on a triumphant note with the form-
ing of Adam and proceeded on a descending scale to that of
Eden, plants, rivers, animals, and, finally, woman, we
should view it as a creation that evolved from Adam to woman, with the intermediate creations serving to establish the
stage for the higher creation that was attained with the
modeling of woman. [116]

George Tavard spells out this understanding of the
Yahwist's description of the prelapsarian state of woman as
humanity's (i. e. , adam, man in the generic sense) perfection: as far as humankind as a whole is concerned, there
is only one creation, that of adam. The next step is not a
second process of creation, but rather a step within the total
process, a further development of what began with the fa-
shioning of Adam. We should therefore understand woman
not as an addition to the humankind that already was in the
person of Adam; rather, Adam himself (in that part of him
which was his rib) is built up into woman. Adam becomes
a person, aware of himself, reaching consciousness as humankind with the disclosure of woman. For woman also is
humankind. She is not other than adam; but she is adam as
bringing to perfection what had first been imperfect. She is
humankind as fully aware of its status, as the goal and perfection of man. Thus, woman is not made to be Adam's
helpmate just because he is lonely; she is created as the
perfecting element, to the revelation of which he aspired
when he refused companionship with the animal world. In
one way, Ishah was made for mankind, as she was to bring
it perfection, to be its perfection. In another, mankind was
made for Ishah, the less perfect, the uncompleted, the un-
differentiated being preparatory of the more perfect, the
fullness, the being-in-relation. In the oneness of man and
woman, it is woman who brings perfection. [117]

Thus in Genesis 2 the Yahwist pictured the state of
woman as it was in the beginning, before the Fall. But he
knew from experience that that was not the state of woman
in contemporary society. Present reality was the opposite
of that in Eden. The curse of woman evoked a reversal of
the order of the universe attained in Eden. While woman in
innocence was creation's acme, woman in experience, following her initiation to sexuality, would be dominated by her
sexual "desire for her husband," indeed, by her husband
himself, and by pregnancy's pains. "The higher aspect of
mankind becomes enslaved, and the ruder aspect, the man,
takes over leadership. "[118]

Thus, seen in the light of the earlier analysis of the
events in the Garden, this story of the curse provides the
key to the entire meaning of the Yahwist tradition about the
origins of humanity. The author, of course, belonged to
postlapsarian history, to the order of the curse. Yet he
was convinced that it was not always thus. And the poet re-
constructed a prelapsarian state which was the exact reversal

of everyday life as he experienced it.  When throughout centuries the Hebrews heard these stories and later read them,
it was recalled to them that they were experiencing the am-
biguity of living East of Eden, while they yet longed to return to Paradise.  They were thus fed by two conflicting
traditions, the postlapsarian, which governed their daily lives
and the structure of society, and the dream of the prelapsarian, which they hoped to return to at the end of their
cycle in life--eventually to be called the messianic era.

Tavard summarizes this explanation when he says
that we are thereby invited to read the whole Hebrew biblical
tradition in this light: "There were two traditions about
woman.  The one corresponded to the order of society, in
which woman, though protected by many laws, was inferior
to man.  The other echoed the legends of the origins as recorded in the Yahwist text:  originally, woman was the higher
and better part of mankind. "[119]

These two traditions do indeed continue to run from
Hebrew society to beyond the Exile into inchoative and ma-
turely formed Judaism (and into Christianity as well), but,
as the subsequent study will clearly show, the prelapsarian
tradition will tend to fade, be distorted, and even be suppressed at times.  But it recurs, as, for example, with the
prophets, who see Israel as the espoused of the Lord; with
the wisdom literature where Wisdom is pictured as the pri-
mordial woman antecedent to the creation of the world; with
some poetry, like the Song of Songs, where the love depicted
is humanist and egalitarian (this erotic humanism was later
rejected by Ben Sira, e.g., 9: 8), and even when it was interpreted, beginning with Rabbi Akiba, first century C.E.,
allegorically, whereby the union of love between man and
woman became a symbol of the relationship between God and
his bride Israel; indeed, with the understanding of Israel as
humanity, humanity as loved by God, for here humanity itself is feminine vis-à-vis God.  It continues to recur throughout later Jewish history, as with the medieval Kabbalah,
where the feminine is projected into the divinity.  But most
important, this prelapsarian tradition of woman as man's
equal, indeed, his completion, is there at the source, waiting to renew the tradition.

CHAPTER II


ATTITUDE TOWARD WOMEN IN WISDOM
AND PSEUDEPIGRAPHICAL LITERATURE


1.  WISDOM LITERATURE

Most of the Wisdom literature was written after the
return of the Jewish people from the exile (587-537 B. C. E.);
a small portion of it--the central section of the Book of Proverbs, e. g. --was pre-exilic.   In the Wisdom literature we
find the two traditions about women reflected.   First, it
must be noted that these books which include some most
disparaging remarks about women also project the feminine
into a personification of divine Wisdom.   In the Book of
Proverbs, Wisdom is described as the highest and first
creature of God, identical with the Law, and this Wisdom
is a woman.   In Ben Sira, Wisdom, Sophia, is also a feminine creature, though an eternal one, that is identified as
the spirit of the Lord and the glory of Yahweh.   In the Book
of the Wisdom of Solomon the personification of the feminine
Sophia attains its acme; she is no longer a creature, but an
eternal emanation from God: "She is a breath of the Power
of God, pure emanation of the glory of the Almighty" (7:25).
Wisdom takes part in all the powers of God.   She is divine,
yet not God, who, as in all biblical texts, remains the Un-
knowable One.   Wisdom is what humans can know of God's
glory, that of God which can be communicated to humans.
Said differently, Wisdom is the "good and evil" which the Ishah
of Genesis 2 desired to know but never learned.   It is the
image of Ishah as transformed by the true knowledge of benediction and malediction, the divine antitype of Ishah.   "It
shows what Ishah would have been had she waited for God's
self-unveiling instead of attempting to grasp the secrets of
God by herself. "[1]

It should also be noted that although it is doubtless
accurate to see the persistence of the prelapsarian, more
positive tradition about woman in this personification of

29

Divine Wisdom as the feminine <u>Hokmah</u> or <u>Sophia</u>, such a
projection can also often become a device to further shunt a
suppressed individual or group out of the path of power; it
can serve as a sop of tokenism, a safety valve which drains
off potential rebellion.    Placing someone, or some group,
on a pedestal clearly takes that person or group out of the
real order of affairs where decisions are made; it is like
"kicking someone upstairs" to get her out of the way.    Thus,
even the persistence of the positive tradition about woman is
ambiguous, though, to be sure, its positive power does per-
sist.

Almost parenthetically, it would also be proper at
this point to discuss in a little detail the image of woman and
of female-male relations projected in the Song of Songs, since
it is classified with the wisdom books in the Septuagint and
the Vulgate, though not in the Massoretic Hebrew Bible.

The book as we have it probably comes from the
third century B. C. E. , though much of the material is considerably older.    It is simply love poetry of a woman and a
man for each other with no particular "religious" content.
Perhaps it was attributed to Solomon, who obviously was not
the true author, because he had the reputation of being a
great lover.    Perhaps the reason it was included in the canon
of sacred Scriptures was because it was interpreted allegorically, that is, as reflecting the love of Yahweh for Israel,
as some rabbis supposedly argued at Jamnia around 100
C. E. , although that does not tell us why it was already included in the Septuagint (third-second century B. C. E. ).    In
any case, it is love poetry, and it reflects an image of woman and female-male relations that fits in the more positive,
prelapsarian Hebrew tradition.

To begin with, attention focuses immediately on the
woman:  the book begins and closes with the woman speaking.    Furthermore, the woman initiates most of the action
and has most of the dialogue; she is active in love-making
(e. g. , "On my bed, at night, I sought him whom my heart
loves," 3:1).    Mother is referred to seven times in the
Song, whereas father is not referred to at all.    The mothers
of both the woman and the man are mentioned:  she is
called the "darling of her <u>mother</u>" (6:9); of the man reference is made to "where your <u>mother</u> conceived you" (8:5);
King Solomon is said to wear the crown "with which his
<u>mother</u> crowned him" (3:11); the woman's brothers are men-
tioned once as "my <u>mother</u>'s sons" (1:6); in two places the

woman takes the initiative by taking the man "into my <u>mother</u>'s house" (3:4, 8:2) for love-making.

One scholar notes that in light of the stress on woman's role as wife and mother in Hebrew society, it is remarkable that the Song is not interested in these ways of identifying a woman. The Song does not tell us whether the lovers are married or not; marriage is not an issue here. Moreover, "the woman is <u>not</u> a mother, and there are no references to her procreative abilities or interest in childbearing."[2]

Some of the most interesting work on the meaning of the Song of Songs has been done by Phyllis Trible, who, among other things, sees the Song as, if not in intent, then at least in fact, a midrash on the Adam and Eve story, a sort of theme and variations. She concludes by saying:

> In many ways, then, Song of Songs is a midrash
> on Genesis 2-3. By variations and reversals it
> creatively actualizes major motifs and themes of
> the primeval myth. Female and male are born to
> mutuality and love. They are naked without
> shame; they are equal without duplication. They
> live in gardens where nature joins in celebrating
> their oneness. Neither couple fits the rhetoric of
> a male-dominated culture. As equals they con-
> front life and death. But the first couple lose
> their oneness through disobedience. Consequently,
> the woman's desire becomes the man's dominion.
> The second couple affirm their oneness through
> eroticism. Consequently, the man's desire be-
> comes the woman's delight. Whatever else it may
> be, Canticles is a commentary on Genesis 2-3.
> Paradise Lost is Paradise Regained.[3]

Thus, we have in the Song of Songs an image of woman that is positive, egalitarian, prelapsarian. However, excepting the Song of Songs and the feminine personification of <u>Hagia Sophia</u>, in general it is accurate to say the Wisdom literature exhibits an attitude that is quite antithetic towards women. Even the oldest of the material, the book of Proverbs (probably put in its present form in the third or fourth century B. C. E.), is filled with negative sentiments toward women.[4]

Perhaps part of the reason for this negative attitude

toward women is that this literature was written by and for
men, although this fact by itself surely would not <u>necessitate</u>
the negative stance.  Moreover, the negative fact that no
such (extant) biblical literature was written by and for women
(with the possible exception of the Song of Songs) also speaks
loudly of the lesser status of women in the later biblical
period.  Even the books of Esther and Judith do not really
offer a counterpoint to this dominant male theme.  (See
Chapter III--1, Pharisees.)

If there is a sexual transgression it is usually assumed that the woman was the cause of it, whether she was
an alien woman or a neighbor's wife:  "Keeping you also
from the alien woman, from the stranger,[5] with her wheedling words ... towards death her house is declining, down
to the Shades her paths go.  Of those who go to her not one
returns, they never regain the paths of life" (Prov. 2: 16-
19).  Shortly afterward the thought is repeated:

> Take no notice of the loose-living woman, for the
> lips of this alien drip with honey, her words are
> smoother than oil, but their outcome is as bitter
> as wormwood, sharp as a two-edged sword.  Her
> feet go down to death, her steps lead down to
> Sheol; far from following the path of life, her ways
> are undirected, irresponsible ... set your course
> as far from her as possible, go nowhere near the
> door of her house, or you will surrender your
> honour to others, your years to one who has no
> pity, and strangers will batten on your property,
> your labors going to some alien house, and, at
> your ending, when body and flesh are consumed,
> you will groan (Prov. 5:2-11).

Again it is presumed that the woman is the source of the
evil, and especially the alien woman, who will alienate the
innocent male's honor, years, property, labors and even
consume his body and flesh.

Then follow a group of rather striking metaphors that
first project the native woman (or lawful wife) not only as a
more prudent choice but also clearly as the property of the
male, existing for his "refreshment":  "Drink the water from
your own cistern, fresh water from your own well.  Do not
let your fountains flow to waste elsewhere, nor your streams
in the public streets.  Let them be for yourself alone, not
for strangers at the same time.  And may your fountain head

be blessed!" (Prov. 5: 15-18). The following chapter again
warns against evil women: "Preserving you from the wicked
woman, from the smooth tongue of the woman who is a
stranger" ... and so on for the next eleven verses (Prov.
6: 24-35). [6] But the author cannot yet leave the topic of the
evil woman, particularly the alien woman (this is all in the
post-exilic prologue, chapters 1-9), even repeating his
earlier phrases: "To preserve you from the alien woman,
from the stranger, with her wheedling words." Then come
twenty verses describing the ways of evil women vis-à-vis
innocent men, ending with the familiar dire warning: "Her
house is the way to Sheol, the descents to the courts of
death" (Prov. 7: 5-27). [7] Thus far this is the post-exilic
material of the book of Proverbs.

The rest of the material of Proverbs (with the exception of the final poem, 31: 10-31, which cannot be dated)
is most probably much older, surely pre-exilic, some going
back perhaps to the time of Solomon (tenth century). Sexual
transgression, particularly with the alien woman, was also
warned against here, again in metaphors whose sexual symbolism is hardly veiled: "The mouth of the alien woman is
a deep pit, into it falls the man whom Yahweh detests" (22:
14). "A harlot is a deep pit, a narrow well, the woman
who is a stranger. Yes, like a robber she is on the watch
and many are the men she dupes" (23: 27-28). "This is
how the adulteress behaves: when she has eaten, she wipes
her mouth clean and says, 'I have done nothing wrong'" (30:
20). The rest of the ancient sayings of Proverbs--save the
general remarks about indiscreet women: "A golden ring
in the snout of a pig is a lovely woman who lacks discretion"
(11: 22), and the enervating effect of all women, with language approaching a semen "cult": "Do not spend all your
energy on women, nor your loins on these destroyers of
kings" (31: 3)--all refer to the non-virtuous wife, replete
with repetitions and near-repetitions: "A gracious woman
brings honour to her husband, she who has no love for justice is dishonour enthroned" (11: 16). "A good wife her
husband's crown, a shameless wife, a cancer in his bones"
(12: 3). "A woman's scolding is like a dripping gutter" (19:
13). "The steady dripping of a gutter on a rainy day and a
scolding woman are alike. Whoever can restrain her, can
restrain the wind, and with right hand grasp oil" (27: 15-16).
"Better the corner of a loft to live in than a house shared
with a scolding woman" (21: 9 and 25: 24). "Better to live
in a desert land than with a scolding and irritable woman"
(21: 19). The misery of living with a husband with compar-
able faults is not mentioned.

There are, however, several places where reference
is made to honoring father and mother, or not dishonoring
them (e. g. , 15: 20; 17: 25; 19: 26; 23: 25; 30: 11, 17)--
though in a number of places honoring the father alone is
mentioned, but never the mother alone.   Then finally comes
the capstone, of an unknown date, the oft-quoted paean of
praise of the perfect wife, in the form of an alphabetic poem, each verse beginning with the next letter of the Hebrew
alphabet.

> A perfect wife--who can find her?
> She is far beyond the price of pearls.
>
> Her husband's heart has confidence in her,
> from her he will derive no little profit.
>
> Advantage and not hurt she brings him
> all the days of her life.
>
> She is always busy with wool and with flax,
> she does her work with eager hands.
>
> She is like a merchant vessel
> bringing her food from far away.
>
> She gets up while it is still dark
> giving her household their food,
> giving orders to her serving girls.
>
> She sets her mind on a field, then she buys it;
> with what her hands have earned she plants a
>     vineyard.
>
> She puts her back into her work
> and shows how strong her arms can be.
>
> She finds her labour well worth while;
> her lamp does not go out at night.
>
> She sets her hands to the distaff,
> her fingers grasp the spindle.
>
> She holds out her hand to the poor,
> she opens her arms to the needy.
>
> Snow may come, she has no fears for her house-
>     hold,
> with all her servants warmly clothed.

She makes her own quilts,
she is dressed in fine linen and purple.

Her husband is respected at the city gates,
taking his seat among the elders of the land.

She weaves linen sheets and sells them,
she supplies the merchant with sashes.

She is clothed in strength and dignity,
she can laugh at the days to come.

When she opens her mouth, she does so wisely;
on her tongue is kindly instruction.

She keeps good watch on the conduct of her household,
no bread of idleness for her.

Her sons stand up and proclaim her blessed,
her husband, too, sings her praises:

'Many women have done admirable things,
but you surpass them all!'

Charm is deceitful, and beauty empty;
the woman who is wise is the one to praise.

Give her a share in what her hands have worked
   for,
and let her works tell her praises at the city gates.
                                   --(Proverbs 31: 10-31)

The "virtuous" wife described here is truly an extraordinary human being. However, the effectiveness of this
poem as a testimony of post-exilic Hebrew appreciation of
womanhood is somewhat weakened by the fact that the Hebrew
gloss, incorporated and developed by the Greek into the final
two verses, "seems to show that the scribes understood this
whole passage allegorically as a description of Wisdom personified (cf. 8: 22 ff.). This would make it an apt conclusion to the book. "[8]  In regard to the appreciation of womanhood it is much more important to note that, like the few
scattered positive remarks about women earlier in the book
(the references, for example, to the good wife being the
husband's crown, honoring one's mother), they are really
not about women as such, about women as human beings,

but only about women in their relationship to men, i. e. , as
a man's wife or a son's mother.   (Men are not similarly
treated solely in relational terms. )   The book of Proverbs
knows almost nothing good about women except insofar as
they are for the advantage or profit of men;[9] this is especially true of the poem on the perfect wife, which is always
referred to when an attempt is made to show that the Wisdom literature was not always depreciative, but sometimes
even appreciative of womanhood. [10]   The husband "will de-
rive no little profit from her.   Advantage and not hurt she
brings him all the days of her life" (31:11-12).   She works
uncommonly hard, exercising a great deal of business judgment and responsibility; the result is not that she is given
some religious or civic responsibility or honorific title or
position--rather her husband is:  "Her husband is respected
at the city gates, taking his seat among the elders of the
land" (31:23).   It is no wonder such a woman is appreciated; she is the best model for the perfect servant.   Indeed,
the impression given by this poem is that thanks to the dili-
gence of the wife, the husband is a man of leisure.   The
model of the perfect wife held up by the rabbis[11] is still
seen today in Mea Shearim, an ultra-Orthodox sector of
Jerusalem.   In return for her complete self-sacrifice she is
given praise by the men:  "Her sons [children in RSV] stand
up and proclaim her blessed, her husband, too, sings her
praises" (31:28), and by those gathered at the city gates:
"let her work tell her praises at the city gates" (31:31).
She is allowed to share in the fruits of her labor:  "Give
her a share in what her hands have worked for"[12] (31:31).

    The rest of the biblical Wisdom literature is all post-
exilic, coming down to within a little more than a generation
of the Common Era.   Ecclesiastes was written around the
middle of the third century B. C. E. ;  Ecclesiasticus, or Ben
Sira, about the middle of the second century B. C. E. ;[13] and
the Wisdom of Solomon, the middle of the first century
B. C. E.   Like Proverbs before them, all three of these
books are addressed solely to men, apparently presuming
that they alone needed to be instructed in wisdom.   Time
and again phrases like "happy the man who..." or "wretched
the man who..." or "my son, do not..." occur throughout
this literature, and it is really the man, the male, that is
in the author's mind.

    In the latest of the books, the Wisdom of Solomon,
outside of the feminine personification of Wisdom discussed
above, there is nothing at all of significance about women.

Ecclesiastes is an unusually short book, twelve brief chapters, and also has unusually little to say about women. Outside of a few metaphorical references to women and an exhortation to marital fidelity (9: 9), the only reference to women is an especially vitriolic and bitter one: "I find woman more bitter than death; she is a snare, her heart a net, her arms are chains" (7: 26). Here the remarks are not like the statements praising women; that is, they are not directed toward them as relationships, as mothers or wives of men. Rather the statements are directed toward women as such: "I find woman," not "my woman." This would seem to fulfill the definition of misogynism, of woman-hating. The author then raises misogynism to the level of a religious virtue: "He who is pleasing to God eludes her, but the sinner is her captive" (7: 27). Here there is no pretence of a virtuous rejection of woman as a prostitute or adulteress; all women have been reduced to essential evil. Of course, in general Ecclesiastes is very pessimistic, as is reflected, among other places, in his remark that only one man in a thousand is "better than the rest." This is surely a relatively low estimate of men; but his condemnation of women is absolute: "but never a woman" (7: 29).

Ecclesiasticus, or Ben Sira, is a deuterocanonical book (also referred to as one of the apocrypha, as is also the Wisdom of Solomon) of the second century B. C. E.; it is therefore found in the Catholic Bible but not the Hebrew or Protestant Bibles. However, it was quoted by the rabbis (the New Testament Epistle of James borrows many expressions from it, and, next to the Psalms, it is the "Old Testament" book most frequently quoted in the Christian liturgy). The author, Ben Sira, lived in Palestine at a time of expanding Hellenist influence, and opposed it vigorously. As a defense he emphasized the Jewish tradition, the Law, Torah. He was conscious and proud of the abilities of the man learned in the Law, the scribe. Wisdom was the privilege of the scribe (39: 1 ff.), whose supremacy in wisdom was described in the most enthusiastic terms. However, the apogee of his enthusiasm was reached in the description of Simon, the son of Onias, the high priest, who was described in all his priestly array as he appeared in the temple at the great festivals. "Ben Sira represents a phase of development in which the wise man has become the scribe, the man learned in the Law of Moses.... In his attitude toward the Law and its observance he seems to belong to that group which later became the Sadducees rather than to the Pharisees."[14]

Ben Sira's opposition to expanding Hellenism by emphasizing Jewish particularity would automatically lead him to an anti-feminist position on two counts: one, since a growing freedom and equality for women was a part of Hellenism,[15] a rejection of Hellenism would tend to include a rejection of this more positive attitude toward women; two, the need to shelter Jewish women from the malign influences of Hellenism (especially its feminism), would tend to reinforce the restrictions on Jewish women--who could not be fortified by the study of the Law. Moreover, this exclusion of women from the study of Torah,[16] coupled with Ben Sira's exaltation of its study, would also incline him toward an anti-woman attitude. In fact, in this regard, Ben Sira fits perfectly the women-denigrating and even, at times, misogynist patterns in other authors of Wisdom literature. The quality of woman-hating of the century older and brief Ecclesiastes is easily matched by Ben Sira. But in the quantity of misogynism the older author is far outstripped by the later one.

Ben Sira discusses women from various aspects: as mothers, daughters, wives, sexual sinners, and as women as such. Only in the first category and partly in the third are his statements in any way positive. There are two brief passages reinforcing the commandment, "Honor thy father and mother" (3:3-6; 7:27-28). But for Ben Sira the great value of mothers is to bear sons; daughters are obviously undesirable: "The birth of a daughter is a loss!" (22:3). The only concern for daughters, it would seem, is to maintain their physical virginity and get them married, the proper age for marriage for girls being twelve and half years old: "Have you daughters? Take care of their bodies, but do not be over-indulgent. Marry a daughter off, and your cares will vanish; but give her to a man of sense.... A sensible daughter will obtain her husband, but a shameless one is a grief to her father. An insolent daughter puts father and mother to shame and will be disowned by both" (7:24-25 ... 22:4-5). (In contrast to this is the care exhibited for sons: "A man who educates his son will be the envy of his enemy" 30:3.)

For Ben Sira daughters are, from one point of view, nothing but painful burdens; from another view they are totally creatures of sex:

> A daughter is a deceptive treasure for her father,
> the worry she gives him drives away his sleep: in

> her youth, in case she never marries; married,
> in case she should be disliked; as a virgin, in
> case she should be defiled and found with child in
> her father's house; having a husband, in case she
> goes astray; married, in case she should be bar-
> ren. Your daughter is headstrong? Keep a sharp
> look-out that she does not make you the laughing-
> stock of your enemies, the talk of the town, the
> object of common gossip, and put you to public
> shame. (42:9-11)

There does not seem to be overly much concern about the
evils themselves or the bad effects they will have on the
daughter. Almost the only worry is what will happen to the
man, the father, as a result of the daughter's evil deeds.
Again, the female's existence seems to be summed up in
her relationship to a male.

    Ben Sira goes even further in his rejection of any
kind of independence in a female offspring, describing her
as "headstrong," heaping abuse on her for her putative future behavior, again in language that has a very transparent
sex symbolism--and given the extraordinary restrictions in
girl's and women's contact with men and the very early non-
love match marriages, it was doubtless at times a self-ful-
filling prophecy: "Keep a headstrong daughter under firm
control, or she will abuse any indulgence she receives.
Keep a strict watch on her shameless eye, do not be sur-
prised if she disgraces you. Like a thirsty traveller she
will open her mouth and drink any water she comes across;
she will sit in front of every peg, and open her quiver to
any arrow" (26:10-12). [12]

    Ben Sira has a number of positive things to say about
good wives, albeit such goodness is often enough expressed
clearly in terms of advantage or profit to the husband:
"Happy the man who keeps house with a sensible wife" (25:8).
"Happy the husband of a really good wife; the number of his
days will be doubled. A perfect wife is the joy of her husband, he will live out the years of his life in peace. A
good wife is the best of portions, reserved for those who
fear the Lord" (26:1-3). The "feminine" qualities of submissiveness are then praised highly: "The grace of a wife
will charm her husband, her accomplishments will make him
the stronger. A silent wife is a gift from the Lord, no
price can be put on a well-trained character. A modest wife
is a boon twice over, a chaste character cannot be weighed

on scales.   Like the sun rising over the mountains of the
Lord is the beauty of a good wife in a well-kept house...."
(26:13-16).   Within this submissive context Ben Sira even
knows to praise physical beauty:

> Like the lamp shining on the sacred lamp-stand is
> a beautiful face on a well-proportioned body.   Like
> golden pillars on a silver base are shapely legs
> on firm-set heels....   A woman's beauty delights
> the beholder, a man likes nothing better.   If her
> tongue is kind and gentle, her husband has no
> equal among the sons of men.   The man who takes
> a wife has the makings of a fortune, a helper that
> suits him, and a pillar to lean on.   (26:17-18;
> 36:22-24)

Not all the remarks about wives, however, are positive.   Some are vaguely ominous, as:   "Do not turn against
a wise and good wife....   Have you a wife to your liking?
Do not turn her out; but if you dislike her, never trust her"
(7:19, 26).   Some are rather threatening comparisons:   "A
godless wife is assigned to a transgressor as his fortune,
but a devout wife given to the man who fears the Lord.   A
shameless wife takes pleasure in disgracing herself, a modest wife is diffident even with her husband.   A headstrong
wife is a shameless bitch, but one with a sense of shame
fears the Lord.   A wife who respects her husband will be
acknowledged wise by all, but one who proudly despises him
will be known by all as wicked" (26:23-26).

In many instances pure vitriol is poured on the wife
(reminiscent of Proverbs 21:9, 19; 25:24; 27:15):

> I would sooner keep house with a lion or a dragon
> than keep house with a spiteful wife.   A wife's
> spite changes the appearance of her husband and
> makes him look like a bear.   When her husband
> goes out to dinner with his neighbours, he cannot
> help heaving bitter sighs.... [18]   Low spirits,
> gloomy face, stricken heart:   such the achieve-
> ments of a spiteful wife.   Slack hands and sagging
> knees indicate a wife who makes her husband
> wretched....   A bad wife is a badly fitting ox yoke,
> trying to master her is like grasping a scorpion.
> A drunken wife will goad anyone to fury, she makes
> no effort to hide her degradation.   (25:16-18, 23;
> 26:7-8)

Sometimes the scorn comes in the form of "humor": "As
climbing up a sandhill is for elderly feet such is a garrulous
wife for a quiet husband.... A loud-mouthed, gossiping
wife is like a trumpet sounding a charge, and any man sad-
dled with one spends his life in the turmoil of war" (25:20;
26:27). The wife as breadwinner is bitterly rejected: "Bad
temper, insolence and shame hold sway where the wife sup-
ports the husband" (25:22).

Ben Sira, like Proverbs and other biblical writers
before him, delivers admonitions for the would-be wise man
to be on the outlook against women who will lead him astray
sexually. Also like Proverbs (31:3) Ben Sira issues dire
warnings against the alien women in language that uses very
plain sexual metaphors and at times approaches a semen
"cult": "My son, preserve the bloom of your youth and do
not waste your strength on strangers. Search the whole
plain for a fertile field, sow your own seed there, trusting
in your own good stock. Thus your offspring will survive,
they will grow great, confident of their breeding. A woman
for hire is not worth spitting at, but a lawful wife is as
strong as a tower" (26:19-22). Moreover, every manner of
woman is warned against: prostitutes, married women,
singing women, handsome women, virgins, and just women:

> Do not give your soul to a woman, for her to
> trample on your strength. Do not keep company
> with a harlot, in case you get entangled in her
> snares. Do not dally with a singing girl, in case
> you get caught by her wiles. Do not stare at a
> virgin, in case you and she incur the same punish-
> ment. Do not give your soul to whores, or you
> will ruin your inheritance. Keep your eyes to
> yourself in the streets of a town, do not prowl
> about its unfrequented quarters. Turn your eyes
> away from a handsome woman, do not stare at the
> beauty that belongs to someone else. Woman's
> beauty has led many astray; it kindles desire like
> a flame. Do not have much conversation with a
> married woman, and do not conduct long discus-
> sions with her[19] (9:2-9).

The beauty of any woman is seen as a danger: "Do not be
taken in by a woman's beauty, never lose your head over a
woman" (25:21).

Ben Sira does seem to move in the direction of

placing a moral onus on the man not to commit adultery, or
indeed fornication or masturbation (23:16-17). [20]  However,
a comparison between the warning against the adulterer and
against the adulteress is instructive.  Though Ben Sira goes
beyond most of his biblical predecessors in demanding "moral
uprightness" in sexual matters from husbands, there still is
clearly a double standard involved.  Only a general threat
of punishment "in view of the whole town" is leveled against
the man (actually only if the woman involved was married
could the man be punished legally, and that because he had
violated the rights of the other husband over his property,
his wife).  The threat against the adulteress is overwhelm-
ing--adulteresses apparently were still to be put to death
regardless of the marital state of the man they consorted
with; [21] even her children and her memory were to be punished and forever stained (23:21-26).

It is not just prostitutes, adulteresses, daughters in
general and all but submissive wives that receive invective
from Ben Sira.  Women in general are bitterly abused by
him with an intensity that surpasses previous biblical misogynism.  It would also seem that for Ben Sira all women
are nymphomaniacs, [22] at least in a passive sense: "A woman
will accept any husband, but some daughters are better than
others" (36:21).  For Ben Sira it also seems that all women
were spiteful by nature: "Do not let water find a leak, do
not allow a spiteful woman free rein for her tongue.  If she
will not do as you tell her, get rid of her....  For a moth
comes out of clothes, and woman's spite out of woman"
(25:25-26).  He pushes the matter further: "Any spite rather than the spite of a woman!" (25:13).  And still further:
"A man's spite is preferable to a woman's kindness; women
give rise to shame and reproach" (42:13-14).  Indeed, to
Ben Sira women are the greatest evil in the world by far!
"No wickedness comes anywhere near the wickedness of a
woman, may a sinner's lot be hers!" (25:19).  Woman is
not only the greatest of evils, but in fact the cause of all
evil: "Sin began with a woman, and thanks to her we all
must die" (25:24).

Note should also be taken here of the attitude toward
women reflected in other Near Eastern wisdom literature.
Such literature was widespread in the ancient Near East, including especially Egypt.  Since there was a considerable
mutual awareness of this wisdom literature, [23] a great deal
of similarity can be expected. [24]  It appears that the Egyptian
wisdom literature was, like the Hebrew, written by and for

men; the image of women in it consequently is likewise that of a relationship to men. The pertinent passages are as follows:[25]

> If thou desirest to make friendship last in a home to which thou hast access as master, as a brother, or as a friend, into any place where thou mightest enter, beware of approaching the women. It does not go well with the place where that is done. The face has no alertness by splitting. A thousand men may be distracted from their [own] advantage. One is made a fool by limbs of fayence, as she stands [there], become [all] carnelian. A mere trifle, the likeness of a dream--and one attains death through knowing her.... Do not do it--it is really an abomination--and thou shalt be free from sickness of heart every day.

> If thou art a man of standing, thou shouldst found thy household and love thy wife at home as is fitting. Fill her belly; clothe her back. Ointment is the prescription for her body. Make her heart glad as long as thou livest. She is a profitable field for her lord. Thou shouldst not contend with her at law, and keep her far from gaining control.... Her eye is her stormwind. Let her heart be soothed through what may accrue to thee; it means keeping her long in thy house.

> Take to thyself a wife while thou art (still) a youth, that she may produce a son for thee. Beget [him] for thyself while thou art (still) young. Teach him to be a man.

> Be on thy guard against a woman from abroad, who is not known in her (own) town. Do not stare at her when she passes by. Do not know her carnally: a deep water, whose windings one knows not, a woman who is far away from her husband. 'I am sleek,' she says to thee every day. She has no witnesses when she waits to ensnare thee. It is a great crime (worthy) of death, when one hears of it.

> Thou shouldst not supervise (too closely) thy wife in her (own) house, when thou knowest that she is efficient. Do not say to her: 'Where

is it?   Fetch (it) for us!' when she has put (it) in
the (most) useful place.   Let thy eye have regard,
while thou art silent that thou mayest recognize
her abilities.   How happy it is when thy hand is
with her!   Many are here who do not know what a
man should do to stop dissension in his house....
Every man who is settled in a house should hold
the hasty heart firm.   Thou shouldst not pursue
after a woman; do not let her steal away thy
heart.

        The image of woman in this Egyptian wisdom litera-
ture is that of a wife or mother or harlot, i. e., she is always seen in relationship to a man.   As in the parallel
Hebrew wisdom literature, men are warned to avoid adultery,
and particularly to avoid the alien woman, and urged to take
a good wife who will produce sons, taking care to deal with
their wives with care and concern.   But nothing like the
outpouring of anger and misogynism on bad wives and all
manner of women which appears in the Hebrew wisdom literature is to be found in this parallel Egyptian wisdom literature.   This is doubtless a reflection of the relatively
high status women enjoyed at various times in Egyptian history discussed above; at the same time this literature likewise reflects the fact that women in Egypt also experienced
a relatively lower status for long periods of time, and even
in the "higher" periods never attained complete equality
with men in all areas of life.

        In the area of Babylon where, after the ancient Sum-
erian period, the status of women was quite uniformly low,
it is not surprising that we find both a warning against harlots, very like that found in Proverbs 7:6-27:

        Do not marry a harlot whose husbands are six
            thousand.
        An Ishtar-woman vowed to a god,
        A sacred prostitute whose favors are unlimited,
        Will not lift you out of your trouble:
        In your quarrel she will slander you.
        Reverence and submissiveness are not with her.
        Truly, if she takes possession of the house, lead
            her out.
        Toward the path of a stranger she turns her mind.
        Or the house which she enters will be destroyed,
            her husband will not prosper. 26

Also the one reference found in Pritchard's Ancient
Near Eastern Texts which focuses on woman as such rather
than on woman as wife, mother, or harlot, and which ex-
presses a deep misogynism:

> 'Servant, obey me. '  Yes, my lord, yes.  'A
> woman will I love. '  Yes, love, my lord, love.
> The man who loves a woman forgets pain and
> trouble.  'No, servant, a woman I shall not love. '
> [Do not love, ] my lord, do not [love].  Woman is
> a well, woman is a iron dagger--a sharp one!--
> which cuts a man's neck. [27]

It appears that with the passage of time there was a
clear movement in the attitude of the authors of the Hebrew
Wisdom literature toward women.   In the earlier materials
from Proverbs the attitude was androcentric, exploitative,
often set in a broader framework of anti-foreign racism.
In the later literature, Ecclesiastes and Ben Sira, the attitude of the authors, without necessarily abandoning those
earlier qualities, shifts toward an explicit misogynism, a
hatred of women as such.   Whether or not this progressively
more repressive stance vis-à-vis women in the post-exilic
biblical period was continued in the pseudepigraphical and
rabbinic literature will be investigated in the following pages.
(Whether the late post-exilic materials also represent a de-
generation of the Hebrew attitude toward women when compared with all the rest of the pre-exilic biblical materials--
as at first blush they would seem to do--is a judgment that
will have to await a careful analysis of the earlier materials. )

It is clear, however, that the two traditions about
women, the prelapsarian, positive one, and the postlapsarian, negative one, are expressed in the Wisdom literature:
there is the humanistic, egalitarian male-female love of the
Song of Songs, the feminine personification of divine Wisdom
(despite its pedestal-pusher problematic), and the positive
sayings about women in relation to men--i. e. , good daughters, good wives, good mothers.   Nevertheless, under the
force of evidence, it must be concluded that the prelapsarian
tradition tends to fade and the postlapsarian to come to the
fore, and that the attitude toward women expressed in the
biblical Wisdom literature is very strongly, even overwhelmingly, negative, reaching at times the peaks of hatred.   Such
evidence cannot, of course, automatically be taken by itself
as absolute proof that the general attitude of the Jewish

population toward women was also so strongly negative.
But in conjunction with other evidence to be discussed below, it must at least be said that it tends in that direction.
At the same time it should be noted that aside from the
question of whether the Wisdom literature's misogynism was
reflective of the population's attitude toward women or not,
because this literature was widely read, studied, commented
on, and quoted, it had a great influence which consequently
tended to make its misogynism in fact reflective of reality. [28]

## 2.  PSEUDEPIGRAPHA

Judaism did not cease producing religious literature
after the last canonical book of the Bible was written (whether in the Hebrew or Septuagint canon).   In the period from
the end of the second century B. C. E. to the end of the first
century C. E. a large number of religious writings welled
forth from Jewish pens; they are usually referred to as
pseudepigraphal (or apocryphal in Catholic tradition) writings,
because they were often attributed to an earlier writer to
lend them a greater authoritative quality. [29]   They were all
written in about a century or so just before or after the beginning of the Common Era and provide us with continuing
evidence on the status of women in the formative period of
Judaism. [30]

The Letter of Aristeas was composed between 130 and
70 B. C. E. by an Alexandrian Jew.   In only one place does
the author speak about women, and there in the traditional
deprecatory manner: "Womankind are by nature headstrong
and energetic in the pursuit of their own desires, and subject to sudden changes of opinion through fallacious reason-
ing, and their nature is essentially weak" (vs. 25).   Here
another small, but very solid, link in the chain of misogynism is forged.

Aristeas makes another remark which, although it is
not directly about women, nevertheless provides a psychological insight helpful in understanding how, side by side
with the already broadly evidenced deep-seated misogynism
in ancient Jewish culture, there could also exist customs
and sayings praising the good wife as the husband's crown,
etc.   Aristeas states:  "for it is a recognized principle
that ... the human race loves those who are willing to be
in subjection to them" (vs.  257). [31]

Another pertinent work, The Book of Adam and Eve, was probably composed in the first century C. E. by a diaspora Jew, perhaps an Alexandrian.[32] The already prevalent idea that sexual sin was the "mother of all evils,"[33] was continued in this work: "Lust is the beginning and root of every sin."[34] In speaking of the action of the serpent in tempting Eve, the Book of Adam and Eve said that the serpent "poured upon the fruit the poison of his wickedness, which is lust, the root and beginning of every sin, and he bent the branch on the earth and I took of the fruit and I ate." (It is interesting to note that a rabbi of the first century C. E., Johanan ben Zackai, apparently expressed a similar idea so forcefully that it was recalled at least three different times in the Babylonian Talmud. He made the first woman, the symbol of all women, guilty of bestiality-- the devil did not pour his semen of sin, lust, on the fruit, but rather injected it directly into Eve via sexual intercourse: "For Rabbi Johanan stated: When the serpent copulated with Eve, he infused her with lust."[35] "Rabbi Johanan said: When the serpent came unto Eve he infused filthy lust into her."[36] "For when the serpent came upon Eve he injected a lust into her."[37] Modern psychologists were not the first to see the serpent as a phallic symbol.)

But here a new dimension is added; in re-telling the story of Adam and Eve, the author makes it very clear that Eve, not Adam, was the primary sinner in the garden of Eden: "And Eve said to Adam: 'Live thou, my lord,[38] to thee life is granted, since thou hast committed neither the first nor the second error. But I have erred and been led astray for I have not kept the commandment of God; and now banish me from the light of thy life and I will go to the sunsetting, and there will I be, until I die."[39] In another place Eve again confesses, rather magnanimously, to being the primary cause of suffering and pain in the world: "And Eve wept and said: 'My lord Adam, rise up and give me half of thy trouble and I will endure it; for it is on my account that this hath happened to thee, on my account thou art beset with toils and troubles.'"[40] A variant version has it: "And when Eve had seen him weeping, she also began to weep herself, and said: 'O Lord my God, hand over to me his pain, for it is I who sinned? And Eve said to Adam: 'My lord, give me a part of thy pains, for this hath come to thee from fault of mine.'"[41] Adam was less magnanimous; he made it very clear that he thought that Eve was the cause of all his--and our--sin and suffering: "And Adam saith to Eve: 'Eve, what hast thou wrought in us? Thou hast brought

upon us great wrath which is death, (lording it over all our
face). '"[42]   A variant version is even more explicit in
Adam's condemnation of Eve:  "And Adam said to Eve:
'What hast thou done?   A great plague hast thou brought
upon us, transgression and sin for all our generations:  and
this which thou hast done, tell thy children after my death,
(for those who rise from us shall toil and fail but they shall
be wanting and curse us and say, All evil have our parents
brought upon us, who were at the beginning).'   When Eve
heard these words, she began to weep and moan."[43]

If it were not already clear that Eve was thought of
as the source of death,[44] the author has Adam state the
claim again quite bluntly:  "And Adam said to him [his son
Seth]:  'When God made us, me and your mother, through
whom also I die.... '"[45]   The same notion of Eve as the
cause of death occurs even more blatantly in another pseudepigraphal diaspora Jewish work, probably of the first century C.E., The Book of the Secrets of Enoch:  "And I put
sleep into him and he fell asleep.   And I took from him a
rib, and created him a wife, that death should come to him
by his wife."[46]

According to the author of the Book of Adam and Eve
it is not only the sin, suffering and death of humanity that
is to be laid at the feet of woman, Eve, but also the whole
revolt of the animal kingdom against man:

>  And Eve saw her son, and a wild beast assailing
>  him, and Eve wept and said:  'Woe is me; if I
>  come to the day of the Resurrection, all those who
>  have sinned will curse me saying:  Eve hath not
>  kept the commandment of God.'   And she spake
>  to the beast:  'Thou wicked beast, fearest thou
>  not to fight with the image of God?   How was thy
>  mouth opened?   How were thy teeth made strong?
>  How didst thou not call to mind thy subjection?
>  For long ago wast thou made subject to the image
>  of God.'   Then the beast cried out and said:  'It
>  is not our concern, Eve, thy greed and thy wail-
>  ing, but thine own for (it is) from thee that the
>  rule of the beasts hath arisen.   How was thy
>  mouth opened to eat of the tree concerning which
>  God enjoined thee not to eat of it?   On this ac-
>  count, our nature also hath been transformed.'[47]

Two of the most important and influential of the

pseudepigraphal books were probably written by Pharisees.
These same two documents also dealt in some detail with
relations to women, and hence help set the tone for the
Pharisees' attitude toward women that persisted to the end
of the Second Temple period (70 C. E. )--and afterward
through the "successors" of the Pharisees, the rabbis (to
be discussed in detail below).

The Book of Jubilees was written between 109 and
105 B. C. E. [48] and in certain limited aspects is extremely
important for the student of religion.  Without it we could
of course have inferred from Ezra and Nehemiah, the
Priests' Code, and the later chapters of Zechariah the
supreme position that the Torah had achieved in Judaism,
but without Jubilees we could hardly have imagined such an
absolute supremacy of the Law as is expressed there.
"Jubilees represents the triumph of the movement, which
had been at work for the past three centuries or more. "[49]
For the author of Jubilees the Torah was of eternal validity.
It was not the expression of the religious consciousness of
one or a number of sages, but the revelation in time of
what was valid from the beginning and for always.  "The
ideal of the faithful Jew was to be realized in the fulfillment
of the moral and ritual precepts of this law:  the latter were
of no less importance than the former. "[50]  Hence what is
portrayed here as part of the Torah or the background to it
is of the first importance, insofar as this book was read and
had an influence--which was widespread. [51]

The matter that seemed to be uppermost in the mind
of the author(s) of Jubilees--and also the Testament of the
Twelve Patriarchs--in their dealings with women was the
avoidance of fornication, particularly with foreign women.
In their symbolic representation as the Canaanite wives of
Esau (The Book of Jubilees is cast in the form of a re-
telling of the story of Genesis), such women are described
as evil and lustful--a combination of the extremely negative
attitude toward foreign women and the notion that every
woman is a nymphomaniac:  "For all their deeds are fornication and lust, and there is no righteousness with them, for
(their deeds) are evil" (25:1).

But this attack on any kind of sexual contact, even,
or rather, especially in legal marriage with foreign women,
reached an extraordinarily extreme point later in the book.
There it was stated, and repeatedly re-stated, that it was a
shameful sin for Jews and non-Jews to inter-marry; all

involved were to be killed, including the Jewish father who
gave his daughter in (mixed) marriage: "And if there is
any man who wishes in Israel to give his daughter or his
sister to any man who is of the seed of the Gentiles he
shall surely die, and they shall stone him with stones; for
he hath wrought shame in Israel; and they shall burn the
woman with fire, because she has dishonoured the name of
the house of her father, and she shall be rooted out of
Israel" (30:7).   (That it would be almost impossible for a
thirteen year old girl to resist the decision of her all-pow-
erful father was apparently not considered important by the
author.)   The author continued:

> For Israel is holy unto the Lord, and every man
> who has defiled (it) shall surely die: they shall
> stone him with stones ... regarding all the seed
> of Israel: for he who defileth (it) shall surely
> die, and he shall be stoned with stones.... And
> do thou, Moses, command the children of Israel
> and exhort them not to give their daughters to the
> Gentiles, and not to take for their sons any of
> the daughters of the Gentiles, for this is abomin-
> able before the Lord.... And it is a reproach to
> Israel, to those who give, and to those that take
> the daughters of the Gentiles; for this is unclean
> and abominable to Israel.   And Israel will not be
> free from this uncleanness if it has a wife of the
> daughters of the Gentiles, or has given any of its
> daughters to a man who is of any of the Gentiles.
> For there will be plague upon plague, and curse
> upon curse, and every judgment and plague and
> curse will come upon him: if he do this thing, or
> hide his eyes from those who commit unclean-
> ness (30:8-15).

Here the effort to maintain the Israelite "seed" undefiled resulted in demands of punishment far in excess of those recorded in Ezra, Nehemiah and the Wisdom literature.[52]

It was not just with foreign women that the observant
Jew was to avoid sexual intercourse, but with all women
(other than his wife).   Through the figure of Abraham it is
advised that "we should keep ourselves from all fornication
and uncleanness (and renounce from amongst us all fornication and uncleanness)" (20:3).   In the immediate context the
charge is repeated again: "And guard yourselves from all
fornication and uncleanness" (20:6).   It is also there

recalled that the giants and Sodomites "died on account of their fornication, and uncleanness, and mutual corruption through fornication" (20:5). If there was any question concerning the seriousness and fundamental quality of sexual intercourse outside of wedlock (even "spiritual" fornication was forbidden: "Let them not commit fornication with her after their eyes and their hearts"--20:4), it was laid to rest a little later when it was stated unambiguously that "there is no greater sin than the fornication which they commit on earth" (33:20). The one who was to suffer most of all from such sins was the woman: "And if any woman or maid commit fornication amongst you, burn her with fire" (20:4). (There is no mention here of any punishment whatsoever to be meted out to the man involved.)[53] Such a fundamental grounding of evil in sex and meting out of punishment to women tended to imply and further a misogynist attitude in males--and in females by way of self-hatred.

The second important pseudepigraphal book perhaps written by a Pharisee, The Testaments of the Twelve Patriarchs, was composed at almost the same time as the Book of Jubilees, that is, between 109 and 106 B. C. E. [54] It too was greatly concerned with fornication as the "mother of all evils" (5:3), but it exhibited a much more generous attitude toward the Gentiles than did Jubilees; the author of the Testaments of the Twelve Patriarchs held a basically universalistic view of salvation: "And the twelve tribes shall be gathered together there, and all the Gentiles, until the Most High shall send forth His salvation."[55] As a consequence there is none of the diatribe of Jubilees against sexual contact with foreign women, though there is a slight residue of the feminine xenophobic attitude in the Testament of Judah (14:7).

However, as noted, fornication was viewed with such a repeatedly expressed horror that the author's attitude approached that of an idée fixe: "For a pit unto the soul is the sin of fornication, separating it from God, and bringing it near to idols, because it deceiveth the mind and understanding, and leadeth down young men into Hades before their time" (T. of Reuben 4:6). Here fornication was seen as a fundamental sin, leading to death. The next verse says much the same: "For many hath fornication destroyed; because, though a man be old or noble, or rich or poor, he bringeth reproach upon himself with the sons of men and derision with Beliar" (T. of Reuben 4:7). [56] Again the author said: "Beware, therefore, of fornication" (T. of Reuben 6:1).

And still further: "For in fornication there is neither understanding nor godliness, and all jealousy dwelleth in the
lust thereof" (T. of Reuben 6:4).

        In the author's "rule of truth" the avoidance of for-
nication was <u>primary</u>: "And now my son I will show the rule
of the truth.... First, take heed to thyself, my son against
all lust and uncleanness, and against all fornication."[57]  The
author added elsewhere that fornication has grave, massive
consequences: "He that committeth fornication is not aware
where he suffers loss, and is not ashamed when put to dis-
honor.  For even though a man be a king and commit fornication" (T. of Judah 15:1-2).  This description of the consequences of fornication still did not satisfy the author.  He
found it necessary a short while later to spell out in great
detail the effects he saw flowing from fornication--and there
seemed to be little missing:

> Beware, therefore, my children, of fornication ...
> (for they) withdraw you from the law of God, and
> blind the inclination of the soul, and teach arro-
> gance, and suffer not a man to have compassion
> upon his neighbor.  They rob his soul of all good-
> ness, and oppress him with toils and troubles,
> and drive away sleep from him, and devour his
> flesh.  And he hindereth the sacrifices of God;
> and he remembereth when he speaketh, and re-
> senteth the words of godliness.  For being a slave
> to the passions contrary to the commandments of
> God and because they have blinded his soul, he
> walketh in the day as in the night.  (T. of Judah
> 18:2-6)

Still later the author again took up the specific question of
fornication and bluntly labeled it the fountainhead of all evil
--sex is the source of sin: "Beware, therefore, of fornication, for fornication is the mother of all evils, separating
from God, and bringing near to Beliar" (T. of Simeon 5:3).
Indeed, as in the Wisdom literature,[58] there was even a
strong hint of a sort of "sacred semen": "Defile not thy
seed with harlots; for thou art a holy seed, and holy is thy
seed like the holy place" (T. of Simeon 5:17).

        The author moved a step further and urged not only
the avoidance of illicit sexual intercourse, but also "spiritual" fornication, that is, with the eyes or mind:[59]  "Do you,
therefore, my children, flee evil-doing and cleave to

goodness.   For he that hath it looketh not on a woman with view to fornication, and he beholdeth no defilement" (T. of Benjamin 8:1-2). [60]   In the Testament of Issachar the author claimed, "I never committed fornication by the uplifting of my eyes" (7:2).   This step of urging the avoidance of sexual fantasy is, of course, psychologically understandable, but the matter did not remain there.   The conclusion of the author was to see in the beauty of women a source of evil which at all costs should be avoided: "And now, I command you, my children, not to ... gaze upon the beauty of women" (T. of Judah 17:1).   "Pay no heed to the face of a woman, nor associate with another man's wife, nor meddle with the affairs of womankind" (T. of Reuben 3:10).   Again: "Pay no heed, therefore, my children, to the beauty of women, nor set your mind on their affairs" (T. of Reuben 4:1).   And still again: "And the spirits of deceit have no power against him, for he looketh not on the beauty of women, lest he should pollute his mind with corruption" (T. of Issachar 4:4).

From this attitude of the need to avoid women out of fear, it is but a brief step to outright misogynism, of seeing women as such as evil; every woman leads the essentially "good" man down to evil.   The author takes that step: "For women are evil, my children; and since they have no power or strength over man, they use wiles by outward attractions, that they may draw him to themselves.   And whom they cannot bewitch by outward attractions, him they overcome by craft" (T. of Reuben 5:1-2).   Somewhat as in Ben Sira, the author proceeded to describe how women in general went about spreading their evil: "By means of their adornment they instil the poison, and then through the accomplished act they take them captive.   For a woman cannot force a man openly, but by a harlot's bearing she beguiles him" (T. of Reuben 5:3-4).   The "logical" conclusion is then drawn by the author, namely, that all women should reject attractive clothing, jewelry and cosmetics: "Command your wives and daughters, that they adorn not their heads and faces," and woe to the woman who nevertheless does, "because every woman who useth these wiles hath been reserved for eternal punishment" (T. of Reuben 5:5).   (At this point the author described how the women allured the angels to their fall, that is, to fornication; they did so by adornments and cosmetics.) [61]   In the end the principle, which was already seen in Ben Sira, was put forth, namely, that every woman is a nymphomaniac.   It was expressed in the Testament of Reuben in the strongest possible form: "Moreover,

concerning them (women), the angel of the Lord told me,
and taught me, that women are overcome by the spirit of
fornication more than men, and in their heart they plot
against men" (T. of Reuben 5:3).

Conclusion? "Guard your senses from every woman.
And command the women likewise not to associate with men"
(T. of Reuben 6:1-2). Contact between men and women,
"even though the ungodly deed be not wrought," was seen as
"an irremediable disease" for the women and as a "destruction of Beliar and an eternal reproach" for the men (T. of
Reuben 6:3-4).

The misogynism of the (Pharisee?) author of the
Testaments of the Twelve Patriarchs seems rather complete. [62]

This then is basically all the pertinent material about
women to be found in the pseudepigraphical, or apocalyptic,
literature--other than the Dead Sea materials, which will be
treated separately later. As can be seen, it is all quite
negative in its estimate of women (other than the neutral,
purely narrative portions); it does not even contain the few
positive evaluations of "good" wives found in some of the
Wisdom literature. The prelapsarian, positive, tradition
seems to be nowhere in evidence. Thus, the developing
misogynism was sustained, and even intensified.

The question needs to be asked at this point why the
status of women in post-exilic Judaism, at least as far as
this is reflected in the literature of the period, appears to
have declined, especially when women in Hellenistic culture
appeared to be improving their status throughout a similar
period. Perhaps what was suggested above (p. 38) concerning Ben Sira's anti-woman attitude is at the basis of the
increasingly repressive attitude taken toward women by
Jewish writers throughout the post-exilic period. Positively,
there was the need to stress the identity, the unity of the
Jewish people; negatively, it was important to ward off outside influences which could confuse and dilute that identity
and unity.

The need to develop such in-group/out-group defenses
in the early centuries after the Exile, in view of the return
of such a relatively small group of Jews, is patent. The
traditional stress within a patriarchal society, like that of
the Hebrews, on continuing the male line in general leads to

the sexual restriction of women far beyond that of men (e. g. , polygyny but not polyandry being allowed). But the condition of the embattled remnant obviously forced the Jews to take even more drastic measures to retain group identity and unity, as is evidenced by the radical negative actions of Ezra and Nehemiah. After the conquest of the area by Alexander the Great toward the end of the fourth century B. C. E. and the subsequent spread of Hellenistic culture, the repressive Jewish attitude intensified even more, as can be seen in Ben Sira, the Book of Jubilees and the Testament of the Twelve Patriarchs. The Hellenistic culture proved increasingly attractive and pervasive, and those Jews who saw it as a threat to Jewish identity felt that they had to insulate the Jewish community from its enervating influences. By increasing restrictions half the population, the female half, was thereby more surely removed from Hellenism's baleful blandishments; such moves would also tend to lessen the Hellenizing influence non-Jewish women would have on the male half of the Jewish community. Such an approach was also doubtless reinforced by the knowledge that a significant element in the to-be-rejected Hellenistic culture was the relatively much higher status women held in religion and society.

CHAPTER III

ATTITUDE OF MAJOR JEWISH GROUPS TOWARD WOMEN

1.  PHARISEES

As noted, of the last two pseudepigraphal books just
analyzed, one most probably, and the other perhaps, was
written by early Pharisees.  Outside of the teachings of the
Pharisees reflected in the rabbinic documents (and to some
extent the New Testament), they are, along with Josephus,
our best sources of information concerning their attitude
toward women.  Since the rabbinic writings will be treated
at length later and since the pertinent material in Josephus
is brief, it would be helpful to present Josephus' material
here so as to provide, along with the completed analyses of
the Book of Jubilees and the Testaments of the Twelve
Patriarchs (realizing that the latter's relevance here is quite
tentative), a basis for an initial evaluation of the attitude of
the Pharisees toward women:  Josephus described himself
as having been a Pharisee entrusted with considerable leadership.  Concerning women he said: "The woman, says the
Law, is in all things inferior to the man."  He drew the
consequence from this position:  "Let her accordingly be
submissive," and added a slightly ameliorative phrase--
which changed nothing: "not for her humiliation, but that
she may be directed; for the authority has been given by
God to the man."[1]

The evidence of these sources indicates that the
Pharisees thought of women as "in all things inferior to the
man," as "evil," as "overcome by the spirit of fornication
more than men," as ones who "in their heart plot against
men," and that every man should "guard (his) senses from
every woman."  Such an attitude could hardly be without wide
social effects in the areas which came under the influence
of the Pharisees.

Joseph Klausner[2] would seem to argue that the

opposite is the case, not only for the early Pharisees, but also for the whole Hasmonean period, i.e., the first and second centuries before the Common Era:

> The social position of women in any land is evidence of the country's cultural state.... In general, the status of women in Judea was improved under the Hasmoneans. The legend about the mother and her seven sons during Antiochus' persecution shows that the nation knew how to appreciate the dignified and patriotic stand taken by the Jewish woman. Mention should also be made of the fine relationship depicted in the Book of Tobit (the father) and his wife Anna, between Tobiah (the son) and Sarah, and between Raguel and Edna, whom he calls 'my sister,' just as the 'beloved' calls his love in the Song of Songs. All this is reliable evidence that the general attitude towards women took a turn for the better in Hasmonean Judea. The position of Queen Salome constitutes further proof of this. Also worthy of note is the fact that not a single Hasmonean king had more than one wife, in contrast to Herod, for example, who took many. The regulations which Simeon ben Shetah introduced regarding the woman's kethubah (wedding contract) simply lent religious and juridical sanction to this satisfactory situation which already prevailed in fact.

Klausner said the same thing, using almost identical words, over forty years earlier in his Jesus von Nazareth;[3] there he also added a reference to the book of Judith, and ended with the statement: "This position of the Jewish woman in the centuries before Jesus is a witness therefore to the high level of the Hebrew culture of that time."

The evidence offered by Klausner unfortunately appears to be quite incommensurate with the conclusion drawn, especially in view of all the counter evidence already put forth.

First, the story about the "mother and her seven sons" is extremely moving, but when one asks what the image of the woman in this story is, the answer is rather stereotypical: she was a mother (of sons!), and suffered; hardly "reliable evidence" that the "general attitude toward women took a turn for the better" (which language would indicate that it had been even worse previously). The evidence of the Book of Tobit seems even weaker. The events of the story, which can hardly be true, were supposed to have taken place in the seventh century B. C. E. , and in this sense evidence nothing concerning the Hasmonean period; moreover, the book was written before 200 B. C. E. , hence considerably before the Hasmonean period; in this sense it likewise can have no bearing on that latter period. Further, it is quite likely that the book was composed in Egypt,[4] or Syria,[5] and hence it could hardly reflect Hasmonean Palestinian Judaism. The fact that all three wives were addressed by their husbands as "sister" (which was an Egyptian custom at the time the book was written) does not seem to prove much. Likewise, the fact that a real human affection appeared to exist between the husbands and wives in the story[6] shows that marriages with affection existed (where or when?) within Judaism; but doubtless there have been many such instances everywhere and at all times.

The message of the Book of Judith is that God will protect his People; it is hardly that of high esteem for women. Again, when it is asked what the image of woman is, this time in the Book of Judith, the answer, again, is stereotypical: woman accomplishes her end by adorning her physical beauty and seducing men, and, in this instance, killing men.[7] As in the Wisdom literature and elsewhere, the implicit message to men is to beware of beautiful women--they will un-man you and lead you to death. The redeeming factor here of course is that Judith puts her evil womanly wiles at the service of her nation. But Judith was hardly held up as a model of the typical Jewish woman; though she was a widow from her youth and was extremely beautiful, she did not take another husband either before her killing of Holofernes or afterwards; perhaps placing her seductive sexual powers at the service of her nation, and God, demanded, in this obviously fictional story, both that she not be "defiled" by Holofernes, or by any other man subsequently.[8] The moral of the book is not that women are good creatures of God, but that God is so great that He can bring good out of evil; the moral is not that women are to be valued greatly, but that God is so great that He can humble Israel's enemies even through the lowliest of instruments, women. "And the Lord struck him down by the hand of a woman!" (13:16).

A brief discussion of the Book of Esther might well be parenthetically inserted here, for although Klausner does

not refer to it, it is nevertheless often pointed to, along
with Judith, as evidence of a high evaluation of women in the
late biblical period.   Actually it also provides evidence of
the opposite thesis.   After a seven-day-long celebration King
Ahasuerus was drunk and ordered his eunuchs to fetch Queen
Vashti, "in order to display her beauty to the people and
the officers" (1:11).   She declined to come, an understandable decision given the probably riotous condition of what by
then must have been a somewhat sodden drinking bout.   This
infuriated the king and disturbed his advisers, for they
thought that when word got abroad among the other wives in
the kingdom, "there will be endless disrespect and insolence!"   Hence, Queen Vashti had to be deposed, so that
"all the women will henceforth bow to the authority of their
husbands ... ensuring that each man might be master in
his own house" (1:20-21).

One contemporary Jewish woman writes that,

> Further, in order to insure that we really have
> no shred of sympathy left for Vashti, several
> sources credit her with responsibility for prevent-
> ing the king from giving his consent to the re-
> building of the Temple.   These legends are very
> significant, for they reflect popular and rabbinic
> feeling.   And it is very clear that in no way was
> Vashti's refusal to debase herself seen by suc-
> ceeding Jews as noble or courageous.   Quite the
> contrary.   The Rabbis must have found themselves
> in somewhat of a bind initially.   On the one hand
> they couldn't possibly approve the demand Aha-
> suarus makes on Vashti.   On the other hand, to
> support her would be to invite female disobedience
> in other situations, an idea they apparently could
> not tolerate.   They solve this by condemning Aha-
> suarus as foolish and by creating legends whereby
> Vashti is shown as getting exactly what she de-
> serves. [9]

The later chosen queen, Esther, a Jew, saved her
people by a certain bravery, but basically through her physical beauty, the result being that tens of thousands of people
were killed at her behest.   Again the image of women in the
Wisdom literature was substantiated:   "good" women are
beautiful and submissive; but the beauty of women is danger-
ous and leads to the death of many.   Here again, as with
Judith, the redeeming factor was that Esther put this

death-dealing female power at the service of her people. [10]
The point of this whole, fictional, story concerns the Providence of God which preserves his people from annihilation--
and by the most unlikely means, a woman, just as happened
with Judith.  The fact that in both these stories the "heroines" were women indicates not that women were often heroines or highly thought of in Jewish society at that time, [11]
but just the opposite, that women were not heroines or highly
thought of in that society; otherwise the stories would not
have been interesting or worth recording.  They were of interest exactly because they displayed God's Providence for
his people by having them saved by the most unlikely and
despised means available--women.

In comparing Vashti and Esther, Mary Gendler wrote:

> Ahasuerus can be seen not only as an Ultimate
> Authority who holds vast power over everyone, but
> more generally as male, patriarchal authority in
> relation to females.  As such, Vashti and Esther
> serve as models of how to deal with such author-
> ity.  And the message comes through loud and
> clear:  women who are bold, direct, aggressive
> and disobedient are not acceptable; the praise-
> worthy women are those who are unassuming,
> quietly persistent, and who gain their power
> through the love they inspire in men.  These wom-
> en live almost vicariously, subordinating their
> needs and desires to those of others.  We have
> only to look at the stereotyped Jewish Mother to
> attest the still-pervasive influence of the Esther-
> behavior-model. . . .  What I am interested in here,
> however, is pointing up typical male and female
> models of behavior and, at that level, it is clear
> that society rewards men for being direct and ag-
> gressive while it condemns women, like Vashti,
> for equivalent behavior.  For, in a sense, Morde-
> cai and Vashti have behaved identically:  both re-
> fuse to debase themselves by submitting to illegiti-
> mate demands.  For this Mordecai is praised and
> Vashti is condemned. [12]

The reigning of Queen Salome (did the Hellenist example of reigning queens have an influence here?) and the
"monogamy" of the Hasmonean kings (remember of course
also the multiple concubines some of them had) and the
small reforms in the marriage contract by Rabbi Simeon ben

Shetah[13] are perhaps items favoring the position of women.
But in the face of the flood of opposite evidence, they hardly
warrant the conclusion that "The position of woman ... was
from the time of the Hasmoneans onward one of thorough-
going esteem,"[14] nor could any similar claim be made for
the position of women in the view of the early Pharisees.


## 2.  SADDUCEES

Besides the Pharisees there were three other groups
of men who had an important influence on the customs and
everyday life of Palestinian Judaism: the priests, the Essenes, and the scribes or rabbis.  Each of these groups
will have to be analyzed somewhat further, but the last is
overwhelmingly more important than the first two.  As can
be seen in the cultic restrictions placed on women by the
priestly writers in Leviticus, and elsewhere, the priestly
party tended throughout the biblical period to be restrictive
of the role women were allowed to play in religion and society.  In the late biblical times this was reinforced by the
strongly negative attitude toward women expressed by Ben
Sira (second century B. C. E.), who was at least vigorously
supportive of the priestly party.  Hence, it has been suggested that he was a forerunner of the Hellenized upper-
class priestly party, the Sadducees.

The Sadducees gathered their support not only from
the aristocratic priestly families but also from the merchants
and middle-class Jews who would benefit from association
with the ruling, or at least powerful, class.  They were adherents of the written Torah, but recognized no oral Torah,
and hence were in opposition to the Pharisees.  Unfortunately, almost nothing about their attitude toward women is
known; it can only be speculated that perhaps Hellenist influence led them to give women more freedom than was otherwise customary, but on the other hand, the priestly tradition would have bent them in the opposite direction.  In any
case, their influence, at least insofar as they deviated from
tradition, was doubtless relatively meager among the masses,
who cared little for "foreign" ways, which were associated
with the hated foreign rulers--earlier the Seleucid Greeks
and later the Romans.  Since these upper classes often
joined in oppressing their own people, they were also often
hated--which is reflected in the fact that they were frequently
attacked and looted by their own people during the disastrous
Jewish rebellion, 66-70 C. E.

## 3. ESSENES--QUMRAN

Until recently what we knew of the Essenes came
from three contemporary sources: the Roman writer Pliny,
the Alexandrian Jew Philo, and the Palestinian Jew Josephus.
Then at the end of the nineteenth century the Damascus
Document was discovered; it is a copy of a document written by and about a Jewish sectarian group around the beginning of the Common Era which most scholars identify with
the Essenes of the three traditional sources.  Still further
discoveries came with the finding of the Dead Sea Scrolls;
these are original manuscripts from around the beginning
of the Common Era, most of which came from or were connected with the Essene-like settlement at Qumran on the
Dead Sea.  Though there is some dispute, most scholars
also identify Qumran with the Essenes, and for the purposes
of this study they can be so treated.  Concerning the Essenes' attitude toward women, it must be said that they followed in the tradition of the misogynism of the Wisdom,
apocryphal, and pseudepigraphical literature, and the attitude of the Pharisees.

The Essenes were in many ways closely related to
the Pharisees, and came into existence about the same time
in Palestine, namely, the second century B. C. E.  In fact,
Schürer says "Essenism is first of all only Phariseeism in
the superlative."[15]  In the matter of their relation with
women, they went considerably farther than the Pharisees,
however:  the central group were male celibates.[16]  Pliny
stated the matter bluntly: "The solitary tribe of the Essenes is remarkable beyond all the other tribes in the whole
world, as it has no women and has renounced all sexual desire."[17]  This description of the Essenes' celibacy is neutral
enough in regard to women, but the more detailed information from Josephus, who claimed he was an Essene novice
for a number of months,[18] is not so neutral.  To begin
with, women are considered a source of dissension: "They
neither bring wives into the community nor do they own
slaves, since they believe that the latter practice contributes
to injustice and that the former opens the way to a source
of dissension."[19]  The almost ubiquitous concern in this
period with sexual immorality as a--if not the--primary sin
is also reflected in the Damascus Document, which states:
"Meanwhile, however, Belial will be rampant in Israel, the
son of Amoz: 'Terror and the pit and the trap shall be upon
thee, O inhabitant of the land!' (Isa. 24:17).  The reference
is to those three snares, viz., whoredom...."[20]  In another

place Josephus noted that the Essenes "Disdain marriage, but they adopt other men's children, while yet pliable and docile, and regard them as their kin and mould them in accordance with their own principles."[21]

Philo also attributed to the Essenes much the same derogatory attitude toward women, but spelled it out in much greater detail, and misogynism again rang through clearly:

> They eschew marriage because they clearly dis-
> cern it to be the sole or the principal danger to
> the maintenance of the communal life, as well as
> because they particularly practice continence.  For
> no Essene takes a wife, because a woman (gyne)
> is a selfish creature, excessively jealous and an
> adept at beguiling the morals of her husband and
> seducing him by her continued impostures.  For
> by the fawning talk which she practices and the
> other ways in which she plays her part like an
> actress on the stage she first ensnares the sight
> and hearing, and when these subjects as it were
> have been duped she cajoles the sovereign mind.
> And if the children come, filled with the spirit of
> arrogance and bold speaking she gives utterance
> with more audacious hardihood to things which be-
> fore she hinted covertly and under disguise, and
> casting off all shame she compels him to commit
> actions which are all hostile to the life of fellow-
> ship.  For he who is either fast bound in the love
> lures of his wife or under the stress of nature
> makes his children his first care ceases to be the
> same to the others and unconsciously has become
> a different man and passed from freedom into
> slavery. [23]

Some scholars argue that this opinion concerning wom-
en is not really that of the Essenes, but rather Philo's own.
However, Colson is most likely right when he says, "This
diatribe must not, I think, be taken as Philo's definite opinion, but rather as what might be plausibly argued by the
Essenes."[24] What the Essenes, through Philo, say about
women is more detailed than what is found in Josephus, but
it surely is in line with it.  Moreover, it is very similar
to the lengthy descriptions of the wily ways of women depicted in the Wisdom and pseudepigraphal literature quoted
above,[25] and a similar diatribe found among the Qumran
literature, quoted below;[26] this factor is especially

significant when it is realized that all this literature was
kept, copied, and studied at Qumran. "The association of
women with trouble-making belongs quite naturally to the
Wisdom of the OT. At Qumran, not only the OT Wisdom
literature, but also Ben Sira and even properly Essene Wisdom texts were copied; and one of the unpublished texts
from Cave IV attests, among other things, that the sapien-
tial depreciation of women was not forgotten but developed
startlingly."27 It should also be noted that what Philo's
Essenes have to say here about the sinful seductiveness of
women is not predicated of the wanton woman or the prostitute, but rather of women as such, or at least of wives!

   The text from Cave IV referred to by Strugnell is
doubtless the lengthy description of the wayward ways of the
harlot. The previous descriptions of the ways of prostitutes
from Proverbs and elsewhere, or indeed any description of
the seductive ways of women from ancient Jewish literature,
is far outstripped by this Essene diatribe. There is obviously
a fascination here with that forbidden thing, sex, and its
personification, woman; but since it is forbidden, there is
also expressed a deep hatred of the unattainable, woman,
here in the form of a harlot. Here is the fountainhead of
misogynism.

> (The har)lot utters vanities,
>     and [...] errors;
> She seeks continually [to] sharpen [her] words,
>     [...] she mockingly flatters
> and with emp[tiness] to bring together into derision.
>     Her heart's perversion prepares wantonness,
> and her emotions [...].
>     In perversion they seized the fouled (organs) of
>         passion,
> they descended the pit of her legs to act wickedly,
>     and behave with the guilt of [transgression...
> ...] the foundations of darkness,
>     the sins in her skirts are many.
> Her [...] is the depths of the night,
>     and her clothes [...].
> Her garments are the shades of twilight,
>     and her adornments are touched with corruption.
> Her beds are couches of corruption,
>     [...] depths of the Pit.
> Her lodgings are beds of darkness,
>     and in the depths of the nigh[t] are her [do]-
>         minions.

From the foundations of <u>darkness</u> she takes her
     dwelling,
  and she resides in the tents of the underworld,
in the midst of everlasting fire,
  and she has no inheritance (in the midst of)
     among all who gird themselves with light.
She is the foremost of all the ways of iniquity;
  Alas! ruin shall be to all who possess her,
And desolation to a[ll] who take hold of her.
  For her ways are the ways of death,
and her path[s] are the roads to sin;
  her tracks lead astray to iniquity,
and her paths are the guilt of transgression.
  Her gates are the gates of death,
in the opening of her house it stalks.
  To Sheol a[l]l [ ... ] will return,
and all who possess her will go down to the Pit.
  She lies in wait in secret places,
[ ... ]  all [ ... ].
  In the city's broad places she displays herself,
and in the town gates she sets herself,
  and there is none to distur[b her] from [ ... ].
Her eyes glance keenly hither and thither,
  and she wantonly raises her eyelids
to seek out a righteous man and lead him astray,
  and a perfect man to make him stumble;
upright men to divert (their) path,
  and those chosen for righteousness from keeping
     the commandment;
those sustained with [ ... ] to make fools of them
     with wantonness,
  and those who walk uprightly to change the
     st[atute];
to make the humble rebel from God,
  and to turn their steps from the ways of
     righteousness;
to bring <u>presumptuousness</u> [ ... ],
  those <u>not arraign[ed]</u> in the tracks of upright-
     ness;
to lead mankind astray in the ways of the Pit,
  and to seduce by flatteries the sons of men. [28]

However, apparently not all who wished to follow the
Essene principles were able or willing to give up married
life.  Josephus said:

There is yet another order of Essenes, which

while at one with the rest in its mode of life, customs, and regulations, differs from them in its
views on marriage.  They think that those who decline to marry cut off the chief function of life,
the propagation of the race, and, what is more,
that, were all to adopt the same view, the whole
race would very quickly die out.  They give their
wives, however, a three years' probation, and
only marry them after they have by three periods
of purification given proof of fecundity.  They
have no intercourse with them during pregnancy,
then showing that their motive in marrying is not
self-indulgence but the procreation of children. [29]

In sum it must be said that there is no significant
evidence of a positive attitude among the Essenes toward
women as such; at most there seems to be a tolerance
among some for marriage for the sake of offspring.  But
there is a great deal of evidence of an extremely negative
attitude on the part of the Essenes toward women;  the
misogynist tradition was continued here vigorously.  The
celibate way of life apparently did not continue beyond the
destruction of the temple in 70 C.E. , but the Essenes did
have a significant impact on the Palestinian Judaism of
their time.  Pliny's remarks in this regard are dramatic:
"Day by day the throng of refugees is recruited to an equal
number by numerous accessions of persons tired of life and
driven thither by the waves of fortune to adopt their manners.
Thus through thousands of ages (incredible to relate) a race
in which no one is born lives on for ever; so prolific for
their advantage is the other men's weariness of life. "[30]
Something so basic and pervasive as their misogynism could
not help but be spread with their influence in general.

4.   THERAPEUTAE

Mention should be made at this point of the Therapeutae, a group of Egyptian, Essene-like Jewish ascetics
who shared a common life.  They provide an interesting
study in similarity and contrast with the customs of their
contemporaries, the Essenes, in Palestine.  What is known
about them is from Philo; therefore they were in existence
in the first century C.E.  The Therapeutae community lived
near Alexandria and had both men and women members,
though for the most part they were separate, each having
his or her own cell.  They came together every Sabbath in
their synagogue, which was divided into two sections:

> being separated partly into the apartment of the
> men, and partly into a chamber for the women;
> for the women also, in accordance with the usual
> fashion there, form a part of the audience, having
> the same feelings of ardor as the men, and having
> adopted the same sect with equal deliberation and
> decision; and the wall which is between the houses
> rises from the ground three or four cubits[31] up-
> ward, like a battlement, while the space above up
> to the roof is left open ... on two accounts: first
> of all, in order that the modesty which is so be-
> coming to the female sex may be preserved; and
> secondly, that the women may be easily able to
> comprehend what is said, being seated within ear-
> shot. [32]

Here is exhibited a mingling of Jewish and Hellenist
influences--which one would expect in the then perhaps most
flourishing of Hellenist cities (founded by Alexander the
Great) which was at the same time perhaps the then most
flourishing Jewish city in the world.   The men and women
were separated in the synagogue, according to the Jewish
custom;[33] even today one can see in the synagogue in the
very orthodox section of Jerusalem, Mea Shearim, the same
kind of wall (though higher) between the room for men and
the room for women, with a separate entrance for each
room; a somewhat similar division exists at the Western,
or "Wailing" wall.   That meant, of course, that the women
could only listen, but not speak in the services.   However,
it was untraditional that the women would have committed
themselves with a devotion equal to that of the men to the
life of this sect, for that meant devoting the greatest part
of their lives to being in their cells studying allegorical
interpretations of the Scriptures; women traditionally did not
devote themselves, like men, to a study of the Scriptures,[34]
whereas in Hellenist Mystery religions and the Egyptian Isis
cult women did take prominent and even priestly roles. [35]

There was, however, one regular occasion when the
female Therapeutae did take an active part in a religious
service.   Every seventh week there was a sacred feast day
with a meal.   The men would recline at one side of the
table and women on the other; with the meal there were
readings, prayers and hymn-singing--and the women participated in the latter.   Afterwards the men and women
grouped themselves in two separate choirs and sang in alter-
nating fashion, accompanied with various hand and body

movements, like a sacred dance.  At the end the men and
women mixed to form a single choir.  Philo said: "Then,
when each choir has separately done its own part in the
feast, having drunk as in Bacchic rites of the strong wine
of God's love they mix and both together become a single
choir, a copy of the choir set up of old beside the Red Sea
in honor of the wonders there wrought ... the men led by
the prophet Moses and the women by the prophetess Miriam."[36]  Thus they prayed, sang and danced, filled with
pious enthusiasm, until morning, when they returned to their
cells.  Leipoldt noted that the Therapeutae were "outsiders
of Judaism," that their general asceticism, their eremitical
life-style (which one finds in Greek thinkers), their philosophical critique of slavery,[37] and especially their night
feast every seven weeks, which had all the characteristics
of a Greek Mystery religion feast, clearly reflected the influences of Hellenism.  Concerning the last matter Leipoldt
continued: "When the Greeks reflected a past fateful event
by imitation, men and women participated equally--in Mystery
religions something accepted as obvious.  When the Therapeutae take this over they may not exclude the women Therapeutae, so much more so may they not since in the Old
Testament model the prophetess Miriam steps forward so
decisively.  Hence, one may not view the participation of
the women Therapeutae in the worship service as indicative
of the Jewish manner,"[38] but rather the Greek manner.  It
should be noted that if, despite all the massive Hellenistic influences present in Alexandria and among the
Therapeutae, the women were still so strictly separated
in the weekly synagogue service and relegated to listen-
ing, then the force of the Jewish custom must have been
very strong.

Thus we find a blending of Jewish and Greek traditions in the Therapeutae, and, as far as women are concerned, the stronger influence of Greek customs--in contrast
to the apparently relatively weaker Greek influence among the
Essenes--worked to their advantage:  they were full-fledged
members, "having adopted the same sect with equal (to the
men) deliberation and decision"; they spent their time studying the Scriptures; they took an active part in the sacred
banquet, vigil and dance every seven weeks.  None of these
things was true of the position of women in the Essenes.
Nevertheless, all women Therapeutae were segregated in the
Sabbath synagogue, did not have the right to speak there,
and in other ways appeared subordinate to men, which
was not the case with women in many contemporary

Greek Mystery religions. The misogynism of much of contemporary Palestinian Judaism seemed to have been greatly
modified by Greek influence in the Therapeutae, though we
know from other evidence that this modifying influence on
the restrictions in the lives of married Jewish women in
Egypt was not so effective. [39]


## 5.  ELEPHANTINE WOMEN

At some point in this study a brief description of the
status of women in the fifth century B. C. E. Jewish colony
at a Persian military outpost at Elephantine, far up the Nile
near Aswan, should be given.  In time this material falls
beyond the main confines of the study; likewise, this distant
outpost apparently remained isolated and without influence
on the rest of Judaism.  Nevertheless, as a Jewish community with an extraordinarily different attitude toward the status of women from what was prevalent elsewhere in Judaism
in either the biblical or rabbinic periods, it deserves to be
mentioned here, however briefly.

Perhaps the best guide in this matter is Reuven
Yaron, Introduction to the Law of the Aramaic Papyri (Oxford, 1961).  He states that the position of women in the
Elephantine compared favorably with that in other parts of
the ancient Near East and that one ought to look to Egyptian
law for an explanation.  In the law of procedure he noted
that women at Elephantine did not attest documents, but that
they could be parties to litigation, and were capable of taking an oath.  In the field of the law of property and obligations women enjoyed full equality; they went about their
transactions in the same manner as men, no trace of inferiority or male supervision of any kind being discernible,
although in the field of succession women may have been in
an inferior position.  Outside the sphere of private law,
women were apparently enlisted in the military units which
made up the population of the Elephantine.  Equality of property rights also involved the duty to share in the burden of
taxation.  In C 22 women are conspicuous among the contri-
butors to the temple fund, paying two shekels each, just like
the men.  The most interesting feature of divorce at Elephantine is the equal capacity of the spouses, as far as the
power of dissolution of the marriage is concerned.  "This
is in striking contrast to the situation which on the whole
obtains in the ancient East, and also in Talmudic law, where
the husband alone is entitled to dissolve the marriage...."

The equality at Elephantine is probably due to the Egyptian environment. "[40]

In most of these matters Jewish women elsewhere in both late biblical and rabbinic times labored under grossly contrasting disabilities, perhaps most dramatically so in the essential area of marriage and divorce; outside of Elephantine it was the Jewish man who acquired the woman, and he alone could effect a divorce. [41]  However, the privileges enjoyed by Jewish women at Elephantine did not effect mainstream Judaism.


6.   THE RABBIS

The scribes, as their name partially indicates, were those men who were responsible for the copying, protection, understanding and explanation of the sacred books, the Scriptures.   By the beginning of the Common Era they commanded tremendous respect from the masses of the people, who were over the years convinced that they were first of all Jews and that to be a Jew meant to live according to the Torah, the Scriptures; but it was only the scribes, those learned in the Law, the Torah, who could properly explain what that meant.   Beyond this dependence of the masses on the scribes for instruction and explanation of what the Law was and how it was to be lived, was the tendency to see in the scribes the bearers of a secret knowledge, of an esoteric tradition.   The replete apocalyptic literature of the time is evidence of such an esoteric tradition, as also is the fact that for hundreds of years the knowledge of the scribes, the rabbis, was handed down orally--committed to writing in the Mishnah, which was produced in the second century C. E. -- in an archaic, holy language, Hebrew, that was not understood by the masses (it was only in the first century of the Common Era that the leading rabbis promoted the translation of the Bible into vernacular versions, called Targums). [42]

It should be noted that the scribes of the first century C. E. were not all of one religious party.   There were scribes who belonged to the Sadducees, but the majority belonged to the party of the Pharisees.   It should also be observed that not all priests were necessarily members of the Sadducees.   Many were adherents of the Pharisees (both the Pharisees and Sadducees, as well as the Essenes, were closed brotherhoods; not just everyone who claimed to live according to their principles could claim the name of and

membership in the fraternity--a period of probation had to
be passed before acceptance or rejection was decided upon),
which is not at all strange when it is recalled that the
Pharisees in effect wished to raise the biblically required
stipulations for priests on Temple duty concerning purity and
food regulations to the norm for the everyday life of the
priest and the entire people.   (Rabbi Meir--about 150 C. E. --
once defined a non-Pharisee as someone who "did not eat
his profane food in levitical purity.")[43]   At the same time,
not all Pharisees (there were perhaps something over 6,000
in Palestine in the first century, as compared to 7,000-
9,000 priests)[44] were priests or scribes.   They came from
all parts of society, though in the main they were lower
middle class laymen who were also not scribes.

Succinctly put, the Pharisees were a sect of men who
lived according to certain levitical rules of ritual purity,
etc. that were derived from the written Torah and the Oral
Law as handed down from the time of Moses by the scribes.
(The term "Rabbi" was originally a form of address meaning
"my master," but by the first century it had become a title
for one learned in the Law; in other words, the scribes, or
as the Germans more descriptively put it, the "learned in the
Scriptures," Schriftgelehrten, came to be called not scribes
but rabbis.)   The scribes were those who studied and taught
what this correct way of living was.   As a consequence,
many Pharisees became scribes and were doubtless as a
consequence the most important and influential members of
their brotherhood.

It is important to recall that in the first century C. E.
the party of the Pharisees completely attained the upper
hand in Palestine and after the destruction of the Temple in
70 C. E. the Sadducees as a party disappeared.   Particularly
interesting for the question concerning the status of wom-
en in the early formative period of Judaism is the Tannaitic
tradition which recalls that the wives of the Sadducees followed the ritual purity regulations of the Pharisees, "since
otherwise in the eyes of the Pharisees they would have been
considered tainted with the impurity of a menstruant and
their husbands would then, in their eyes, have been constantly impure."[45]   Josephus confirmed this overwhelming
influence of the Pharisees when he wrote: "They are, as a
matter of fact, extremely influential among the townspeople;
and all prayers and sacred rites of divine worship are performed according to their exposition.   This is the great
tribute that the inhabitants of the cities, by practising the

highest ideals both in their way of living and in their dis-
course, have paid to the excellence of the Pharisees. "[46]

Of the Sadducees Josephus said: "Whenever they
come to officiate they follow the prescriptions of the Pharisees, even if it be in an involuntary and forced manner; the
masses would not tolerate its being otherwise. "[47] As a
consequence, very little of the thought of the Sadducees or
their scribes has been recorded. The work of the rabbis
of the Mishnah and Talmud, and subsequent work, has been
overwhelmingly influenced and dominated by the Pharisaic
tradition. Moreover, most scribes were Pharisees. Therefore it is very important to learn the attitude of the Pharisees, particularly the Pharisaic scribes, the rabbis, toward
women, since they handed on and developed traditions that
not only often went back hundreds of years, but also exercised a wide influence at that time and subsequently.

As noted above, there is a wealth of material to document this attitude, particularly as found in the Mishnah and
Talmud. Since the scope of the influence of the rabbis covered every aspect of life, methodologically it would seem
best to deal with the rabbinic material in each area as it is
treated systematically below. However, it would be helpful
to quote and analyze a number of rabbinic statements which
reflect the general attitudes of the ancient rabbis toward
women, keeping in mind that the body of rabbis of course
did not present a homogeneous attitude toward women.

a)   Positive Evaluations of Women

In the rabbinic writings there are a number of positive evaluations of women. For example, "It was taught:
He who has no wife dwells without good, without help, without joy, without blessing, and without atonement. "[48] There
is a series of sayings gathered together in one place in the
Talmud, mostly concerning the sadness caused by the death,
or divorce, of one's wife: "Rabbi Alexandri said: The
world is darkened for him whose wife has died in his days
(i. e. , predeceased him).... Rabbi Jose ben Hanina said:
His steps grow short.... Rabbi Johanan also said: He
whose first wife has died, (is grieved as much) as if the
destruction of the Temple had taken place in his days....
Rabbi Samuel ben Nahman said: For him who divorces the
first wife, the very altar sheds tears. "[49]

In modern discussions of the status of women in rabbinic Judaism, lists of such positive rabbinic sayings about women will frequently be put forward to prove that women were very highly valued by the rabbis, or at least that this positive evaluation balanced, or even outweighed, the negative statements found in rabbinic literature. A judgment about whether the positive or negative attitudes of the ancient rabbis predominated can wait until the evidence on both sides has been presented and analyzed. But two things should be kept in mind in evaluating the positive statements. First, as with the Wisdom literature noted above,[50] almost all the positive things said about women by the rabbis are not about women as such, but rather about women as they are related to men, namely, as wives. In fact, at the same place in the Talmud as the above appreciative statements about the loss of one's wife it is also stated: "Rabbi Samuel ben Unya said in the name of Rab: A woman (before marriage) is a shapeless lump, and concludes a covenant only with him who transforms her (into) a (useful) vessel."[51] Secondly, although a good wife is highly valued and receives deep affection, this appreciation very frequently is expressed, as in the Wisdom literature,[52] in terms of what the wife does for the husband and family.

This attitude was expressed well by a modern rabbi writing on the subject of the Jewish woman: "Only the life of the woman contains even more renunciation. Her whole life is a self-denying devotion to the welfare of others, especially of her husband and children. The true woman is the performance of duty personified ... renunciation, sacrifice for the joy of her husband and children becomes her joy." On the next page is a further comment about the subordination of wives to their husbands: "This will-subordination of the wife to the husband is a necessary condition of the unity which man and wife should form together. The subordination cannot be the other way about, since the man ... has to carry forward the divine and human messages."[53]

This essay on Jewish women, written by Rabbi Samson Hirsch in German in the latter part of the nineteenth century and translated and published in English in the middle of the twentieth century, contains about as thorough a listing of the positive rabbinic statements about women as might be found,[54] and hence will serve as a convenient check-list for analysis here. Rabbi Hirsch claims "full equality of status" for women in Judaism and speaks of placing "the woman forthwith on a footing of equality with the man."[55] The last

portion of this rather lengthy essay is devoted to "The Jewish Woman in the Talmudic Tradition," and here the list of
rabbinic statements is brought forward.

In addition to the laudatory statements already mentioned, the ancient rabbinic literature also contains the following rabbinic teachings which are likewise in praise of
women, or rather, of wives and marriage. "Rabbi Eleazar
said:  Any man who has no wife is no proper man," that
is, as Rabbi Eliezer is recorded in the same place as having taught: "Anyone who does not engage in the propagation
of the race is as though he sheds blood." Also in the same
place Rabbi Hiyya taught about wives that, "It is sufficient
for us that they rear up our children and deliver us from
sin," i. e. , satisfy the male's sexual drive. "Our Rabbis
taught:  Concerning a man who loves his wife as himself,
who honors her more than himself...."[56]  "Rabbi Hama
ben Hanina stated:  As soon as a man takes a wife his sins
are stopped up," that is, his concupiscence is allayed. A
man was advised to "be quick in buying land, but deliberate
in taking a wife. Come down a step in choosing your
wife"; since the wife was to be in the subordinate position it
was thought important that she come from a lower social
position.  In the same place in the Talmud there is also the
appreciative saying: "Happy is the husband of a beautiful
wife; the number of his days shall be double," which is immediately followed by a warning against all other beautiful
women: "Turn away thy eyes from (thy neighbor's) charming
wife lest thou be caught in her net. Do not turn in to her
husband to mingle with him wine and strong drink; for,
through the form of a beautiful woman, many were destroyed
and a mighty host are all her slain."[57]

If a good wife was appreciated by the rabbis, a bad
wife was equally unappreciated: "Raba said:  (If one has a)
bad wife it is a meritorious act to divorce her." "Raba
further stated:  A bad wife ... (should be given) a rival at
her side"; that is, a second wife should be taken. "Raba
further stated:  A bad wife is as troublesome as a very
rainy day; for it is said, A continual dropping on a very
rainy day and a contentious woman are alike." "How bane-
ful is a bad wife with whom Gehenna is compared." "Behold I will bring evil upon them, which they shall not be
able to escape. Rabbi Nahuan said in the name of Rabbah
ben Abbuha:  This refers to a bad wife, the amount of whose
kethubah is large."[58]

In demonstrating the high estimation of women held
by the ancient rabbis, Rabbi Hirsch referred to the rabbinic
teaching about the beneficent or maleficent influence a wife
has on a husband: "It once happened that a pious man was
married to a pious woman, and they did not produce children. Said they, 'We are of no use to the Holy One, blessed
be He,' whereupon they arose and divorced each other. The
former went and married a wicked woman, and she made him
wicked, while the latter went and married a wicked man, and
made him righteous. This proves that all depends on the
woman."[59] However, the fact that this truly appreciative
story about a pious wife is immediately followed by a whole
series of rather deprecatory statements about women in general somewhat modifies the force of that story as evidence
of high appreciation of women by the rabbis as a group (although clearly individual rabbis at least at times expressed
themselves more positively about women):

> And why must a woman use perfume, while a man
> does not need perfume?... And why has a woman
> a shrill voice but not a man?... And why does a
> man go out bareheaded while a woman goes out
> with her head covered? She is like one who has
> done wrong and is ashamed of people; therefore
> she goes out with her head covered. Why do they
> (the women) walk in front of the corpse (at a
> funeral)? Because they brought death into the
> world, they therefore walk in front of the corpse....
> And why was the precept of menstruation given to
> her? Because she shed the blood of Adam (by
> causing death), therefore was the precept of men-
> struation given to her. And why was the precept
> of the 'dough' given to her? Because she cor-
> rupted Adam, who was the dough of the world,
> therefore was the precept of dough given to her.
> And why was the precept of the Sabbath lights
> given to her? Because she extinguished the soul
> of Adam, therefore was the precept of the Sabbath
> lights given to her. [60]

Similarly weakened, or at least put in an ambivalent
light as evidence concerning the rabbis as a group, are
several sets of rabbinic teachings quoted by Rabbi Hirsch:
"Rabbi Helbo said: One must always observe the honor due
to his wife, because blessings rest on a man's home only
on account of his wife," and "Thus did Raba say to the
townspeople of Mahuza, Honor your wives, that ye may be

enriched," and again, "Rab said:  One should always be
heedful of wronging his wife, for since her tears are frequent she is quickly hurt. "61   These are all truly sensitive
sentiments, but in the same place the same "Rab also said:
He who follows his wife's counsel will descend into Gehenna. "
At this the Talmud adds the part which Rabbi Hirsch only
partially quoted as proof of the rabbis' high estimation of
women:  "Rabbi Papa objected to Abaye:  But people say,
If your wife is short, bend down and hear her whisper!"
He did not include the following resolution of what the rabbis
saw as a contradiction between the teachings of Rab and Papa
just quoted:  "There is no difficulty:  the one refers to general matters; the other to household affairs.   Another version:  the one refers to religious matters, the other to
secular questions. "62   Apparently the translator of the English Soncino edition was somewhat embarrassed by this
teaching for he noted:  "A man should certainly consult his
wife on the latter, but not on the former,--not a disparage-
ment of woman; her activities lying mainly in the home,"
which means that rabbinic "high estimation of women" was
here limited to a valuing of women as housekeepers.

        The noble statement:  "Who is wealthy?...   He who
has a wife comely in deeds,"63 takes on a somewhat in-
timidating quality when it is realized that it was made by
Rabbi Akiba, who allegedly allowed his wife to spend twenty-
four years in living widowhood while he studied Torah, who
was "the founder of the peculiar institution of married
'monasticism'....   After marriage they would devote themselves completely to their studies while their wives supported them"64 (not unlike what happens in the Mea Shearim
section of Jerusalem today), and who also taught that a man
may divorce his wife merely on the grounds that "he finds
another woman more beautiful than she is. "65

        It also says in the Talmud:  "The Holy One ... en-
dowed the woman with more understanding than the man. "66
However, since this statement comes in the midst of a discussion about the age at which vows can be made and is
used as an argument that girls can make vows a year earlier
than boys because they mature sooner, its intended meaning
seems to be limited to this particular case.   This is clearly
confirmed in an early midrash where the very same discussion is taken up and carried further as follows:  "Some reverse it, because a woman generally stays home, whereas
a man goes out into the streets and learns understanding
from people. "67

The evidence presented by Rabbi Hirsch from the early rabbinic writing, Sifra commentary on Leviticus 26:13, is at best of doubtful value.  He writes:  "Like the men, so the women are through the deliverance and election of Israel called to the highest spiritual and moral elevation of which mankind is capable (Sifra on Leviticus 26:13)."[68] The commentary referred to reads:  "'And I make you to walk tall.'  Rabbi Schimon says:  two hundred cubits.  Rabbi Jehuda says:  one hundred cubits, as Adam, the first.   I have only men.  Whence women?  Because it says:  'our daughters as corner columns, hewn according to the pattern of the Temple.'  (Ps. 144, 12)  And how high is the temple pattern?  One hundred cubits."[69]  This quotation would not seem to indicate a "high" estimate of women by the rabbis-- at least not in the usual sense.

Rabbi Hirsch also notes that the Talmud says that women are promised greater bliss--after death--but he does not note what it then says about how women are to merit this bliss.  The following first sentence Rabbi Hirsch refers to; the rest he does not:  "(Our Rabbis taught):  Greater is the promise made by the Holy One, blessed be He, to the women than to the men; for it says, 'Rise up, ye women that are at ease; ye confident daughters, give ear unto my speech.' Rab said to Rabbi Hiyya:  Whereby do women earn merit? By making their children go to the synagogue to learn Scripture and their husbands to the Beth Hamidrash to learn Mishnah, and waiting for their husbands till they return from the Beth Hamidrash."[70]  The latter half of this pas- sage would seem to at least dilute somewhat the strength of the former half as evidence of the rabbis' high estimation of women.

Also brought forth as evidence is the talmudic state- ment[71] that "only if the husband has preserved his own fidelity to his wife and has allowed himself no excesses does the water test the fidelity of his wife."[72]  According to this rabbinic teaching, if the husband has been faithful, the wife will either miscarry as a result of the ordeal if she is guilty of adultery, or not miscarry if she is not guilty; whereas, if the husband has not been faithful, she would pre- sumably not miscarry in either case.  But no matter what, the woman must go through the humiliating ordeal merely on the demand of her husband; that is, she must be brought before the priest in the temple, in public, have her head dress and hair disheveled and her cloths ripped off her to the waist, and be forced to drink water mixed with dirt from

the floor.  In no case does the husband suffer any disabilities. [73]  The need of the husband to be faithful so as to
make his wife's ordeal effective on the one side, and the
obligation of a wife suspected even by a groundlessly jealous
husband to go through the ordeal on the other would not
seem to bespeak an especially high estimation of womanhood
by the rabbis.

Rabbi Hirsch likewise maintained that "the Sages expect from the husband the most tender consideration and the
most loving and respectful treatment for his wife,"[74] and
offered as one piece of evidence of this the statement that
"if a man goads his wife to insult him by refusing her ornaments and finery, he becomes poor (Shabbath 62b)."  The
statement referred to is as follows:  "Three things bring
man to poverty, viz., urinating in front of one's bed naked,
treating the washing of the hands with disrespect, and being
cursed by one's wife in his presence. . . .  Raba said (that
is when she curses him) on account of her adornments.  But
that is only when he has the means but does not provide
them."  Hirsch further added as proof that, "even if a man
has to deny his wife something or reprove her, his right
hand should draw her near him while his left hand repels
(Sota 47a)."[75]  The pertinent quotation is:  "It has been
taught:  Rabbi Simeon ben Eleazar says:  Also human nature
should a child and woman thrust aside with the left hand and
draw near with the right hand."  The English Sorcino edition
notes:  "One must not be too severe in chiding a child or
reproving a wife lest they be driven to despair."  As still
further evidence Rabbi Hirsch stated that "reminders of duty
should also be given by the husband softly and gently
(bGitten 6b)."  The talmud passage reads:  "Rabbi Hisda
said:  A man should never terrorize his household . . . the
three things which a man has to say to his household just
before Sabbath commences . . . should be said by him gently,
so that they should obey him readily."  Since these statements are all very much like advice to treat servants well
so that they will obey properly, they are not very effective
testimony of the high value the rabbis placed on women.

Here Hirsch also added the quotation from bB. M.  59a
about bending down to consult one's wife if she is short, already discussed above, and the differing treatment of wives
by various types of men, including those who lock them up
whenever they leave the house, discussed below (see chapter
V--4, "Women Appearing in Public"),[76] and also the reference to the fidelity of the husband and the trial by ordeal

for his wife. He then wrote: "Nowhere do we meet among Jews such a seclusion and isolation of women as is usually assumed on the analogy of oriental custom," which is a less than accurate statement if one simply recalls, as one example, Philo's description of the harem-like existence of Jewish women in first century C. E. Alexandria (see chapter V--4, "Women Appearing in Public," for a detailed discussion of the seclusion of Jewish women). As still further evidence of the "most tender consideration and the most loving and respectful treatment" of the wife by the husband, Rabbi Hirsch wrote: "If women are not allowed to move about much in public, this is from fear of misbehaviour not on their part but on the part of the men (Genesis Rabbah 8, 12)."[77] The teaching alluded to is as follows: "'Wekibshah' (and subdue her) is written: the man must master his wife, that she go not out into the market place, for every woman who goes out into the market place will eventually come to grief." This would appear to be a rather domineering "most tender consideration." Moreover, women were often seen as lustful, grasping creatures of sex by many of the Pharisees and other writers of apocryphal and pseudepigraphal literature of the first century before the Common Era and by Philo, as already discussed above.

From these quotations from Rabbi Hirsch and elsewhere it can be concluded that there are a number of ancient rabbinic statements which are appreciative of women, but that they are almost inevitably about women as wives rather than as individual persons; and not a few of the frequently quoted statements do not reflect as much appreciation of women, i. e., wives, as they are often claimed to.

b)  Negative Evaluations of Women

The following is a brief list of rabbinical sayings about women which do not particularly fit into the various categories of Jewish life that will be analyzed below; they give some indication of the widespread negative, and even, misogynist, attitude toward women among the rabbis.

The great rabbi of the first century before the Common Era, Hillel, who had a reputation of generosity and openness, said, "Many women, much witchcraft."[78] In the first century C. E. Rabbi Joshua said: "A woman would rather have a single measure (of food) with wantonness than nine measures with continence."[79] The notion that women

by nature tend toward nymphomania was, of course, already
familiar from the Wisdom and pseudepigraphical literature. [80]
It was continued by the rabbis in the following teaching:
"One glass is good for a woman; two are a disgrace; with
three she opens her mouth (in lewdness); with four she soli-
cits in complete abandon even an ass on the street."[81]

The in-a-way opposite notion, that woman is an irre-
sistible sexual temptation for man, was also taught, in
terms that were not only very slightly veiled sexual symbols
--reminiscent of the Wisdom literature--but were also brim-
ming with hatred of women: a woman is "a pitcher full of
filth with its mouth full of blood, yet all run after her."[82]
Around 150 C. E. Rabbi Simon ben Jochai taught: "The
most virtuous of women is a witch."[83]  He also taught that,
"Women are light-headed,"[84] a teaching reiterated by the
school of Elias. [85]  Also doubly taught and recorded in this
early period is this teaching: "The world cannot exist without male and female children.  It is well for those whose
children are male, but ill for those who are female."[86]  A
similar thought was expressed by Rabbi Simon ben Jochai:
"At the birth of a boy all are joyful ... at the birth of a
girl all are sorrowful."[87]  In the same place like thoughts
of a rabbi from the following century, i. e. , toward the end
of the third century, are also recorded: "Rabbi Jicchaq
said that Rabbi Ammi said:  When a boy comes into the
world, peace comes into the world.... When a girl comes,
nothing comes."  A list of "characteristically female" vices
was also provided, and added to by various rabbis: "The
Rabbis said:  Women are said to possess four traits:  they
are greedy, eavesdroppers, slothful and envious.  Greedy,
as it says ... Rabbi Judah ben Nahman[88] said:  she is also
a scratcher and talkative ... Rabbi Levi[89] said:  She is
also prone to steal and is a gadabout."[90]  This last teaching is also doubly taught. [91]

Perhaps the most widely known rabbinic saying from
this early, mishnaic period which reflects the inferior position of women starkly is the three-fold daily prayer, still
found in many Jewish prayer books: "Praised be God that
he has not created me a gentile!  Praised be God that he
has not created me a woman!  Praised be God that he has
not created me an ignoramus!  Praised that he has not created me a gentile: 'For all gentiles are as nothing before
him,' Isaiah 40:17.  Praised that he has not created me a
woman because the woman is not obliged to fulfill the commandments.  Praised that he has not created me an ignoramus for the ignorant man does not avoid sin."[92]

Because of the blunt attitude of male superiority expressed in this prayer one might be somewhat tempted to discount it as a single hyperbolic statement of an obscure rabbi. Such is not the case. No less than three separate direct quotations of this prayer occur in three of the most ancient rabbinic collections and at least one paraphrase in another later collection, and Paul paraphrases it in his Letter to the Galatians. The ancient collections are the Tosephta--a collection of Tannaitic teaching, i. e. , from rabbis from two hundred before the Common Era to two hundred afterwards; the Jerusalem or Palestinian Talmud; and the Babylonian Talmud. [93] In the first two the order is different--gentile, woman, ignoramus in the Tosephta; and gentile, ignoramus, woman in the Palestinian Talmud--but the wording is basically the same, including the three bases for the prayer. The Babylonian Talmud keeps the order of the Tosephta, but substitutes "slave" for "ignoramus," and also does not repeat the three "justifications" for the prayer.

The somewhat later paraphrase stems from a fourth century rabbi: "I call on heaven and earth as witness: whether Jew or non-Jew, whether man or woman, whether slave or slave woman--each one has according to his actions the holy spirit within him. "[94] The quotation has no context in the text and is hence difficult to interpret completely, but it is apparently based on the earlier formulated prayer.

Paul in his Letter to the Galatians forms his statement in verse 28 of chapter 3 on this prayer: "There is neither Jew nor Greek, there is neither slave nor free, there is neither male nor female; for you are all one in Christ Jesus. " At that time the rabbinic teaching was not yet written down, or at least not in any codified, authoritative fashion; hence there is some variation from each of the later edited forms. In Paul's letter, Greek is used rather than gentile in the contrast with Jew; slave is used in contrast to free, paralleling the text of the Babylonian Talmud; the order he uses--gentile, slave, woman--is the same as that which appears in both the Tosephta and the Palestinian Talmud. [95]

The fact this statement is not simply a teaching, but rather a prayer, increases its significance considerably. Moreover, it was not recommended as a once-a-year or occasional prayer, but rather as a daily prayer--and it has been used by some as such ever since. [96] In the Tosephta Rabbi Judah recommended that this prayer be said daily.

In the Babylonian Talmud the prayer is attributed to Rabbi
Judah's contemporary, Rabbi Meir, who lived in the first
part of the second century C. E. and claimed he faithfully
passed on what he learned from Rabbi Akiba.

There are many more rabbinic statements about wom-
en which reflect a negative, if not a misogynist, attitude on
the part of many rabbis toward women; but they will be
dealt with, as indicated, within the context of the systematic
analysis of the life of Jewish women.  However, on the
basis of the evidence of both the positive and negative rabbinic statements about women thus far analyzed, and prolep-
tically considering the mass of essentially negative evidence
to be discussed below, it would be correct to conclude that
quantitatively and qualitatively the negative attitude vastly
outweighs the positive.  It can be said, therefore, that the
attitude of the ancient rabbis toward women was a continuation of the negative attitude toward women that evolved from
the return from the Exile through the later Wisdom, apocryphal, and pseudepigraphical literature. [97]  In fact, it was in
a way an intensification of it, in that the rabbis, through
their great influence on the masses of Judaism, projected
it most forcefully into the everyday life of the observant
Jew, for example, by the promotion of the three-fold
prayer.

As C. G. Montefiore summed up the matter:

> The Rabbinic literature is written by men and for
> men.  The difference in the relations of men and
> women to each other makes a constant difference
> between the Rabbis and ourselves.  It is always
> cropping up.  Modern apologists tend to ignore or
> evade it.  They quote a few sentences such as
> 'Who is rich?  He who has a good wife'; or they
> tell of a few exceptional women such as Beruria.
> It is quite true that wife and mother played a
> very important part in Rabbinic life; it is true the
> Rabbis were almost always monogamists; it is
> true that they honoured their mothers profoundly,
> and usually honoured and cared for their wives.
> But that is only one side of the story.  'Women,
> children and slaves': that familiar and frequent
> collocation means and reveals a great deal.  Wom-
> en were, on the whole, regarded as inferior to
> men in mind, in function and status. [98]

CHAPTER IV

WOMEN IN RELATION TO CULT AND TORAH

## 1. WOMEN FULFILLING TORAH

The heart of Judaism is Torah, the Law, and the differing status of men and women is reflected here right at the heart, even quite explicitly. There are at least two places in the Mishnah which take up the different standings and obligations men and women have before the Law. The question is asked, "Wherein does a man differ from a woman?" and eight responses are given, of which three are of more interest than the others for they indicate both the greater power of the father compared to the mother and the inferior status of the daughter vis-à-vis the son (only the daughter can be sold by the father, not the son; only the daughter can be betrothed without her consent--if done before she is twelve and a half years old): "The man may place his son under the nazirite vow, but the woman may not impose the nazirite vow upon her son ... the man may sell his daughter, but the woman may not sell her daughter; the man may betroth his daughter, but the woman may not betroth her daughter."[1]

In a second place distinctions are made between positive and negative ordinances, and between those which are bound up with a stated time and those which are not. In effect, women are supposedly obliged to all ordinances other than time-bound, positive ones: "All positive ordinances that are bound up with a stated time are incumbent upon men but women are exempted, but all positive ordinances which are not bound up with a stated time are incumbent upon both men and women; and all negative commandments ... must be observed by men and women alike," except for three specific ritual laws, like trimming a beard.[2] Either the Mishnah elsewhere or the Talmud spelled out specifically to some extent which time-bound religious obligations women were freed from: women did not have to live in the "sukka," or temporary dwelling (the essential action for the week-long feast of Succoth)[3] or carry the festival bouquet;

be present at the sounding of the ram's horn, the shofar,
on the New Year's feast, or put on the cicith or tephillin;[4]
read the Book of Esther on the feast of Purim,[5] or recite
each morning and evening the great prayer of Judaism, the
Shema: "Hear, O Israel, the Lord is our God, the Lord
is One" (Dt. 6:7). [6]  It is difficult to see how in most of
these instances the duties of a housewife or daughter would
be any more inhibiting than those of a householder or son:
since everyone, woman or man, has to get up and go to
bed ("when you lie down and when you rise up"--Dt. 6:8),
the recitation of the Shema at those times would cause no
problem; nor should the living in the sukka, since the men's
meals would have to be served in there anyhow; and the at-
tendance at one New Year's feast per year should cause no
more difficulty for women than for men.

One midrash stated that the reason women--and
slaves and children--were not obliged to fulfill all the Law
was: "Because she has a single heart (for her husband);
likewise, the heart of the slave is directed to his master....
Women and slaves still have a human master over them and
the service of him makes such a claim on their heart that
the time and energy for the service of God is lacking.
Therefore, is a lesser claim in regard to the fulfillment of
commandments made on women and slaves than on men and
freeman. "[7]

Much subsequent explanation, however, including that
of most contemporary Jewish commentators, points out that
the reason for the differing obligations to fulfill the Law was
that women would at times find it impossible to fulfill the
time-bound commandments because of their household obligations and limitations connected with their sex, i. e. , menstruation, pregnancy, nursing, etc. [8]  But, in the same
paragraph of the Mishnah this rule is contradicted when
rules which are not time-bound are said not to oblige wom-
en: "All obligations which devolve upon a father concerning
his son must be observed by men but women are exempt,
and all obligations which devolve upon a son regarding his
father are incumbent on both men and women. "[9]   The Babylonian Talmud observes that these obligations of the father
include:  circumcision, redemption of first born son, teaching Torah, teaching an occupation, marriage, swimming--
and except for circumcision, none of these tasks were bound
to a specific time. [10]   That means that women, mothers,
had no obligation to perform these tasks for their sons; in
fact, in all these instances women also had either no

obligation or, in some instances, no possibility to fulfill these tasks for themselves, i.e., no obligation to learn a trade, no absolute obligation (as a man has) to marriage, or no possibility for circumcision or redemption.

The Talmud itself made a somewhat similar observation: "Women are exempt from the study of Torah, the obligation of producing progeny, and from the redemption of the (firstborn) son, although these are not commands which are bound to a particular time."[11] In the same place the Talmud notes three additional feasts (including Passover) which are connected with a specific time, but which women are nevertheless obliged to observe. Apparently the oft-offered rationale of giving precedence to women's physical weakness and her household duties did not apply here, but only in certain select cases. In such a situation one feels the need to search for a deeper reason behind the one so ambiguously applied:

> Learning was seen as the key to survival--obviously the only way Jews could remain Jews in exile was by learning what it meant to be a Jew and passing this knowledge on from generation to generation. This learning role, however, was open only to men. Women were also excluded from religious or communal activity that was associated with learning or the communal observance of rituals. There were certain mitzvot from which women were exempted. In essence, all the important ways in which Judaism defined what it meant to be a Jew were (and still are) either partially or completely closed to women.

> There are several reasons for this. First, there is always a division of labor in patriarchy: men get the status roles and women get the role of doing everything that men don't want to do, and anything else that enables men to do what they want to do. In addition, the Jews were in exile, and involved in a struggle for survival. In the division of labor, the people who were considered most capable got the most important role. Men, seen (by men) as being most capable of intellectual labor, allocated that role to themselves. Men were also more actively involved in confronting daily overt oppression and hostility as they went out into the world to earn a living. They needed

some sort of compensation to offset their being
treated as inferiors.   They had to have someone
to whom they were superior.   Women had a definite role to play. [12]

The question of obligation concerning meal prayers
is a good example of rabbinic legal distinctions which perhaps obligate women in some instances, perhaps not in others, and forbid them in still others.   Women (along with
slaves and children again) are not exempt from saying the
prayers after meals, [13] but it is disputed whether or not
they can say it for someone else who for some reason cannot say it himself.   Some say women, along with children
and slaves, may, [14] but the Talmud says:   "A curse light
on the man whose wife or children have to say grace for
him"; [15] and with regard to a different prayer reference,
the Talmud repeated the curse:   "May a curse come upon
that man whose wife and (minor) sons have to recite the
benediction for him." [16]   Furthermore, the ancient Mishnah
stated that, "Women or slaves or minors may not be included (to make up the number needed) for the recitation of
Common Grace." [17]   And still further, women (and children
and slaves) may not even extend the ceremonial, and offi-
cially obliged, invitation to say grace (when three or more
are together at meal), the zimmun; in this connection, "a
hundred women are no better than two men." [18]   In this connection a baby boy was considered, at least by some talmudic
rabbis, as more significant than a grown woman, for the
Talmud stated:   "An infant in the cradle may be counted for
the zimmun, but women, of course, could not." [19]

It should also be noted here that there are three commands directed specifically at women, the disregarding of
which, according to the Mishnah, has dire results:   "For
three transgressions do women die in childbirth:   for heedlessness of the laws concerning their menstruation, [20] the
Dough-offering (Hallah), and the lighting of the (Sabbath)
lamp." [21]   The reasons given for these three commands--in
no less than four ancient sources [22]--all lead back to the
charge that Eve caused the death of Adam:

Concerning menstruation:   The first man was the
blood and life of the world ... and Eve was the
cause of his death; therefore has she been given
the menstruation precept.   The same is true concerning Hallah (leaven); Adam was the pure Hallah
for the world....   And Eve was the cause of his

> death; therefore has she been given the Hallah
> precept. And concerning the lighting of the (Sab-
> bath) lamp. Adam was the light of the world....
> And Eve was the cause of his death; therefore
> has she been given the precept about lighting the
> (Sabbath) lamp. Rabbi Jose (early second cen-
> tury) said: there are three causes of death and
> they were transmitted to women, namely, the
> menstruation precept, the Hallah precept, and
> the precept about lighting the (Sabbath) lamp. 23

Though the precept concerning menstruation could be seen
as degrading for women, and the precept concerning Hallah
might be seen as bothersome, the lighting of the Sabbath
lamp at the Friday evening home service would normally be
viewed as an honor; hence, it is somewhat of a surprise to
learn that the ancient rabbinic reason for it is that it is a
punishment for Eve's having caused Adam's death. 24

It might at first blush seem that this double-standard
in men's and women's obligations toward fulfilling the Law
was not really a restricting thing for the women, but rather
a lightening of a burden. However, one result was that
when a woman performed an act that she was exempt from,
it had a lesser value than the same act performed by a man,
who was obliged to perform it. The Talmud makes this
point quite baldly; it discusses, and rejects, the opinion that
a heathen would not receive any merit for his good actions--
that is, for fulfilling the Torah25--but goes on to make the
point that the performance of a good act which is not obligatory has less merit than if it is obligatory:

> Said Mar the son of Rabina: The release from
> those commands only means that even if they ob-
> served them they would not be rewarded. But
> why should they not? ... What is meant, then, is
> that they are rewarded not as greatly as one who
> does a thing which he is bidden to do, but as one
> who does a thing unbidden. For, Rabbi Hananina
> said: He who is commanded and does, stands
> higher than he who is not commanded and does. 26

Given the fact that fulfillment of the Law had more and
more become the way par excellence of the righteous Jewish
life from the time of Ezra on, such a result was natural--
the threefold benediction concerning women expressed this
vividly.

The double-standard Torah obligation often had even greater effect: with the passage of time many non-obligations for women became outright restrictions.  One modern Jewish scholar makes the point bluntly: "A logical consequence of female exemption from the time-geared features of the liturgical round is the ineligibility of women to take an active role in them, for example, as leaders in prayer for congregations including men."[27]  In referring to the exercising of ministerial functions by Lily Montagu in a Liberal Synagogue in England (this century), the same author chides his countrymen: "The appointment was an exceptional one and probably not often, if indeed ever, paralleled within Reform Judaism even in its most radical manifestations. In so far as it was possible at all, it reflects the weakness of the sense of history within Liberal Judaism and a consequent tendency towards a loss of organic cohesion with the main stream of Jewish life."[28]

## 2.   SEGREGATION IN TEMPLE AND SYNAGOGUE

One clear development of an exemption into a prohibition can be seen in the physical separation of men and women that prevailed in the Temple of Herod (started in 19 B. C. E.), but which did not exist in the earlier temples. In Herod's Temple, by far the most grand and imposing of Jewish temples, women were permitted to enter only the first court, the "court of heathens," and the court inside that, the "women's court."  The women's court was five steps above that of the heathens, but also fifteen steps below that of Jewish men, the "Israelite's court," which women were not permitted to enter. [29]  The Mishnah even described the women's court as being enclosed by a gallery: "Beforetime (the Court of the Women) was free of buildings, and (afterwards) they surrounded it with a gallery so that the women should observe from above and the men from below and that they should not mingle together."[30]  Moreover, the women were allowed to enter their own court only by certain gates,[31] and indeed this, as well as the entrance to the court of the heathens, was denied to them if they were within seven days of the end of their menstruation, or forty days of the birth of a boy, or eighty days of the birth of a girl. [32]  (It should be remembered, of course, that this separation of men and women was not only part of a broader set of distinctions between men and women, but a part also of another pattern of distinctions, for "separation was the principle upon which Temple worship was founded;

it emphasized the distinction between man and God, Jew
and Gentile, men and women, priests and people. These
various separations were symbolized by the different courts
of the Temple"[33]--beyond the Israelites' court was the
Priests' court, and beyond that the Holy Place and the Holy
of Holies).

Each Jewish community in Palestine and throughout
the Diaspora usually had at least one synagogue, an institution whose origins go back to the time of Ezra, and possibly to the Exile. As a building, the synagogue was a meet-
ing place for prayer and for the study of the Law; at least
by the time of the Roman emperor Augustus the synagogues
tended to have two separate areas: the "sabbateion," for
worship services, and the "andron," for lectures on and
discussion of the Law by the scribes and their students.
The latter room, as the name makes clear, was exclusively
for males. [34] But even in the prayer hall the sexes were
separated,[35] either by some sort of barrier or grillwork[36]
or moderately high wall, as with the Therapeutae discussed
above, or in a separate adjoining room, as in the synagogue
of Delos (from the first century B. C. E.), or, later, in a
gallery around the two sides and the rear, complete with a
separate entrance, as can be seen from the oldest extant
ruins in Palestine, those at Capernaum. The latter stem
from the third century C. E.; presumably all earlier synagogues were destroyed by the Romans after the 70 C. E. and
135 C. E. rebellions.

For a rather thorough discussion and documentation
of the existence of a separate women's section in ancient
synagogues see the work of Eliezer L. Sukenik. [37] Among
other things, he says:

> The ancient literature nowhere mentions a specific
> regulation to the effect that the men and women
> must be kept separate at public worship; still less
> is it prescribed that the women's section shall be
> built in the form of a gallery. That the sexes
> were in fact kept apart in synagogues, however,
> is already attested by Philo (apud Eusebius,
> Praep. Evang. 8:12), the custom having probably
> been taken over by the synagogue from the Jeru-
> salem Sanctuary.... There is therefore every
> reason to suppose that the galleries of which re-
> mains have been found in several of the ancient
> synagogues of Palestine served, as in modern

> synagogues, as a women's section.... The stair-
> cases leading up to the gallery are always situated
> outside the basilica proper, leaning against either
> the outer or inner walls of one of the annexed
> chambers.

Sukenik then notes that the Palestinian Talmud (fourth century C. E.) described a scene in 116 C. E. when Trajan destroyed the famous Diplostoon synagogue in Alexandria which
proved that the women occupied the gallery above the men;
after having killed the men Trajan offered mercy to the
women at the price of their honor--they replied: "Do to
those above as you have done to those below. "[38]

In the same place[39] there appears the following even
more explicit and detailed rabbinic statement, probably about
the temple primarily, but also doubtless influencing synagogue customs:

> In what does the 'disposition of a large display at
> a feast' consist? In a separation between the
> men's area and the gallery reserved for women.
> That is therefore something which has been taught
> elsewhere. Originally the court had been undi-
> vided: then a balcony was erected; the women
> viewed the ceremony from above and the men re-
> mained below so that there was no mixing of the
> sexes. That virtuous act was taught in the words
> of the Law, saying (Zechariah 12:12): The coun-
> try will be in mourning, each family separate,
> etc. , the women apart. There are two different
> ways of explaining this verse. According to the
> one the prophet deplores the future death of the
> messiah; according to the other the matter con-
> cerns the destruction of the evil inclination (from
> henceforth overcome). The former justifies itself
> thus: if during the mourning the Law prescribes
> the separation of the men and the women, how
> much more therefore would this be so at a mo-
> ment of rejoicing. Those who take the other way
> justify it as follows: if for those who no longer
> have the evil inclination the men must be separ-
> ated from the women, how much more is that sep-
> aration necessary for those who have not over-
> come the evil inclination at all.

Slightly later than the time of the codification of the

Palestinian Talmud, the fact that Miriam took out the wom-
en to sing the Song (of the Sea) separately was taken as the
authority for the segregation of the sexes in prayer in the
synagogue. [40]

A somewhat similar picture is offered by the archae-
ological data. Although the remains of the ancient basilical
synagogues of Galilee, with a distinctive Hellenistic stamp,
show unmistakable indications of the existence of galleries,
which probably were the place assigned women, no traces
of a women's gallery have been found in the well-preserved
remains of the non-basilical, more oriental synagogue of
Dura-Europos in Hellenized Mesopotamia. Scholars differ
in interpreting these facts. According to one school, the
silence of earlier rabbinic sources and the absence of a
women's gallery in Dura reflect an earlier, more liberal
attitude toward women, which allowed them to sit in the
main hall, though in a special part, together with the men.
The other school argues that the silence of earlier rabbinic
authorities implies that in those circles no provisions were
made at all for women in the synagogue, because they were
excluded from active participation in public worship. For
a few special occasions, in which women might have access
to the synagogue, a temporary, removable screen would
have been sufficient.

Isaiah Sonne maintains that:

> Only the latter interpretation seems to fit the evi-
> dence that provisions for separation of sexes ap-
> pear mainly in synagogues with a Hellenistic
> tinge.... Another consideration should be borne
> in mind. It is probable that the basilical type of
> synagogue, which adopted architectural features
> of the temple, followed the example of the 'wom-
> an's hall' in separating the sexes--i.e., by erect-
> ing galleries. The communities with a non-basili-
> cal type of synagogue might have taken stricter
> measures of separation, confining the women to a
> separate, adjoining room, as seems to have been
> the case in the earlier building of the Dura-Euro-
> pos synagogue. [41]

3. NO MEN, NO MINYAN

Given the physical separation of women in the synagogue, it is not surprising that they were also "precluded

onstituting units of the necessary quorum of ten
'orm a congregation to worship communally,
irteen being likewise precluded (and also, in
...aves). "[42]

Basically what Loewe says is accurate; already in
the Mishnah it is clearly indicated that ten men constitute
a minyan, [43] but it is not totally precise to say that boys
under thirteen or slaves were never counted toward a minyan:  the Encyclopaedia Judaica article on Minyan states
that "the accepted custom in emergency cases is nine adults
and a boy," and gives rabbinic references.  Already in the
Babylonian Talmud it was noted that an infant boy "can be
counted to make up ten," and that "nine and a slave may be
joined (to make up ten). "[44]  In a reference to the Mishnah
and Talmud references, Meg. 1, 3 and bMeg. 5a, the above
Encyclopaedia Judaica article notes:  "In talmudic times a
community was regarded as a 'city' if there were at least
'ten idle men ... who could come to each synagogue service
to make up the minyan ... in traditional congregations, especially in Eastern Europe, when it was customary to pay
a few old or idle men to be present twice a day at the services.  These people were called 'minyan men. '  In the
Reform ritual women are counted in the minimum quorum
of ten persons to constitute a public prayer service since
they have full religious equality with men. "  Since late 1973
counting women toward a minyan is to be allowed in Conservative American synagogues, but this has not been done
in Orthodox synagogues.

4.   WOMEN READING TORAH

It is also not surprising to read in the ancient
Tosephta:  "Everyone is reckoned among the seven persons
(who are called forward to read from the Torah in the Sabbath synagogue service), even a child and even a woman. [45]
But a woman is not to come forward to publicly read (from
the Torah). "[46]  A talmudic quotation of the same teaching
added, "out of respect for the community. "[47]  I. Elbogen[48]
argues that women were originally called to Torah, but then
were later forbidden in practice from carrying out the reading; Billerbeck, [49] on the other hand, insists that women
were called to the Torah merely in appearance in order
honor them, but in keeping with the general custom they always had to forego actually carrying out the reading.

A similar explanation is often given to the somewhat anomalous facts that a three-year old child was once named the president of the synagogue in Venosa, and the same happened to a woman in Smyrna and once in Myndos, and that a woman proselyte was called the mother of two synagogues. These events took place in the Diaspora where foreign pressures were strong and it was sometimes important to adapt to the Hellenist environment (with its women's liberation movement) at least in language; hence, these honorary titles, with no real powers, were handed out to important personages--including patronesses. [50]

Thus, at the beginning of the Common Era, and subsequently, women were not only not individually active participants in the synagogue services; they could also often not be spectators--only listeners, who might also join in the congregationally recited prayers.

## 5.  WOMEN STUDYING TORAH

In the time after the destruction of the temple (70 C.E.) there is no question but that the central element in Jewish life was the study of Torah, the Law, oral and written.  But even in the immediately preceding centuries the study of the Law was at least a close second to temple worship.  Indeed, with the ever-increasing significance of the scribes after the return from the Exile in the sixth century B.C.E., and especially with the appearance of the Pharisees in the second century B.C.E., the study of the Law became as important as temple worship, and at times more important, as with the Essenes and some Pharisees, like the author of the Book of Jubilees (second century B.C.E.). Given, then, the extraordinary prominence in Jewish life held by the study of the Law,[51] it is important to see what relationship women had to it.

The fact is that Jewish women of ancient rabbinic days, i.e., the formative centuries just before and after the beginning of the Common Era, did not study Torah, the Law. [52]  There was no outright command forbidding women to study Torah, but there were statements that came very close to it, and in fact went considerably beyond a simple negative command.  In the first century C.E., Rabbi Eliezer, who claimed he taught only what he learned from his teachers, said: "If any man teach his daughter Torah it is as though he taught her lechery."[53]

The opposing opinion of a contemporary scholar, Ben
Azzai, was also given in the same place, but his opinion
was clearly neither the traditional nor the accepted one.
Ben Azzai, though a widely reputed scholar, was not an ordained rabbi and hence his opinion did not carry as much
weight as an Eliezer, who was an ordained rabbi and who
hence belonged to the "chain of tradition." Moreover, Ben
Azzai wanted to teach daughters enough Torah merely so
that they would know that if they had performed some meritorious deeds, this would result in postponing the deadly effects of the drinking the "Waters of Bitterness" by wives
suspected of adultery: "Hardly has she finished drinking
before her face turns yellow and her eyes bulge and her
veins swell, and they say 'Take her away! take her away!
that the temple court not be made unclean!' But if she had
any merit this holds her punishment in suspense ... Hence
Ben Azzai says...." The commentary of the Babylonian
Talmud completely ignored Ben Azzai's opinion and provided
a reason for Eliezer's position, adding the tiny suggestion
that instead of saying that the teaching of Torah to women
actually taught them lechery, Eliezer, rather, had taught
that it was as though she were taught lechery.[54] The Palestinian Talmud, in the discussion of this portion of the Mishnah, provided an additional story about Rabbi Eliezer that
bore on the same subject--Eliezer said: "The wisdom of
women is only in her distaff.... May the words of the
Torah be burned rather than be given to women!"[55] These
are amazingly strong words for one whose entire life was
devoted to the preservation and study of the Torah.

Hans Kosmala[56] has some very enlightening remarks
on the passage; he noted that Ben Azzai, as we know from
his other statements, made more generous judgments than
his contemporaries. He often maintained a view which was
totally contrary to the interpretation and stand handed down.
Moreover, he was not an ordained rabbi, but only a student
of wisdom. Even though because of his personality he stood
in high esteem, he did not exercise an independent teaching
office. Probably he took part in halachic discussions, but
he did not possess the same authority in decisions, as, for
example, Rabbi Eliezer. From this debate we can conclude
that Ben Azzai's statement was a counter-move against an
ancient custom that had become law. This counter-move
was repulsed. The dictum of R. Eliezer was sustained
throughout the following period. In his debate over the matter, Kosmala concluded:

Farbstein knows all this perfectly well, but apologetical grounds prevented him from presenting us with the true state of affairs. With his (partial) Talmud citation he makes us believe that the opinions on the matter were in fact fundamentally divided. In reality, however, only once in a special situation and in a very special connection was a contrary voice raised, and it sank on the same day in the broad stream of legal tradition. The Torah remained an affair of men.

Another talmudic passage has pertinence here. When commenting on the statement in the Mishnah that if an adulteress had any merit the effectiveness of the test waters would be postponed, the Talmud asked what kind of merit could bring about the postponement of the effects for three years: "'And another for three years, etc.' What sort of merit? If I answer merit of (studying) Torah, she is (in the category) of one who is not commanded and fulfils![57] Rather must it be merit of (performing) a commandment.... Rabina said: It is certainly merit of (the study of) Torah (which causes the water to suspend its effect); and when you argue that she is in the category of one who is not commanded and fulfils, (it can be answered) granted that women are not so commanded, still when they have their sons taught Scripture and Mishnah and wait for their husbands until they return from the Schools, should they not share (the merit) with them?"[58] It is clear from this teaching that the rabbis did not expect any women to be studying Torah; the only connection with the study of Torah that women could be expected to have was to send their <u>sons</u> and husbands off to study and to wait for them.

Although it was not absolutely forbidden to teach women Torah (if Rabbi Eliezer's dictum and its widespread echo is not seen as an absolute negative), there also was no obligation to do so either, as there was for sons: "The father is obliged to teach his son Torah."[59] When it is recalled how important the obligation to fulfill a command was, and how the mere lack of obligation led to positive restrictions in other instances, such as women not being counted in a minyan, it will be apparent that this lack of obligation to teach women Torah, or for women to study Torah, was likely to have a very negative effect. This likelihood was confirmed by the fact that this obligation--or lack of it--was specifically discussed at length in the Talmud, with the result that it was clearly stated that women were not obliged

to study Torah: "and how do we know that she (mother) has
no duty (to teach her children)?... Because it is written
'And ye shall teach them your sons'--but not your daughters."[60]

      Still another story about Rabbi Eliezer corroborated
the presumption that women did not study Torah: "Rabbi
Eliezer was asked, 'Is it permissible to drink from the
hand of the bride so long as her husband is sitting with her
at the festive table?' He replied, 'Whoever drinks from
the hand of a bride is as though he drinks from the hand
of a harlot.' (His colleagues) said to him, 'Are not all the
daughters of Israel possessed of good manners?' He answered, 'God forbid! who is not familiar with the Torah
cannot be possessed of good manners.'"[61]

      The assumption that men are to learn Torah, but
not women, was further mirrored in the "difference in formulation, according to sex, of a prayer for the prosperity
of a new-born infant. In the case of a boy, the conclusion
asked that his parents may be granted to bring him up to
'Torah, marriage, and good works';[62] for girls, a current
modification of the formula runs 'to reverence, marriage,
and good works.' ... Reference to the Torah is conspicuous-
ly absent."[63] It should be added that in the recitation of
the Shema, Deuteronomy 6:7, is quoted: "You shall repeat
them to your sons." That this very ancient precept, with
its sole focus on men, persisted through much later times
is seen by the fact that it was listed as the eleventh commandment (of the total of 613) to which Maimonides remarked: "Women are not obliged thereto."[64]

      Thus, if no women were obliged to study Torah, and
if no one was obliged to teach them, there was not much
possibility that they would in fact study Torah. For who
taught Torah? The rabbis, and their attitude toward women
would have made it impossible for them to have women students. As the modern Jewish scholar C. G. Montefiore
notes:

> Very few women were students of the Law: it was
> not intended that they should be. Yet the highest
> and most adorable thing in the world was to study
> the Law. The greatest and purest joy in the
> world was to fulfil all the commandments and or-
> dinances of the Pentateuch and Rabbinic codes.
> But women need not, and could not, observe them

all.  It was not for nothing that the daily blessing
was said (the blessing which the modern orthodox
Jews have not had the courage and good sense to
remove from their prayer books):  'Blessed art
thou, O Lord our God, who hast not made me a
woman. '  This blessing was as sincerely said as
the two previous ones:  'Blessed art thou, O Lord
our God, who hast not made me a gentile or a
slave. '[65]

## a)  Beruria:  The Exception that Proves the Rule

Montefiore said, "they tell of a few exceptional wom-
en such as Beruria," who apparently had some knowledge
of Torah.  In fact, whenever some kind of evidence is put
forth which is counter to the above documentation, that wom-
en in reality did not study Torah, Beruria is always mentioned.  When one finds in this connection a reference to
Beruria everywhere, and very often only to Beruria,[66] one
is tempted to see this as a classical case of the exception
proving the rule.

Because Beruria was such an exceptional woman in
early Jewish history, she is deserving of a more detailed
discussion.  The Encyclopaedia Judaica (vol. 4, col. 701)
emphasizes that "she is famous as the only woman in talmudic literature whose views on halachic matters are seriously reckoned with by the scholars of her time."  Beruria
was the daughter of a rabbi and the wife of the very important Rabbi Meir (early and middle second century).  There
are various spellings of her name, the usual alternates being Valeria, or possibly Valuria.  In his 1921 book, Jesus
und die Frauen, Johannes Leipoldt referred to these alternate spellings and described her as the daughter of Rabbi
Chanina ben Teradion (p. 120).  Twenty years later in
Jesu Verhältnis zu Griechen und Juden, he referred to her
as a proselyte: "The proselyte Veluria[67] is probably the
same woman as Meir's wife Veluria because of the rarity
of the name" (p. 20).  However, in 1954, in Die Frau in
der antiken Welt und im Urchristentum Leipoldt again simply
referred to Beruria as the daughter of Rabbi Chanina ben
Teradion (p. 100).  Since the Talmud itself[68] identifies
Beruria as the daughter of Rabbi Chanina ben Teradion, it
is not likely the identification between her and the proselyte
Valeria can be made.[69]

Beruria became an avid student of Torah, although
we do not know who taught her to read or with what rabbi
she studied; she may have studied with her father, but perhaps also with other rabbis. Apparently she went through
the intensive three-year course of study customary for disciples of rabbis at the time:

> Rabbi Simlai came before Rabbi Johanan and re-
> quested him: Let the master teach me the Book
> of Genealogies.... Let us learn it in three
> months, he proposed. Thereupon he (Rabbi Joha-
> nan) took a clod and threw it at him, saying: If
> Beruria, wife of Rabbi Meir and daughter of Rabbi
> Hananya ben Teradyon, who studied three hundred
> laws from three hundred teachers in one day could
> nevertheless not do her duty in three years, yet
> you propose to do it in three months![70]

Beruria not only put in the canonical three-year program of
study, but also did it in such an exemplary manner that she
was held up as an example of how to study Torah. Indeed,
her reputation as an avid student was so great that it
spawned legends about her studiousness, as in the clearly
hyperbolic reference to the three hundred laws studied from
three hundred teachers every day for three years. Such a
legend was quite a compliment to her reputation, and triply
so when it is also recalled that Beruria was being held up
to be emulated by Rabbi Simlai who himself was a very re-
knowned rabbi, and that Rabbi Simlai lived over a hundred
years after Beruria.

Beruria also took part in the discussions and debates
among the rabbis and their more able followers. In one
such a debate over a very technical matter of ritual purity
she opposed, and bested, her brother: in refering to Beruria, Rabbi Judah ben Baba said, "His daughter has answered more correctly than his son."[71] Another debate
was recorded in which two rabbinical schools were ranged
on opposite sides, whereupon Beruria gave her solution.
"When these words were said before Rabbi Judah, he commented 'Beruria has spoken rightly. '"[72] The striking thing
about these reports, and others elsewhere in the Talmud,
is that a woman's opinion on Torah became law, halacha.
At least one woman penetrated to the heart of Judaism,
Torah, and not only as an absorbent student, but also as a
rabbinical disputant and a decisive maker of law.

Beyond these accomplishments Beruria also followed
the path of all other really able students of Torah and became a teacher of Torah: "Beruria once discovered a student who was learning in an undertone.  Rebuking him, she
exclaimed: Is it not written, 'ordered in all things and
sure?' If it (the Torah) is 'ordered' in your 248 limbs it
will be 'sure,' otherwise it will not be 'sure. '"73  The then
common mode of studying Torah was to recite it aloud to
memorize it more effectively.  Here Beruria not only drilled
the student as a schoolmistress, but did so in a peculiarly
rabbinic fashion:  she quoted from the Torah and argued her
position by explaining and applying the scriptural passage.
Her rebuke of the student was gentle; she tried to lead him
more deeply into his studies.  As one modern Jewish woman
scholar states, "One gets the impression that Beruria had the
personality of a master-rebbe who was seriously concerned
with the spiritual and educational welfare of people. "74
That this story of Beruria, together with one of her teaching
the famous rabbi Jose the Galilean on the road to Lydda, is
grouped with a number of other rabbinical stories about
teaching, indicates that the editors of the Babylonian Talmud
were aware of her teaching prowess as late as the fifth cen-
tury--three centuries after her death.

Still another story recorded in the Talmud portrays
Beruria teaching Torah in the customary rabbinical manner--
quoting, explaining, and applying Scripture:

> A certain min (Sadducee) said to Beruria:  It is
> written:  'Sing, O barren, thou that didst not
> bear. '  Because she did not bear, she should
> sing?  She said to him:  Fool!  Look at the end
> of the verse, where it is written, 'for more are
> the children of the desolate than the children of
> the married wife, saith the Lord. '  Rather, what
> is the meaning of 'O barren, thou didst not bear'?
> --Sing O community of Israel, who resembles a
> barren woman, for not having borne children like
> you, who are damned to hell. 75

Beruria clearly did not suffer fools gladly, as this story and
the one about Rabbi Jose the Galilean, related below, indicate.  She could also be extremely sympathetic and sensitive
to those she felt were sincere, but here she faced a man
she thought was helping to destroy true Judaism (min is to
be understood here either as a Sadducee opponent of the
Pharisees/rabbis or as a Jewish-Christian) and who

apparently was expounding Scripture in an ignorant way.    If
there was anything Beruria could not tolerate, it was a man
being pretentious about Torah.

Beruria likewise had an intense moral fervor and sensitive concern for persons, as illustrated by the following
story about her and her famous husband, Rabbi Meir:

> Certain highwaymen living in the neighborhood of
> Rabbi Meir annoyed him greatly, and Rabbi Meir
> prayed for them to die.  His wife Beruria said to
> him:  What is your view?  Is it because it is
> written:  'Let the sinners be consumed'?  Is 'sin-
> ners' written?  'Sins' is written.  Moreover, look
> at the end of the verse:  'and let the wicked be no
> more. '  Since the sins will cease, the wicked will
> be no more.  He prayed for them and they re-
> pented.

This is clearly high moral advice, presented with the usual
scriptural quotation, analysis and application of its meaning.
Beruria here showed herself the superior of the best male
rabbinical mind and moral spirit; the hard proof of that is
that Rabbi Meir took her advice, with success.  A modern
male Jewish scholar has commented on this passage:  "Students sufficiently familiar with Hebrew would profit greatly
by following Beruria's argument in the Talmud's original
text, also looking up the Hebrew of the verse.... "[77]

If Beruria was a brilliant student and teacher of
Torah, a decider of halacha, and one who lived and taught
an intensely moral life, did she not have all the qualities
of a rabbi?  Rabbi, after all, simply meant master or
teacher; it was a term of respect given to the teachers of
Torah who were expected to decide the law and live morally.  She clearly did, but in the documents as we have them
she is never referred to as rabbi.  Presumably she never
received the "ordination" (semikhah) to the rabbinate that
promising young men normally received at the completion
of their studies.  (At least one man, as noted above, Ben
Azzai, of the first century, was also learned in the Law,
taught Law, decided Law, and was of high moral character,
and was also not "ordained," and hence not referred to as
rabbi.)  There was no legal reason why she could not have
been "ordained"; rather, the generally very low rabbinic
estimate of women is the most likely reason, though from
the documents which are available we cannot know that for
certain.

Beruria, as she appears in the pages of rabbinic writings, is a person who lived a very full human life with perhaps more than her measure of suffering. Hers was the time of the final destruction of the Jewish homeland in Palestine by the Romans in 135 C. E. , until it was reestablished in the twentieth century. She lost her father Rabbi Hananya ben Teradyon in these same Hadrianic persecutions. Her brother, whom she had bested in a Torah dispute, disgraced the family by turning to banditry and subsequently was murdered by his gang for trying to inform on them. Her sister was forced into a brothel by the conquering Roman authorities, although Beruria contrived to have her husband Rabbi Meir rescue her. But perhaps the most tragic suffering of her life was the death of two of her sons. Her endurance and response to their sudden deaths is recalled in the following rabbinic story:

> When two of their sons died on Sabbath, Beruria
> did not inform Meir of their children's death upon
> his return from the academy in order not to grieve
> him on the Sabbath! Only after the Havdalah
> prayer did she broach the matter, saying: Some
> time ago a certain man came and left something
> in my trust; now he has called for it. Shall I
> return it to him or not? Naturally Meir replied
> in the affirmative, whereupon Beruria showed
> him their dead children. When Meir began to
> weep, she asked: Did you not tell me that we
> must give back what is given on trust? 'The
> Lord gave, and the Lord has taken away. '[78]

In the midst of extraordinary suffering we see her rabbinic style coming to the fore once more, as she tells a story and applies it to the present situation with a Scripture quotation. Likewise, the stereotypical sex roles are reversed as the strong Beruria takes the more intellectual approach and Rabbi Meir weeps.

In all the stories recorded about Beruria, she is always set over against a man; the only story involving another woman is really not a tale about Beruria but about her husband, who was asked by Beruria to rescue her sister from the brothel. [79] In the rabbinic writings Beruria is seen only as a rabbinic student, disputant, halachic decision-maker, and above all a teacher--always with men. Moreover, she is always superior to the men, whether as a model of studiousness, a teacher, or as a superior and even at times

triumphant disputant and exegete.   This is the case even in
regard to her husband, the most learned and renowned rabbi
of his age.   If such a strong and positive image comes
through even the totally male memorized, written and edited
rabbinic materials, what must Beruria have been like?

Beruria had to be an unusual--a rabbinical--woman
to make a broad mark on that massive male work, the Talmud.   Clearly she did not fit the female stereotype of her
day.   But she was more than that.   She very keenly felt the
oppressed, subordinate position women held in the Jewish
society around her, and struck out against it.   Her consciousness was extremely sensitized: "Rabbi Jose the Galilean was once on a journey when he met Beruria.   'By what
road,' he asked her, 'do we go to Lydda?'   'Foolish Galilean,' she replied, 'did not the Sages say this:  Engage not in
much talk with women?   You should have asked:  By which
to Lydda?'"[80]  What is irritating Beruria is woman's second-
class status, here reflected in the rabbinic law that a man
should not speak much with women, who are too "light-
headed" to waste time on, and sexually tempting besides.
Here was a chance to throw verbal acid in the face of one
of her "oppressors."   A student she treated gently; the rabbi she called a fool.   But with her keen wit she did not simply vituperate the rabbi (one wonders if he had earlier delivered himself of some pompous sage quotation on the frivol-
ity and inferiority of women to have earned this breathtaking
attack); instead, she carefully followed the traditional rabbinic pattern of disputation by rebutting a statement with a
quotation from the written or oral Law.   Always she remained the intellectual.

What a weight Beruria's reputation must have had in
talmudic times for this vitriolic putdown of a rabbi to be
noted, remembered for hundreds of years, and finally made
permanent in the final redaction of the Talmud.   That there
was obviously also a counter-feeling among the early rabbis
is reflected only in a shadowy fashion in the last line of the
talmud story about Rabbi Meir's rescue of Beruria's sister
from a brothel.   There was a backlash to his rescue efforts
and "He then arose and ran away and came to Babylon; others say because of the incident about Beruria."[81]  No further
information about the "incident" is given in the Talmud.
There is merely this dark reference, sheer innuendo.

A thousand years later, we find a full-blown legend
about the incident in the commentary on this passage by the

famous Jewish medieval talmudic scholar Rashi:

> Beruria once again made fun of the saying of the
> Sages that women are lightheaded.  Then Meir
> said to her:  With your life you will have to take
> back your words.  Then he sent one of his stu-
> dents to test her to see if she would allow herself
> to be seduced.  He sat by her the whole day until
> she surrendered herself to him.  When she real-
> ized (what she had done) she strangled herself.
> Thereupon Rabbi Meir ran away (to Babylonia) on
> account of the scandal. [82]

There is nothing at all in the intelligence, perceptiveness
and moral character of Beruria to make this in any way
credible.  Would she not have perceived that her husband
had set a trap for her?  Is it not incomprehensible that the
great Rabbi Meir could have commissioned his rabbinic student to commit one of the three deadly sins[83] in its most
serious form:  sexual immorality with a married Jewish
woman?  Finally, why would it take a thousand years for
this story, so out of character with all of the previously
known documentation, to surface?[84]  It clearly was invented
simply to morally annihilate Beruria, the one woman of
superior stature in the Talmud, Beruria the feminist--for it
was exactly on that point that she was attacked.  Because
she took an overtly feminist stance of rejecting the rabbinic
stereotyping of women as intellectually inferior she was told
she would have to give up her life.  Feminism was a capital
crime!  In male chauvinist fashion the moral destruction
planned for her would reduce her to the female stereotype,
a weak sexual creature who could not resist a determined
Don Juan.

    Despite the historical bankruptcy of this late legend,
it does underline Beruria's towering reputation in her life-
time and for centuries afterwards.  The very attempt to
destroy it is evidence of its power.  Although the opposition
was already there in talmudic times, as is seen in the innuendo about the "incident," the later hatchet job suggests
that the enemies of what she stood for grew stronger in time.
Fortunately, the character assassination attempt was far
from completely successful, for the clearly historically based
evidence of the earlier talmudic stories remains today.
Less fortunately, the fact that the talmudic evidence was not
erased bears witness not only to the vigorous reputation of
Beruria, but also to the faithful honesty of the generations

of rabbis who memorized, handed on and finally wrote down,
collected and edited the stories about Beruria.  This latter
means that there were no other women who entered and advanced in the heartland of Judaism, the study of the Torah,
otherwise we would have talmudic stories of them as well.
Beruria was the "exception that proves the rule" that in
talmudic days women did not study Torah.

### b)  Imma Shalom:  No Exception

The one other woman of the early Rabbinic period
who, along with Beruria, is at times mentioned by name as
one who knew Torah, if not exactly as an example of "many
women recorded as being Torah scholars in the fullest
sense,"[85] is Imma Shalom.  She was the sister of Rabbi
Gamaliel II and the wife of Rabbi Eliezer ben Hyrcanus--
both famous first century C. E. rabbis, the latter being the
one who, among other things, said "Whoever teaches his
daughter Torah, it is as though he taught her lechery."[86]
Imma Shalom could not qualify as a Torah scholar in any
sense of the word.  There are several references to her in
rabbinical writings, but only two have importance for us
here.  One story is about a dispute she was involved in with
her brother (whether the recorded dispute is real or fictitious
is difficult to determine definitely, but that has no bearing
on its significance--or lack of significance--here), during
which she bribed the (Christian?) judge, but lost anyhow because her brother put up a larger bribe.  No scriptural or
rabbinic argumentation was presented by Imma Shalom, nor
was an ethical principle propounded or exemplified. [87]

The second story about Imma Shalom also hardly
proves that women were learned in Torah or were highly
esteemed by the rabbis.  It relates that when she once
heard a sceptic mocking her brother, saying, "Your God
is not strictly honest, or He would not have stolen a rib
from sleeping Adam," she asked him to fetch a police official, whereup he asked her why.  "We were robbed last
night of a silver cruet and the thief left in its place a golden
one. "  He responded, "If that is all I wish that thief would
visit me every day!"  Imma retorted, "and yet you object
to the removal of the rib from sleeping Adam!  Did he not
receive in exchange a woman to wait on him?"[88]  Perhaps
the last line helps explain why the story was recorded. [89]

## c)  Other Non-exceptions

The article on "Woman" in the Universal Jewish Encyclopedia[90] refers to the ubiquitous Beruria, then to the
wife (no name given--a revealing fact) of Jacob ben Judah
Mizrahi, who "continued to direct his Yeshiva after his
death," and to the "daughter (again no name) of the exilarch
Samuel ben Eli of Baghdad, and Miriam Sapira (who) both
taught Torah to male students from whom they were separated by a curtain"--also a "revealing" fact.  Again, outside
of Beruria, none of these cases has any bearing on the topic
at hand, the status of women in the period of formative
Judaism, i. e., 200 B. C. E. -500 C. E.; the latter two women
lived during the High Middle Ages and the wife of Mizrahi
lived in the sixteenth century.

A different list of "learned women" of this early period is given by Shalom Ben-Chorin.[91]  He grants that such
women were the exception, but insists that there were some.
Again none of them, with the exception of Beruria, can in
any way be said to be learned in Torah, and in fact there
is some difficulty with the general term "learnedness"
(Gelehrsamkeit) used in reference to some of them.  Ben-
Chorin does not include Imma Shalom in his list of learned
women because he has just referred to her in a somewhat
derogatory fashion as a bluestocking.[92]  He begins his list
with Beruria and then mentions "Homa the daughter of Rabbi
Chisda from Kaphri."

It is puzzling why Homa the daughter of Rabbi Chisda
should be listed as learned in Torah.  In the Babylonian
Talmud she does not even have a name, but is constantly
referred to simply as the daughter of Rabbi Chisda.[93]  As
a child she was once taken upon her father's lap and was
asked which of his two prize pupils she wanted for a husband; she said, both.  This was recorded because she did
eventually marry one, Rami, and after his death, the second,
Raba.[94]  It is also recorded that she had a hole made in the
wall of the "court" so that she could stick her hand through
above the head of her husband, presumably to ward off maleficent spirits,[95] and that once she burst into the courtroom
to denounce a woman as a liar.[96]

The last story about her in the Talmud is largely
about another woman whom the Talmud names Homa.  In the
story this other Homa, who was reputed to be very beautiful
but who also had the ill-fortune of having three husbands die

one after the other, went to the rabbinical court, and in the
course of her visit her beauty apparently "became visible"
to the court:

> As she was shewing it to him her arm was uncov-
> ered and a light shone upon the court.   Raba
> arose, went home and solicited Rabbi Chisda's
> daughter [his own wife].   'Who has been to-day at
> the court?' enquired Rabbi Chisda's daughter.
> 'Homa the wife of Abaye,' he replied.   Thereupon
> she followed her, striking her with the straps of
> a chest until she chased her out of all Mahuza.
> 'You have,' she said to her, 'already killed three
> (men), and now you come to kill another (man)!'[97]

Here Rabbi Chisda's daughter (Homa) appears either as a
very jealous woman or one superstitiously fearful of the evil
power of a thrice-widowed woman--or both.   From all of
the evidence, Homa (Rabbi Chisda's daughter) can in no way
be said to exhibit learnedness in Torah, or anything else.

A third learned woman, according to Ben-Chorin, is
Yalta, the wife of Rabbi Nahman, a fourth century C. E.
Babylonian rabbi.   Although there are a number of references to Yalta in the early rabbinical writings, none of
them indicate that she was in any way learned.   She exhibited a sharp temper when a guest refused to send her a
glass of wine with a blessing over it--women were not present when guests were at meals.[98]   She also once said to
her husband: "The Torah has permitted something of a
similar taste for everything it has forbidden; I would like to
eat meat in milk"; whereup she listed a number of things
that were forbidden and other things somewhat similar which
were allowed.[99]   The list, however, shows no more "gelehrsamkeit" than any Jewish wife would have if she tried to
keep a kosher home; that is, if she followed the rules her
"learned" husband laid down.

Two other women are also referred to by Ben-Chorin.
One is the foster mother of Rabbi Abaye, mentioned above,[100]
who possessed medical knowledge and is credited with some
pedagogical statements--but this of course does not qualify
her as one learned in Torah.   The last reference is more
interesting: "Also a maid of Rabbi Judah (second century
C. E. ) is described as learned; she commented on Bible
verses which were difficult to understand."[101]

Perhaps the first thing to notice about this maidservant of Rabbi Judah (the codifier of the Mishnah) is that she
is nameless; in the five, or possibly six, places in the
Babylonian Talmud where she is mentioned she is always
referred to only as Rabbi Judah's maidservant or domestic.
Our evidence concerning her is very meagre.  We do know
that she had learned at least some Hebrew, something of the
symbolic style of speaking current among rabbis and their
students, and was an imposing and responsible enough member of Rabbi Judah's household to be able to levy an excom-
munication and exercise a powerful prayer at the death of
the Rabbi--no mean accomplishments for a woman servant.
However, given the slimness of the documentation one must
be careful to neither unduly expand nor contract its significance.  It is necessary to look at each portion separately
before attempting an over-all evaluation.

If the reference in bShab. 152a, about a ninety-two
year old domestic of Rabbi Judah's household serving as a
food taster, refers to the female domestic in question, as
seems reasonably likely, and if it is coupled with the stories
of her exercising sign..icant household responsibilities, one
gets the picture of an intelligent, perceptive woman servant
who for many decades must have heard the great Rabbi
Judah, and perhaps even his father, Rabbi Simon III, teaching his students and discussing halachic matters with his
colleagues.

> She even had charge of the tables reserved by the
> patriarch for the numerous pupils who received
> free board at his house; and as circumstances or
> her whims dictated, she would either immediately
> dismiss the students after the meals were over or
> invite them to remain a while longer.  In such
> company she adopted the technical language known
> only to the initiated, and employed exclusively by
> the Rabbis, who scarcely ever expressed the prin-
> cipal idea literally, but nearly always resorted to
> symbols and figures of speech:[102]
>
> When Rabbi's maid indulged in enigmatic speech
> she used to say this:  The ladle strikes against
> the jar [all the wine in the jar has been used up];
> let the eagles fly to their nests [the students may
> now leave the dining room for their lodgings]; and
> when she wished them to remain at table she used
> to tell them, The crown of her friend [the bung of

the adjoining jar] shall be removed and the ladle
will float in the jar like a ship that sails in the
sea. 103

That such a woman in that setting would have learned
some Hebrew is not at all surprising, especially those terms
dealing with kitchen and domestic matters.    However, when
looking at the passage in bMeg. 18a it is a little difficult to
conclude with Ben-Chorin that she "commented on Bible
verses which were difficult to understand." The passage
reads as follows:

> The Rabbis did not know what was meant by seru-
> gin, until one day they heard the maidservant of
> Rabbi's household, on seeing the Rabbis enter at
> intervals, say to them, How long are you going to
> come in by serugin?
>   The Rabbis did not know what was meant by
> halugelugoth, til one day they heard the handmaid
> of the household of Rabbi, on seeing a man peel-
> ing portulaks, say to him, How long will you be
> peeling your portulaks? (halugelugoth).
>   The Rabbis did not know what was meant by,
> salseleah and it shall exalt.   One day they heard
> the handmaid of the house of Rabbi say to a man
> who was curling his hair, How long will you be
> mesalsel with your hair?... [Then comes a sim-
> ilar example which does not involve Rabbi Judah's
> maidservant.]
>   The Rabbis did not know what was meant by
> we-tetethia bematate of destruction, til one day
> they heard the handmaid of the household of Rabbi
> say to her companion, Take the tatitha (broom) and
> tati (sweep) the house. 104

To be sure, Ben-Chorin is not alone in making the
sort of claim he does: "She used to help the great scholar
and his students to interpret difficult biblical passages by
muttering clues to their interpretations as she cleaned the
room."105   Likewise: "In almost one breath this sensible
woman once explained the meaning of four separate rabbinical expressions in the presence of the learned.   The ingenious, roundabout way in which this was done, and her half
playful manner of concealing the act, are matters not without interest."106

There are difficulties with these explanations of this

passage.   First, those who were aided by the maidservant's
Hebrew utterances did not include Rabbi Judah himself.
Secondly, that these word difficulties all occurred and were
solved "in almost one breath" is quite unlikely.   What is
likely is that several different occasions were involved and
that these four at any rate were remembered and (almost)
brought together in this one passage--after all, they were
also recorded singly elsewhere in the Talmud. 108   The Talmud simply records that a group of rabbis who gathered
around the household of Rabbi Judah the Prince were inad-
vertently assisted in understanding some unusual Hebrew
words when they overheard the maidservant on different occasions using a form of these words--which concerned household matters that a maidservant would deal with.   It is just
possible that the maid was circumspectly passing on some
of her household Hebrew to perhaps relatively newly arrived
rabbis, but there is nothing in the text that positively indicates that this was the case; rather, the contrary is true.
If she was "commenting on Bible verses which were difficult
to understand," then neither the rabbis who overheard her
utterances nor those who recorded them in the Talmud were
aware that she was doing so.   Still, it is possible.

        This same maidservant also wielded an extraordinary
degree of responsibility, as the following story of her ban-
ishing a malefactor from the company of the Rabbi's household indicates:

> Then R. Samuel b. Nahmani got up on his feet and
> said:   Why, even a 'separation' imposed by one of
> the domestics in Rabbi's house was not treated
> lightly by the Rabbis for three years; how much
> more so one imposed by our colleague, Rab
> Judah!...   What (was the incident) of the domestic
> in Rabbi's house?   It was one of the maidservants
> in Rabbi's house that had noticed a man beating
> his grown-up son and said, Let that fellow be un-
> der a shammetha! because he sinned against the
> words (of Holy Writ):   Put not a stumbling-block
> before the blind.   For it is taught:   and not put a
> stumbling-block before the blind, that text applies
> to one who beats his grown-up son (and this caused
> him to rebel). 108

Obviously not only rabbis could "exclude" wrongdoers at that
time, but obviously, too, the maidservant's reputation must
have carried some weight.   It should also be noted that she

also knew the rabbinic style of backing things up with a
Scripture quotation--she doubtless had heard many such ban-
nings issued over the decades.

The final story about Rabbi Judah's maidservant reveals again her strength of character in a most dramatic
manner.

On the day when Rabbi died the Rabbis decreed a
public fast and offered prayers for heavenly mercy.
They, furthermore, announced that whoever said
that Rabbi was dead would be stabbed with a sword.
Rabbi's handmaid ascended the roof and prayed:
The immortals desire Rabbi (to join them) and the
mortals desire Rabbi (to remain with them); may
it be the will (of God) that the mortals may overpower the immortals.  When, however, she saw
how often he resorted to the privy, painfully taking
off his tefillin and putting them on again, she
prayed:  May it be the will (of the Almighty) that
the immortals may overpower the mortals.  As
the Rabbis incessantly continued their prayers for
(heavenly) mercy she took up a jar and threw it
down from the roof to the ground.  (For a moment) they ceased praying and soul of the Rabbi
departed to its eternal rest. [109]

In sum, it is likely that the same maidservant is
spoken of in all the passages quoted, although one cannot be
absolutely certain since no name is ever given--a fact in
itself which reveals a good deal about the inferior status of
women, even those of strong character.  This maidservant
was a strong character who learned at least some Hebrew,
could banter with rabbinic students in the "in" language, and
at least once wielded effectively the "separation" in the ap-
proved manner.  Nevertheless, for all of her strength of
character, she is not evidence that women studied Torah.
In fact she is evidence that they did not, for if such a servant had been male, he would doubtless have eventually been
pulled into the ranks of the rabbinic students and then the
rabbis, and would not have been nameless, or known simply
as a man's servant.

In a further remark Ben-Chorin writes:  "When a
pharisee can even issue a warning about a pharisaical woman
(Sotah 3, 4), that shows that women had already entered into
the theological discussion, if perhaps even only on the

periphery. "[110] The pertinent reference in the Mishnah is
as follows: "A foolish pious man and a cunning wicked man
and a sanctimonious woman and the self-inflicted wounds of
the Pharisees--these ruin the world. "[111] Neither this text
itself, however, nor the comment on it in the Babylonian
Talmud give any indication of women being involved in theological discussion. [112]

In the end, of course, Shalom Ben-Chorin also is
not attempting to maintain that women studied Torah in ancient rabbinic days. As noted, he remarks: "learned women were the exception. "[113] In fact he goes beyond that,
saying: "We must envision the religious life of a Jewish
woman in this time as extremely introverted.... We have
rather indiscriminately chosen several examples here out of
a relatively large time span, but this is legitimate, for in
this time span, from the time of Christ to the later talmudic
period, no real emancipation of the woman took place. Her
status within Judaism did not change. "[114] It does seem
that every time a list of women from ancient rabbinic days
purportedly learned in Torah is put forth, they all seem to
be chimerical--with the exception of Beruria. One can conclude that in misnaic and talmudic times women did not
study, nor were they taught, Torah.


6.   WOMEN DISTRACT FROM TORAH STUDY

A corollary point might well be added here: for the
sake of prayer and the study of Torah, men did well to
avoid contact with women, including their wives. The second
century B. C. E. Testament of Naphtali stated: "There is a
season for a man to embrace his wife, and a season to abstain therefrom for his prayer. "[115] The idea is further
developed in the Mishnah, where it states: "If a man vowed
to have no intercourse with his wife.... Disciples (of the
Rabbis) may continue absent for thirty days against the will
(of their wives) while they occupy themselves in the study
of Torah. "[116] This period is especially noteworthy, for by
contrast the Mishnah adds: "laborers--only for--one week. "

The Talmud expands the opposition between women
and the study of Torah when it states: "Students may go
away to study Torah without the permission (of their wives
even for) two or three years. "[117] But it does not stop
there, for a number of stories are added which indicate that
it was often customary for a man to go off without his wife

for twelve years!   (This was apparently the usual period of
Torah study in the academy.)   This is true not only for the
later rabbinic times but perhaps even for the first century
C. E. , for such a story is also told of Rabbi Akiba. [118]   If
the question is "for how long (may they--disciples--go away)
with the permission (of their wives)?" the response is:
"For as long as they desire. "[119]   In fact, the life of Rabbi
Akiba illustrates this dictum well, for after allegedly spend-
ing twelve years away from his wife he returned to his home
town where he overheard an old man saying to his wife:
"'How long will you lead the life of a living widowhood?'
'If he would listen to me,' she replied, 'he would spend (in
study) another twelve years. '  Said (Rabbi Akiba):  'It is
then with her consent that I am acting,' and he departed
again and spent another twelve years at the academy. "[120]

However, Louis Finkelstein[121] says:  "The time of
separation from his wife, which in reality could hardly have
exceeded three years, is extended [according to the Talmud]
over the full thirteen years.... Incredible as this is, the
Babylonian teachers thought it insufficient, and they created
a legend, according to which, when Akiba came home at the
end of the twelve years, he heard a neighbor...." Nevertheless, even if Finkelstein is accurate, that the rabbis
thought expanding Akiba's three years' absence from his wife
to study Torah to twenty-four years would enhance his reputation, says almost as much about what the rabbis thought
about women and their compatibility with the study of Torah
as does the actual three-year absence or the perhaps legend-
ary twenty-four year absence.

Finkelstein also commented:

> Akiba may thus be regarded as the founder of the
> peculiar institution of married 'monasticism' which,
> while it never became very popular in Judaism,
> has exerted an influence throughout the centuries.
> Many of Akiba's pupils followed his example, and
> hardly more than a generation ago there were
> groups of people in the small Lithuanian communi-
> ties, called perushim, separatists, who resur-
> rected the ancient custom.  [For a record of the
> institution during the Middle Ages, see Moritz
> Guedemann, Geschichte des Erziehungswesens und
> der Cultur der abendländischen Juden, Amsterdam,
> 1960, vol. I, pp. 266 ff. --who refers to the thir-
> teenth century "almost monastic foundation. "]

After marriage, they would devote themselves completely to their studies while their wives supported
them.   Rightly or wrongly, the talmudists believed
that as married men, students were less open to
temptation than as celibates.   'He who has bread
in his basket,' they said in a rather coarse metaphor, 'is safer than he who lacks it. '122

Indeed, elsewhere the Talmud teaches it is good to
neglect one's family and let them go hungry so as to devote
one's time to the study of Torah. 123   The haggadic En
Jacob on Gittlin 1 even records an instance when a man sold
his daughter to gain the means needed to study Torah! 124

Thus, holding to the observance of the scriptural
command for every man to produce progeny, and adhering
to the need for men to allay their sexual drive (as exhibited
by some rabbis in their refusal to instruct an unmarried
young man on the grounds that his entire day was filled with
sin, that is, filled with sinful thoughts of sex), 125 it was
thought best to remove women from Torah, or at least to
subordinate them as much as possible to the study of Torah.
The perfect wife and mother was one who lived so as to allow her husband and sons to spend as much of their lives
as possible in the study of Torah: "Whereby do women
earn merit?  By making their children go to the synagogue
to learn Scripture and their husbands to the Beth Hamidrash
to learn Mishnah, and waiting for their husbands till they
return from the Beth Hamidrash. "126  One "rabbi," Ben
Azzai, even went so far as not to marry at all; he was, he
said, in love with the Torah.   Though strictly speaking not
an ordained rabbi, Ben Azzai was probably the only known
ancient "rabbi" not to marry. 127   Concerning the obligation
for all Jewish men to marry to produce progeny and Ben
Azzai's delinquency in the matter, the Babylonian Talmud
recorded: "They said to Ben Azzai:  Some preach well and
act well, others act well but do not preach well; you, however, preach well but do not act well!  Ben Azzai replied:
But what shall I do, seeing that my soul is in love with the
Torah; the world can be carried on by others. "128

In the end, it was not the brilliant Torah scholar and
ethical thinker Beruria who was held up as the ideal wife,
but rather the wife of Rabbi Akiba, who spent perhaps twenty-four years in living widowhood while Akiba studied
Torah. 129

CHAPTER V

WOMEN IN SOCIETY

1. WOMEN'S EDUCATION

If women did not study Torah, it must also be concluded that they normally received no formal education,
since formal study in ancient Judaism was largely limited
to the study of Torah. Concerning more ancient times it
was said that,

> her protected status was based on a religious and
> moral outlook, sharply contrasting local Canaanite
> custom, as well as in economic and social inter-
> ests that predated the Settlement. These gener-
> ally limited her activity to that of the home and
> kindred occupations and provided the goals and
> limitations of her education, contingent upon her
> father's position in society. The mother was
> naturally the girl's primary teacher and model ...
> the young girl learned the domestic chores and
> special skills of her mother through observation
> and imitation in the informal atmosphere of the
> home. [1]

Raphael Loewe also noted: "Marriage, as far as
concerns the women, took place regularly at the age of
twelve.... Opportunities for the development of maturity of
personality, let alone the acquisition of formal education,
were consequently limited."[2] However, some daughters of
upper class families may have learned Greek, "as a social
accomplishment."[3] But even those who had managed to learn
something were normally forbidden to teach even children;[4]
the reason given by the Talmud was "on account of their
(the children's) fathers"[5]--that is, there was a danger of
sexual immorality between the woman teacher and the children's fathers who brought them to school. [6]

114

## 2.   BEARING WITNESS

Another crucial matter which was somewhat dependent upon the education women had--or did not have--and which was related both to religious and civil life, was that of bearing witness. Basically women were not allowed to bear witness in the Jewish society of the rabbinic period. The ancient Mishnah stated the matter rather clearly: "The law about an oath of testimony applies to men but not to women."[7] There were a very few specific situations when a woman's testimony did carry weight; they were always the same circumstances when the testimony of a gentile slave would also be accepted--for example, a woman could remarry on the strength of the testimony of another woman that her husband was indeed dead.[8] There can be no doubt but that women were disqualified from bearing witness, as is borne out by much discussion in the later Talmud, where, among other places, it says: "For that he (a slave) is disqualified from giving evidence can be learnt by means of an a fortiori from the law in the case of woman: for if woman who is eligible to enter (by marriage) into the congregation (of Israel) is yet ineligible to give evidence...."[9] There is still further evidence from the first century C.E. that women were so disqualified. Josephus wrote: "The testimony of women is not accepted as valid," and then added as a reason, "because of the lightheadedness and brashness of the female sex."[10] On the other hand the midrash compilation Jalqut Schimoni says women were disallowed because they were given to lying.[11]

The midrash Pirke REL 14 (7d, 7) lists women's not being able to bear witness as one of the nine curses visited upon women as a result of the Fall:

> To the woman he gave nine curses and death: the burden of the blood of menstruation and the blood of virginity; the burden of pregnancy; the burden of childbirth; the burden of bringing up the children; her head is covered as one in mourning; she pierces her ear like a permanent slave or slave girl who serves her master; she is not to be believed as a witness; and after everything--death.[12]

In the same place there is also an interesting exegesis put forward to explain on the basis of Scripture why women are not allowed to bear witness. It concerns Gen. 18:9-16, where Sara is told by Abraham that she would bear

a child in her old age--at which she laughed. The rabbis
said: "And then Sara denied it: I did not laugh. It is
from this place that it is taught that women are unqualified
to bear witness."

It is interesting to note that in the middle of the
twentieth century Rabbi Raphael Loewe, consciously or un-
consciously, opted for Josephus' reason rather than that in
the Jalqut Schimoni:

> No reflection on their veracity is hereby intended,
> but merely (to cite an operative phrase) 'because
> they have light, i. e. , flighty minds. ' (bShab. 33b;
> bKid. 80b) The solemnity of oathtaking was
> deemed to be a matter beyond the range of normal
> female appreciation (Shab. 4, 1; bShab. 30a;
> Maimonides, Hilekhoth Eduth 9, 1-2; Shulhan
> Arukh, Hoshen Mishpat 35, 14); and in cases
> where a woman's testimony was indispensable for
> the pursuance of justice, as affecting her personal
> status, evidence was generally taken from her in-
> formally and not in open court. The analogy af-
> forded by certain informalities of procedure intro-
> duced into juvenile courts today, out of considera-
> tions of child psychology, is of relevance here. [13]

It is possible that this disability of women was not
always so stringent in an earlier, biblical time. At least,
so argues one Jewish legal scholar, Boaz Cohen. In speaking of a statement concerning giving testimony from the
Mishnah, B. K. 1, 3,[14] he states: "The quaint formulation
of this hoary halackah seems to suggest the admission of
women as witnesses.... Needless to say that our baraita is
merely the reminiscence of an earlier rule that was later
abandoned.... According to the prevalent Tannaitic view,
women were excluded from testimony."[15] Cohen also notes
that in contrast, in the Hellenistic world "women were accepted as witnesses in Greco-Egyptian Law," although "in
Athenian Law, women were competent witnesses only in
cases of homicide."[16] Whereas the legal position of women
in this regard, and others, improved with the passage of
time from the Greek, to the Hellenistic, to the Roman
worlds, if Cohen is correct it apparently deteriorated in the
Jewish world.

## 3.  WOMEN, CHILDREN, AND SLAVES

In the ancient rabbinic writings, the Mishnah, and
later the Talmud also, there is an extraordinary linking of
women along with slaves and children; they all more or less
suffered the same disabilities in these instances; they were
all less than full Jewish citizens.  The grouping of these
three occurs numerous times; the following is a sampling:
"Women and slaves and minors are exempt from reciting
the Shema and from wearing phylacteries."[17]  "Women,
slaves, and minors are exempt from (the law of) the Suk-
kah."[18]  These first two examples at least apparently re-
lieve women, slaves, and minors of certain burdens--
though it is a mixed blessing.[19]  The following can hardly
make even that claim.

"What is found by a man's son or daughter that are
minors, what is found by his Canaanitish bondman or bondwoman, and what is found by his wife, belong to him."[20]
The following two teachings expand the list of disqualified
persons beyond that of women, slaves and minors; it is an
extraordinary grouping:  "All are subject to the command
to appear (before the Lord) excepting a deaf-mute, an imbe-
cile, a child, one of doubtful sex, one of couple sex, women, slaves that have not been freed, a man that is lame
or blind or sick or aged, and one that cannot go up (to
Jerusalem) on his feet."[21]  "These are they that are ineligible (to bear witness concerning the new moon): a dice-
player, a usurer, pigeon-flyers, traffickers in Seventh Year
produce, and slaves.  This is the general rule:  any evidence that a woman is not eligible to bring, these are not
eligible to bring."[22]  At least one midrash provides a reason why women, slaves and children are grouped together in
exempting them from fulfilling all the Law:  they are all
subordinate to a master.[23]

In the first five articles of the Mishnah tractate Kiddushin women are grouped together, not with slaves and
children, but with slaves, beasts and property.  What they
all have in common is very revealing in regard to the relative status of women; namely, how each of these "items" is
acquired by a man:  "The woman is acquired by three
means....  She is acquired by money, or document, or by
sexual connection."[24]  There are only two ways to acquire
a Jewish slave:  "A Hebrew bondman is acquired by money
or by document";[25] but the parallel is fully restored with
the non-Jewish slave:  "A Canaanite bondman is acquired by

money or by a document or by usucaption."[26] The next
"item" again varies in the manner of acquisition: "A big
beast is acquired by the act of delivery and a small animal
by lifting up."[27] But the parallel of three is again restored
in regard to the next "item": "Property that carries security
can be acquired by money, or by document, or by usucaption."[28]

In going from the mishnaic to the talmudic period the
relative position of women among slaves and children slips
to last place. Whereas the Mishnah says simply: "Women
or slaves or minors may not be included (to make up the
number needed) for the Common Grace,"[29] the Talmud commentary on that mishnah carries the matter further in such
a way that both an infant and a slave take precedence over
women in certain important religious circumstances: "Women, slaves and children are not counted (in the three).
Rabbi Jose said: An infant in the cradle may be counted
for zimmun.[30] But we have learnt: women, slaves and
children may not be counted? He adopts the view of Rabbi
Joshua b. Levi. For Rabbi Joshua b. Levi said: Although
it was laid down that an infant in a cradle cannot be counted
for zimmun, yet he can be counted to make up ten.[31] Rabbi
Joshua b. Levi also said: Nine and a slave can be counted
toward a minyan (and the former perhaps for a zimmun),
but a woman may not.

There can be no doubt that the repeated grouping of
women together with slaves and children, and even other
types of "inferior" persons and animals and property, reflects
very clearly the inferior status of women. As quoted above,
C. G. Montifiore notes: "'Women, children and slaves':
that familiar and frequent collocation means and reveals a
great deal. Women were, on the whole, regarded as inferior
to men in mind, in function and in status."[33]


4.   WOMEN APPEARING IN PUBLIC

The degree to which Jewish women appeared in public
in the first centuries just before and after the beginning of
the Common Era was apparently not only considerably less
than is the case today in Israel, but also less than in the
then contemporary Hellenistic civilization. Here again, however, we should recall the important differences in the
strength of some customs as practiced on the land and in
small villages as compared to the towns and cities, as well

as the distinction between the upper and lower classes.  In
the country the women went about more freely than in the
towns and cities; they had to draw the water at the well;[34]
they worked in the fields,[35] albeit never alone;[36] they sold
olives at their doors,[37] and they were shopkeepers.[38]  At
the feast of Succoth there used to be such a tumult and mix-
ing of men and women in the women's court of the temple
that galleries were erected for the women to keep them separate.[39]

In the wealthier families such contacts between men
and women were apparently not at all customary.[40]  There
is evidence to indicate that both the ideal and, to a large
extent, at least in the towns and cities, the reality as well
was that unmarried women were very secluded.  A telling
bit of evidence to this effect was recorded in III Maccabees
1:18-19, where, when Ptolomy IV (217 B. C. E.) was about
to desecrate the Holy of Holies by entering it, it was related: "The virgins who had been shut up in their chambers
rushed forth with their mothers, and covering their hair
with dust and ashes, filled the streets with groanings and
lamentations."  A similar event took place several decades
later (176 B. C. E.) when Heliodorus, the chancellor of Seleucid IV, attempted to rob the treasury of the Temple: "Unmarried girls who were kept in seclusion ran to the gates
or walls of their houses, while others leaned out from the
windows; all with outstretched hand made solemn entreaty to
Heaven" (II Mac. 3:19-20).  Around the same time Ben Sira
also gave advice about keeping unmarried daughters out of
sight: "Keep a close watch over a headstrong daughter. . . .
Do not let her display her beauty to any man, or gossip in
the women's quarters."[41]  In a work composed by a Diaspora
Jew shortly before or after the beginning of the Common
Era, but referring to the persecutions of the Jews under
Antiochus IV (167 B. C. E.), it was said of Hannah, the
mother of seven martyred sons:

> Now these are the words that the mother of the
> seven sons, the righteous woman, spake to her
> children:  'I was a pure maiden, and I strayed not
> from my father's house, and I kept guard over the
> rib that was builded into Eve.  No seducer of the
> desert, no deceiver in the field, corrupted me;
> nor did the false, beguiling Serpent sully the purity
> of my maidenhood.[42]

The picture drawn by Philo in Egypt depicts the

physical restriction of Jewish women as even more severe--
at least in Egypt at that time:  "Their women are kept in
seclusion, never even approaching the outer doors, and their
maidens are confined to the inner chambers, who for modesty's sake avoided the sight of men, even of their closest relations. "[43]  In another place Philo confirms this restriction
of women as much as possible to the household, with the unmarried limited even further:  "The women are best suited
to the indoor life which never strays from the house, within
which the middle door is taken by the maidens as their
boundary, and the outer door by those who have reached full
womanhood. "[44]  Women were to stay off the streets, except
to go to pray, and they were only to do that when everyone
else had gone home:  "A woman, then, should not show herself off like a vagrant in the streets before the eyes of other
men, except when she has to go to the temple, and even then
she should take pains to go, not when the market is full, but
when most people have gone home. "[45]

     The evidence given just above from the apocrypha and
the pseudepigrapha refers to unmarried women in Palestine,
and Philo's testimony reflects the restrictive customs concerning both married and unmarried women in Jewish Egypt.
The following mishnaic and tannaitic evidence indicates that
restrictive tendencies concerning married women were also
present in Palestine at the beginning of the Common Era.

     One mishnah states:  "These are they that are put
away without their Ketubah:  a wife that transgresses the
Law of Moses and Jewish custom. ...  And what (conduct is
such that transgresses) Jewish custom?  If she goes out
with her hair unbound, or spins in the street, or speaks
with any man. "[46]  In another discussion of divorce Rabbi
Meir is recorded as saying:

          As men differ in their treatment of their food, so
          they differ in their treatment of their wives.  Some
          men, if a fly falls into their cup, will put it aside
          and not drink it.  This corresponds to the way of
          Papus b. Judah[47] who used, when he went out, to
          lock his wife indoors.  Another man, if a fly falls
          into his cup, will throw away the fly and then
          drink the cup.  This corresponds to the way of
          most men who do not mind their wives talking with
          their brothers and relatives.  Another man, again
          if a fly falls into his soup, will squash it and eat
          it.  This corresponds to the way of a bad man

who sees his wife go out with her hair unfastened
and spin cloth in the street.... Such a one it is
a religious duty to divorce. [48]

Hence, in Palestinian Judaism of the 1st century C. E. some
men even locked their wives in their houses, but "most men"
did not object to their wives talking to their brothers and relatives, although whether within or outside their own households is not stated.

With the passage of time the restrictions on married
women leaving their households in Palestinian Judaism became even more severe. In the rather early Genesis Rabbah[49] there is a very clear statement of this development;
how much it may also precisely reflect the state of affairs
in the first and second centuries is difficult to judge, though
it surely fits in naturally with the other earlier evidence of
Palestinian restrictiveness and the even more rigid Alexandrian limitations: "The man must master his wife, that she
not go out into the market place, for every woman who goes
out into the market place will eventually come to grief."

In sum, it is clear that in Palestinian Judaism at the
beginning of the Common Era unmarried women were kept
indoors; married women were often limited in their appear-
ances in public although apparently many nevertheless did at
times leave their households. [50] In view of these restrictions and those within the household and the head and face
covering of women, both to be discussed below, it would
seem appropriate to speak of a quasi-harem existence in
Palestinian Judaism of the 1st century C. E.;[51] in Alexandrian Judaism the harem existence was full-blown.

## 5. WOMEN'S HEAD AND FACE COVERING

When a Jewish woman did go out in public, she always went out with a head covering[52] which also covered the
whole face,[53] leaving one eye free. [54] Going out without a
head covering was considered so shameful that it was
grounds not only for divorce by the husband,[55] but divorce
without the obligation to pay the ketubah: "These are they
that are put away without their Ketubah ... if she goes out
with her head uncovered."[56] In fact, Rabbi Meir is quoted
as saying that it is a duty for a husband to divorce a woman
who goes out without her head covered. [57] On the other
hand, if a man uncovered the head of a woman in public he

was obliged to pay the large sum of 100 zuz.[58]   Apparently,
when in their own house or own courtyard some women covered their head only minimally, or not at all.[59]   But apparently many women kept their heads covered even when in
their own house or courtyard, for during the early rabbinic
period (17 B. C. E.) the rabbis once asked the mother of the
highpriest Ishmael ben Kimhith what she had done to merit
so much glory (the source of her glory being that two of her
sons had served as highpriest in one day).   She answered:
"Throughout the days of my life the beams of my house have
not seen the plaits of my hair."   Such a statement alone
would lead to the conclusion that such behavior was unusual,
but the rabbis' immediate response confirms the opposite:
"They said to her:   There were many who did likewise and
yet did not succeed."[60]   In the still earlier story of Susanna
in the Book of Daniel (written after 160 B. C. E.) there is
clear evidence that it was customary for women to cover
their heads and faces in public.   When Susanna was brought
to trial by the two lecherous Elders, it was said of her:
"Now Susanna was a woman of great beauty and delicate
feeling.   She was closely veiled, but those scoundrels ordered her to be unveiled so that they might feast their eyes
on her beauty" (Dan. 13:31-32).   Of course, the passage in
Numbers 5:11-31 about the trial of the wife suspected of
adultery provides even considerably earlier evidence (at
least fifth century B. C. E., if not earlier) that women covered their heads in public and that uncovering them was a
great disgrace: "The priest shall bring her forward. . . .   He
shall set her before the Lord, uncover her head. . ." (Num.
5:16-18).

     The head and face covering probably consisted of a
plaited hair-do combined with two kerchiefs, a forehead band
with ribbons hanging down to the chin, and a hairnet with
ribbons and bows on it.[61]   Just how thoroughly this covering
hid the features of the women is documented by many biblical and rabbinic passages,[62] including the following rather
dramatic one: "Once there was a highpriest to whose lot it
fell to administer the water of bitterness (the test for a
suspected adultress of Num. 5:11-31).   The woman was
brought to him and he uncovered her head and took her hair
down.   Then he took the vessel to give her to drink; he
looked at her and saw that it was his mother!"[63]   Billerbeck
comments on this passage: "Here one can see clearly that
the covering and veiling of the woman consisted of her coif-
fure.   As long as her head-dress was in order the priest
did not know who was standing before him, for her hair-do

covered her face.   Only as her head-dress was uncovered
by the undoing of her hair-do did he recognize his mother. "[64]

Jewish women in Palestine before and after the Common Era, and probably also later in Babylonia, then, always
appeared in public with their head and face largely covered,
and very often even maintained this covering, or at least a
somewhat lesser one, within the confines of their own home
and courtyard so that even their own relatives might in
some cases never see their faces.   These customs were
probably less rigidly enforced in the villages.

## 6.   CONVERSATION WITH WOMEN

Jewish women were not only to be seen as little as
possible; they were also to be heard and spoken to as little
as possible.   A general prohibition against superfluous talk
with any women was stated clearly a hundred years before
the Common Era, and was repeated, specified, and extended
subsequently.   The Mishnah recorded that, "Jose b. Johanan
(150 B. C. E.) said ... talk not much with womankind. "[65]
Following tannaitic rabbis developed the text rather dramatically: "This they said of a man's own wife: how much
more of his fellow's wife!   Hence the Sages have said: He
that talks much with womankind brings evil upon himself and
neglects the study of the Law and at the last will inherit
Gehenna. "[66]  The opposition between women and the study of
Torah existed not only in the sense that women did not study
Torah, as discussed above, [67] but also in the sense that women
distracted men from the study of Torah. [68]  The prohibition was
studied in the 2nd century C. E. as confirmed in Beruria's quoting it to Rabbi Jose the Galilean. [69]  It is repeated in the Talmud:
"Do not converse much with women, as this will ultimately lead
you to unchastity. "[70]  In another place it is repeated, paralleling
the mishnaic statement concerning not speaking with one's own
wife, but adding other women relatives as well.   Here, too, the
prohibition is not against "much talk," but apparently against
any speaking with women on the street:

> Our Rabbis taught:  Six things are unbecoming for
> a scholar. ...   'He should not converse with a
> woman in the street. '  Rabbi Hisda said:  Even
> with his wife.   It has been taught similarly:  Even
> with his wife, even with his daughter, even with
> his sister, because not everyone knows who are
> his female relatives. [71]

The matter was carried so far that at times even an indirect
speaking to a woman was forbidden: "'Will you send a greet-
ing to (my wife) Yaltha,' he suggested.   'Thus said Samuel,'
he replied, (to listen to) a woman's voice is indecent.'   'It
is possible through a messenger?'   'Thus said Samuel,' he
retorted, 'One must not enquire after a woman's welfare.'
'Then by her husband!'   'Thus said Samuel,' said he, 'One
must not enquire after a woman's welfare at all. '"[72]   If
there was any question about the seriousness of the prohibition of speaking unnecessarily with women, even one's wife,
the matter was laid to rest by the great Rab (second century
C. E.), who was ordained by Judah ha Nasi, the compiler of
the Mishnah: "Rab said:  Even the superfluous conversation
between a man and his wife is declared to a person in the
hour of his death. "[73]

There is an enlightening passage immediately following the one just cited, which teaches that although a husband
ought not usually to talk much with his wife, he may do so
to cajole her into having sex with him: "Now behold Rabbi
Kahana once lay down beneath the bed of Rab, and he heard
him converse and jest and perform his needs.   (Thereupon)
he said:  The mouth of Rab is like that of one who has not
tasted any food. [74]   Said (Rab) to him:  Kahana, get out,
this is unseemly!--There is no contradiction:  In the one
case (it is) where he has to procure her favor, in the other, where he has no need to procure her favor."   That
there was a tendency for husbands to limit their conversation with their wives to when they had sexual intercourse
with them is reinforced by the story told about the first century C. E. Rabbi Eliezer ben Hyrcanus[75] (but here the story
was told by his wife, Imma Shalom).   What is significant is
the double meaning given to the word "converse" (SPR); here
it obviously means both vocal and sexual intercourse:  "Imma
Shalom ... replied:  He (my husband) 'converses' with me
neither at the beginning nor at the end of the night, but
(only) at midnight; and when he 'converses,' he uncovers a
handbreadth and covers a handbreadth, and is as though he
were compelled by a demon. "[76]

It can be concluded that in ancient Palestinian Judaism men were normally not to speak with women, especially
in public (not even one's own wife or relatives, let alone
other women); in private, conversation with one's wife or
female relatives was to be kept to a minimum concerning
necessary items, although to "procure the wife's (sexual)
favor" this prohibition was relaxed.   In this regard women

seem to have been seen solely as serving and sexual beings.


## 7.  WOMEN'S ABSENCE FROM MEALS

There is an interesting corollary to the restrictions
on conversing with women within the household, which,
among other things, limited their role as a "serving being,"
albeit with a somewhat demeaning motivation.  First, women
did not eat with the men whenever there was a guest.  This
is made clear in two stories about Rabbi Nahman (third century C. E.), who, when at meal with a guest, asked him to
send greetings to his (Nahman's) wife Yaltha.  One story is
quoted just above;[77] the other is as follows:  "Ulla was
once at the house of Rabbi Nahman.  They had a meal and
he said grace, and he handed the cup of benediction to Rabbi Nahman.  Rabbi Nahman said to him:  Please send the
cup of benediction to Yaltha,"[78] but Ulla refused to do so.
At this point Billerbeck comments:  "women normally did
not partake at a meal for guests; in order to honor them,
the cup of benediction with some left over wine was sent
to them."[79]  The same custom persists in the villages of
Palestine today.  While in Israel in 1972 I was in a number
of houses of Arabs, Christian, Druze and Muslim, for meals,
and never met the wives, or any other women; my friends
had many similar experiences.

The separation of women, or rather, females, from
the meals of the men was carried even further; the men
were not even to be served by women.  When the same
Rabbi Nahman wanted to have his daughter, who was only a
child, serve him and his guest a drink, he was rebuked with
the clear quotation of the earlier Rabbi Samuel:  "One must
not be served by a woman."  When Nahman argued that she
was only a child, he was told:  "Samuel said distinctly, that
one must not be served by a woman at all, whether adult or
child."[80]

Again, a similar custom persists among contemporary
Palestinians; at all the meals I was at, we were never
served by girls or women.  The women did all the work of
preparing the food and usually brought it as far as the door
of the dining area, whether it was a room or house roof or
whatever, and there it was taken by the youngest males and
brought to the guests.

# CHAPTER VI

## WOMEN AND SEX

### 1. WOMAN AS SEX OBJECT

Although much of the evidence already discussed indicates that the early rabbis often thought of women as
mainly sexual creatures, there is still further rabbinical
documentation which projects an image of women as almost
totally sex objects.   To begin, on the negative side (that is,
a woman who was not sexually, physically, attractive was
judged negatively), in a discussion in the Mishnah about the
kinds of women who are to be divorced without their kethubah, it was stated that all defects which disqualify priests
also disqualify women (and hence they are to be divorced). [1]
At this point Blackman in his translation notes:  "To these
are added, in the case of women, unpleasant perspiration,
obnoxious breath, unbearable odor, ugly unusual hair, horrid
voice, unsightly scar, ungainly breasts. "

But the rabbis' remarks about women as sex objects
were usually on the "positive" side, i. e. , as stimulating
sexual desire in the male.   The concern for avoiding this
latter was the cause of some unusual prohibitions:   "A man
should not walk behind a woman on the road. "   The editor
of the English Soncino edition here notes:   "To avoid un-
chaste thoughts. "   The prohibition was strengthened:   "Rabbi
Johanan said:   Better go behind a lion than behind a woman. "
And specified:   "Even if his wife happens to be in front of
him on a bridge he should let her pass on one side. "   And
strengthened still further:   "whoever crosses a river behind
a woman will have no portion in the future world. "   The
English Soncino edition notes:   "Because the woman in cross-
ing will naturally lift up her dress. "[2]

Several biblical women were remembered by the rabbis in particularly sexual terms:

126

> Our Rabbis taught: Rahab inspired lust by her
> name; Jael by her voice; Abigail by her memory;
> Mical daughter of Saul by her appearance. Rabbi
> Isaac said: Whoever says, 'Rahab, Rahab,' at
> once has an issue. Said Rabbi Nahman to him:
> I say Rahab, Rahab, and nothing happens to me!
> He replied: I was speaking of one who knows her
> and is intimate with her. [3]

However, it was not just these women who were thought by
the rabbis to stimulate lust, for after admonishing men not
to "converse much with women, as this will ultimately lead
you to unchastity," they added: "Rabbi Aha of the school of
Rabbi Josiah said: He who gazes at a woman eventually
comes to sin."[4] And further: "One should not look intently
at a beautiful woman, even if she be unmarried, or at a
married woman even if she be ugly, nor at a woman's gaudy
garments ... even when these are spread on a wall."[5] It
would seem that every part of a woman's body was an incitement to lust: "Rabbi Isaac said: A handbreadth (exposed)
in a (married) woman constitutes sexual incitement." This
general statement was then specified: "Rabbi Hisda said:
A woman's leg is a sexual incitement." And yet further:
"A woman's voice is a sexual incitement." But perhaps the
crowning sexualizing statement about the body of a woman
is the following: "If one gazes at the little finger of a
woman, it is as if he gazed at her secret place!"[6]

Such looking was thought to have an effect on the offspring when sexual intercourse did actually take place afterwards: "Rabbi Josiah said ... he who looks even at a woman's heel will beget degenerate children. Rabbi Joseph
said: This applies even to one's own wife when she is a
niddah. [7] Rabbi Simeon ben Lakish said: 'Heel' that is
stated means the unclean part, which is directly opposite
the heel."[8] A little later in the same passage a number of
specific birth defects were explained in terms of "deviations"
in sexual practice. Save for the one about conversation,
they all seem to focus on the woman: "Rabbi Johanan ben
Dahabai said: The Ministering Angels told me four things:
People are born lame because they (their parents) over-
turned their table." The English Soncino edition comments
here: "i. e., practiced unnatural cohabitation." What is obviously meant here is that during sexual intercourse the woman rather than the man took the superior position, which
is what the editor of the German edition says. [9] The sperm
had to be deposited in the vagina, since conception took

place.  It is interesting to note, however, that the English
editor apparently still thinks that the woman's having the
superior position is "unnatural."

It is perhaps of sufficient interest to note here parenthetically that the mythical Lilith of early medieval midrash
(the Alphabet of Ben Sira), Adam's first mate, was, like
him, made from the dust of the earth, wanted equality with
him and also wished at times to have the superior position
in sexual intercourse; things did not work out and so the
more docile Eve was made from Adam's rib.  To the medieval author, the things Lilith wanted were clearly "unnatural."
The pertinent portion of the story is as follows: "Adam and
Lilith never found peace together; for when he wished to lie
with her, she took offense at the recumbent posture he demanded.  'Why must I lie beneath you?' she asked.  'I also
was made from dust, and am therefore your equal.'  Because
Adam tried to compel her obedience by force, Lilith, in a
rage, uttered the magic name of God, rose into the air and
left him."[10]  The editors commented:

> It is characteristic of civilizations where women
> are treated as chattels that they must adopt the
> recumbent posture during intercourse, which Lilith
> refused.  That Greek witches who worshipped He-
> cate favoured the superior posture, we know from
> Apuleius; and it occurs in early Sumerian repre-
> sentations of the sexual act, though not in the Hit-
> tite.  Malinowski writes that Melanesian girls
> ridicule what they call 'the missionary position,'
> which demands that they should lie passive and
> recumbent.[11]

Rabbi Johanan ben Dahabai, in the passage quoted
above, went on to say that children are born "dumb, because
they kiss 'that place'; deaf, because they converse during
cohabitation; blind, because they look at 'that place'."[12]
Such prudishness did not go undisputed.  In fact, the re-
sultant decision firmly reestablished the more primitive condition whereby the woman was totally at the disposal of the
man:

> Rabbi Johanan said:  The above is the view of
> Rabbi Johanan ben Dahabai; but our Sages said:
> The halachah is not as Rabbi Johanan ben Dahabai,
> but a man may do whatever he pleases with his
> wife (at intercourse)....  A woman once came

> before Rabbi and said, 'Rabbi! I set a table be-
> fore my husband, but he overturned it.' Rabbi
> replied: 'My daughter! the Torah hath permitted
> thee to him--what then can I do for thee?' A
> woman once came before Rab and complained,
> 'Rabbi! I set a table before my husband, but he
> overturned it.

The answer was the same: the woman belonged to the man
and he could do with her what he would. [13]

Thus, the tradition of woman as a sex object, already firmly founded in the Wisdom literature and the pseudepigraphal writings, was vigorously continued in the rabbinic
literature. C. G. Montefiore noted that social intercourse
with women was usually taboo. They were the source of
moral danger. They were the incitements to depravity and
lust. The evil impulse--the Yetzer ha-Ra--is especially and
mainly the impulse which leads to sexual impurity. "The
result was not entirely healthy.... The lack of healthy,
simple companionship and friendship caused a constant dwelling upon sexual relations and details." For example, concerning levirate marriage the following discussion was held:

> But when he slept? Surely Rab Judah ruled that
> one in sleep cannot acquire his sister-in-law! But
> when accidental insertion occurred? [The English
> Soncino edition comments at this point: "When in
> a state of erection the levirate fell from a raised
> bench upon his sister-in-law who happened to be
> below" (v. Rashi)] Surely Rabbah stated: One
> who fell from a roof and his fall resulted in acci-
> dental insertion, is liable to pay an indemnity for
> four things, and if the woman was his sister-in-
> law no kinyan ['acquisition'] is thereby constituted!
> It is when, for instance, his intention was inter-
> course with his wife and his sister-in-law seized
> him and he cohabited with her.... Raba said: If
> a levir's intention was to shoot against a wall and
> he accidentally shot at his sister-in-law, no kinyan
> is thereby constituted; if he intended, however, to
> shoot at a beast and he accidentally shot at his sis-
> ter-in-law, kinyan is thereby constituted, since
> some sort of intercourse had been intended. [14]

As Montefiore stated, "in the Rabbinic literature sexual allusions are very frequent. Immense are the Halachic

discussions about the details of sex life, and sexual pheno-
mena. " There are six tractates in the Mishnah devoted
specifically to women: Yabamoth (Sister-in-law), Ketuboth
(Marriage Deeds), Sotah (The Suspected Adulteress), Gittin
(Bills of Divorce), Kiddushin (Betrothals), and Niddah (The
Menstruant). (In the Herbert Danby translation of the Mish-
nah into English this amounts to about one hundred pages.)
The corresponding tractates in the Babylonian Talmud in the
English Soncino edition run to eight volumes.

> 'Repel nature, and it recurs.' Repress it, and it
> grows up again, and not always in a healthy form.
> Where we should not dream of thinking that any
> sexual desire could be evoked, the Rabbis were
> always on the watch for it, dwelling on it, sug-
> gesting it. Though they were almost invariable
> married men, they yet seem to have often been
> oddly tormented by sexual desires; perhaps, too,
> the very absence of natural and healthy social in-
> tercourse between men and women drove them to
> dwell theoretically with double frequency upon every
> sort of sexual details and minutiae. [15]

## 2. IMPURE MENSTRUOUS WOMEN

As the Encyclopaedia Judaica points out, the state of
ritual impurity "is considered hateful to God, and man is to
take care in order not to find himself thus excluded from his
divine presence. "[16] The same author also notes that it is
certain that the rabbis did not regard impurities as infectious
diseases or the laws of purification as quasi-hygienic principles; rather, they saw ritual purity as a religious ideal.
It was one of the steps on the way to the spirit of holiness. [17]
Thus, though at times the incurring of uncleanness is involuntary, one of the main results is to somehow separate one-
self from God, to be displeasing to God. The consequences
of ritual impurity can be dire in the extreme. "A polluted
person is always in the wrong. He has developed some
wrong condition or simply crossed some line which should
not have been crossed and this displacement unleashes danger
for someone. "[18]

While the temple in Jerusalem yet existed, the concern of the priestly class about ritual purity became so over-
riding that it was said of them, "to render a knife impure
was more serious to them than bloodshed. "[19] In fact, the

Mishnah notes that "if a priest served (at the Altar) in a
state of uncleanness his brethren priests did not bring him
to the court, but the young men among the priests took him
outside the Temple Court and split open his brain with
clubs."[20]   At the same time it must be remembered that by
the beginning of the Common Era, "the prohibition against
contracting impurity and the obligation of purity extend also
to all Jews and to all localities."[21]

There were three main causes of impurity: leprosy,
dead bodies of certain animals, and particularly human
corpses, and issue from sexual organs (these laws were
based mainly on Leviticus 11-17, composed by priestly writers in the fifth century B. C. E.).  Of the three, the last
is the most important and frequent, and clearly it is the
woman that is mostly involved.  If a man has an emission
of semen outside of intercourse he is unclean; but if a man
has intercourse with a woman, both are unclean--in both instances, however, only until the evening of the day of the
emission.

The Levitical laws concerning the impurity of women
are much more restrictive.  When a woman has a menstruous
discharge of blood, she is unclean for seven days, or as
long as it lasts, whichever is longer.  In addition, whoever
she touches becomes unclean for a day, as does any thing
she touches.  Further,

> whoever touches anything on which she sits shall
> wash his clothes, bathe in water and remain un-
> clean till evening.  If he is on the bed or seat
> where she is sitting, by touching it he shall be-
> come unclean till evening.  If a man goes so far
> as to have intercourse with her and any of her dis-
> charge gets on to him, then he shall be unclean
> for seven days, and every bed on which he lies
> down shall be unclean (Lev. 15:23-34).

In the latter case a further, more severe punishment is
specified: "If a man lies with a woman during her monthly
period and brings shame upon her, he has exposed her discharge and she has uncovered the source of her discharge;
they shall both be cut off from their people" (Lev. 20:18).
In the end, the biblical threat against disregarding these
laws concerning ritual purity was dire: "In this way you
shall warn the Israelites against uncleanness, in order that
they may not bring uncleanness upon the Tabernacle where I

dwell among them, and so die" (Lev. 15:31).   The young
priests referred to above apparently took it upon themselves
to be God's executioners.

     After giving birth a woman was also considered un-
clean for a period of time and in need of still further "purification" for an even longer period.   What is especially interesting is that both periods of "impurity" were twice as
long if a girl was born than if a boy was--which would seem
to indicate that a girl was considered twice as defiling as a
boy:

> When a woman conceives and bears a male child,
> she shall be unclean for seven days, as in the
> period of her impurity through menstruation. . . .
> The woman shall wait for thirty-three days be-
> cause her blood requires purification; she shall
> touch nothing that is holy, and shall not enter the
> sanctuary till her days of purification are com-
> pleted.   If she bears a female child, she shall be
> unclean for fourteen days as for her menstruation
> and shall wait for sixty-six days. . . (Lev. 12:2-5).

Originally, in biblical times, intercourse was forbidden only
during the seven- or fourteen-day period, but by rabbinic
times there were many attempts to expand that restriction
to the entire forty- and eighty-day periods--with substantial
success. [22]

     In the rabbinic period, which began, of course, al-
ready in the late Second Temple period, i. e. , first and
second centuries B. C. E. , "the laws relating to the menstruous woman comprise some of the most fundamental principles
of the halakhic system, while a scrupulous observance of
their minutiae has been one of the distinguishing signs of an
exemplary traditional Jewish family life. "[23]   Already in the
early part of the second century C. E. the rules concerning
menstruation were said to be "essential laws" (gufei Torah). [24]
Judging from the quantity of writing produced, the ancient
rabbis obviously thought the regulation of the "niddah," the
menstruant, to be of extreme importance.   The Mishnah devoted ten chapters to the tractate Niddah, while the contemporary Tosefta had another nine chapters; at least four chapters of additional commentary are still extant in the Palestinian Talmud, while the full text of ten chapters of commentary by the Babylonian Talmud is extant.   It is interesting to note that Niddah is the only tractate out of the twelve

in the more generic "order" of Tohoroth (concerning clean-
ness and uncleanness) that has a gemara (that is, has a
commentary on the Mishnah teachings) in the Babylonian Talmud. The English Soncino edition of Niddah is over 500
pages long.

In connection with a similar point a Jewish woman
editor wrote:

> The laws of niddah raise several issues of concern
> to women.... Perhaps the most vexing is: Why
> were the restrictions imposed upon the menstruat-
> ing woman retained after the destruction of the
> Temple, while all other forms of tu'mah were al-
> lowed to lapse? Women of childbearing age are
> thus the only Jews regularly tameh 50% of the
> time. It is difficult to avoid the implication that
> we are dealing here with the potent residue of an
> ancient taboo based on a mixture of male fear,
> awe, and repugnance toward woman's creative bio-
> logical cycle. Furthermore, is there really no
> stigma attached to the concept of tum'ah, especially
> as practiced in the isolation of the niddah? She is
> treated, after all, as though bearing a rather un-
> pleasant contagious disease. The prolongation of
> her period of tum'ah for seven days after the ces-
> sation of her menstrual flow reinforces the im-
> pression that the menstrual blood itself has power-
> ful contaminating properties which must be guarded
> against. 25

The rabbis fixed the menstrual cycle at 18 days; during the first seven after blood first appeared the woman was
unclean; for the next eleven she was clean, unless blood appeared. The restriction was greatly expanded, however, as
early as the end of the tannaitic period when Jewish women
were accustomed to observe seven "clean" days;26 "if even
a spot of blood as large as a mustard seed appeared,"27
they would be considered unclean for the next seven days.
This practice, of course, could make many women unclean
a majority of the time.

One of the comments of the English Soncino edition
editor, Isidore Epstein, is of special interest:

> Graver in its consequences and in full force to the
> present day [1948] is the law of Niddah. The

reasons for the Niddah ordinances are many and
varied.   They promote sexual hygiene, physical
health, marital continence, respect for womanhood, consecration of married life, and family
happiness.   But over and above these weighty reasons, they concern the very being of the soul of
the Jew.   They safeguard the purity of the Jewish
soul, without which no true religious, moral and
spiritual life--individual or corporate--as Judaism
conceives it, is attainable.[28]

That the niddah regulations would promote marital continence
is apparent; that they necessarily would foster consecration
of the married life and family happiness, or, indeed, sexual
hygiene and physical health, is not.   But to claim that they
promote respect for womanhood is puzzling.   It is difficult
to see how declaring a person unclean and contaminating of
everyone and everything within touch would encourage self-
respect or respect from others.   To go beyond this and say
that the essence of the Jewish soul and the developing of a
true religious, moral and spiritual Jewish life is absolutely
dependent upon the "banishment" (as the word niddah means
in its root) of all women for forty per cent of every year
during thirty years or more of their adult lives is even
more confounding; it would seem to project misogynism into
"the very being of the soul of the Jew."

Perhaps the question of uncleanness resulting from a
discharge from the female sexual organs was fairly straight-
forward in biblical times, but by the rabbinic period the de-
ciding of such questions had become extremely complex and
often of great moment.   Only a rabbi, who of course was always a male, could make the decisions.   Page after page of
the talmudic tractate Niddah is devoted to stories of how
cloths with blood stains would be brought or sent by women
to the rabbis to judge their "purity," normally by color and
smell:   "To decide a law relating to a menstruous woman
demands, besides a profound knowledge of the halakhah, experience in various medical matters, and at times also the
ability to assume the grave responsibility of disqualifying a
woman from pursuing a normal married life and of--at
times--separating her forever from her husband."[29]   Whereas nowadays whether the discharge was "unclean" menstrual
blood or not can be easily resolved, previously this problem
was often one of paramount human significance and an obstacle to married life for many women.   Consequently, the
works of the codifiers in all periods contain hundreds of

responsa dealing with the subject out of a manifest desire to alleviate this hardship, "though with a very scant possibility of doing so."[30]

It cannot be said that persons or things connected with menstruation were considered indifferently in ancient Palestinian Judaism. According to the Mishnah, "heedlessness of the laws of the menstruant" was one of the three transgressions for which women died in childbirth![31]  Further, the uncleanness of a menstruating woman was considered "the most loathsome impurity."[32]  In fact, it was compared with the greatest horror in Judaism, an idol:

> Rabbi Akiba said: Whence do we learn of an idol that like a menstruant it conveys uncleanness by carrying? Because it is written, Thou shalt cast them away like a menstruous thing; thou shalt say unto it, Get thee hence. Like as a menstruant conveys uncleanness by carrying, so does an idol convey uncleanness by carrying.[33]

Israel M. Ta-Shma notes that "this idea was prevalent already in the Bible, where the uncleanness of the menstruous woman occurs as a noun and as a metaphor for the height of defilement (Ezek. 2:19-20; Ezra 9:11; Lam. 1:17; II Chron. 29:5)."[34]  In each of these citations the noun niddah occurs and is usually translated as "impurity" or a synonym of it. It is clear from the Mishnah text Shab. 9,1, quoted above, and others that the early rabbis understood the word niddah to refer primarily to the uncleanness of a menstruous woman, and in a transferred sense to impure things more generally. It is not apparent that in the earlier biblical texts the primary meaning was not basically that which was banished or impure generally; it was also applied in some instances to menstruous women, so that by rabbinic times there occurred a narrowing of the meaning of the word niddah to the uncleanness of a menstruous woman. Whenever the rabbis saw a form of the word niddah in the Bible, they apparently understood it to mean not simply impure, but impure as a menstruous woman is impure. If this analysis bears up under further careful investigation, it would provide an additional bit of evidence that the status of women, at least in some ways, worsened in Judaism from the earlier biblical period to the rabbinic period.

One woman Jewish scholar wrote the following about the relationship between tum'ah (impurity) in general and niddah impurity:

The point at which tum'at niddah was isolated from
the general category of tum'ah and made a special
case was the point at which pathology entered halacha.   At that point, tum'at niddah became divorced from the symbolism of death and resurrec-
tion and acquired a new significance related to its
accompanying sexual prohibitions.   Whereas tum'at
niddah had been a way for women to experience
death and rebirth through the cycle of their own
bodies, it became distorted into a method of con-
trolling the fearsome power of sexual desire, of
disciplining a mistrusted physical drive. [35]

The evil of having intercourse with, or even simply
touching, an unclean, menstruous, woman was apparently
thought so great that this effect could be fatal for the man
as well.  The following story makes that clear and also give
a picture of how "segregated" the Niddah, the menstruating
wife, was:

There was once a certain man who had studied
much Scripture and had studied much Mishnah and
attended upon many scholars, who died in middle
age.   His wife kept asking the rabbis, why did he
die in middle age?   There was not a person who
could answer her.   One time she encountered Elijah, of blessed memory.   My child, he asked her,
why art thou weeping and crying?   Master, she
answered him, my husband studied much Scripture
and studied much Mishnah and attended upon many
scholars, yet he died in middle age.   Said Elijah
to her, During the first three days of thine impurity,[36] how did he conduct himself in thy company?   Master, she replied, he did not touch me,
God forbid! even with his little finger.   On the
contrary, this is how he spoke to me:  Touch
nothing lest it become of doubtful purity.   During
the last days of thine impurity,[37] how did he conduct himself in thy company?   Master, she replied, I ate with him and drank with him and in
my clothes slept with him in bed; his flesh touched
mine but he had no thought of anything.   Blessed
be God who killed him, Elijah exclaimed, for thus
it is written in the Torah, Also thou shalt not approach unto a woman as long as she is impure by
her uncleanness. [38]

According to the Talmud a menstruous woman did not even have to come into contact with a man to have a fatal, physical or spiritual effect on him: "Our Rabbis taught: ... if a menstruant woman passes between two (men), if it is at the beginning of her menses she will slay one of them, and if it is at the end of her menses she will cause strife between them.... When one meets a woman coming up from her statutory tebillah,[39] if (subsequently) he is the first to have intercourse, a spirit of immorality will infect him; while if she is the first to have intercourse, a spirit of immorality will infect her."[40] All this must be understood against the background of various superstitions then current among the Jews concerning menstruating women (similar beliefs, of course, were present elsewhere in the ancient world).[41] It was believed that her breath caused harm, that her glance was "disreputable and created a bad impression," and that menstruous blood was deadly if drunk. If a menstruous woman looked for a long time at a mirror it was thought that red drops resembling blood would appear on it; she polluted the air around her and was regarded as sick and even as afflicted with the plague.[42]

Since a menstruous woman was unclean and contaminated everything and everybody she came into contact with, even indirectly, she really was "banished," at least already in mishnaic times. No food was to be eaten with her: "Rabbi Simeon ben Eleazar [second century, C. E. , a student of Rabbi Meir] said: Come and see how far purity has spread in Israel! For we did not learn, a clean man must not eat with an unclean woman."[43] At this point the English Soncino edition notes: "But there was no need to interdict the first [eating with an unclean woman], because even Israelites ... would not dine together with an unclean woman." In fact she was excluded from her home and stayed in a special house, known as "a house of uncleanness,"[44] and remained there "all the days of her impurity." The tannaitic text of The Fathers According to Rabbi Nathan again makes this, and other restrictions, quite clear:

> What is the hedge which the Torah made about its words? Lo, it says, Also thou shalt not approach unto a woman ... as long as she is impure by her uncleanness (Lev. 18:19). May her husband perhaps embrace her or kiss her or engage her in idle chatter?[45] The verse says, thou shalt not approach. May she perhaps sleep with him in her clothes on the couch? The verse says, thou shalt

not approach. May she wash her face perhaps and
paint her eyes? The verse says, And of her that
is sick with her impurity (Lev. 15:33): all the
days of her impurity let her be in isolation. 46
Hence it was said: She that neglects herself in the
days of her impurity, with her the Sages are
pleased; but she that adorns herself in the days of
her impurity, with her the Sages are displeased. 47

Also Rabbi Akiba in the first century noted that, "when I
went to Gallia, they used to call a niddah 'galmudah. '48
How galmudah? (As much as to say), gemulah da (this one
is isolated) from her husband. "49

The restrictions on menstruous women continued to
expand even after the early rabbinic, tannaitic, period, particularly in the religious sphere. These increasing limitations were brought together in a small work entitled, Baraita de-Niddah, 50 which was probably composed during the
latter part of the geonic period, i.e., circa tenth century
C.E. The menstruous woman was forbidden to enter a synagogue, as was her husband also if he had been made unclean by her in any way, i.e., by her spittle, the dust under
her feet, etc. She was also forbidden to enkindle the Sabbath lights, 51 and no one could inquire after her welfare or
recite a benediction in her presence. A priest whose wife,
mother or daughter was menstruating was not allowed to recite the priestly benediction in the synagogue, nor could any
benefit at all be derived from the work of a menstruating
woman, whose very utterances defiled people! 52 The appearance of the Baraita de-Niddah tended to strengthen greatly the application of its more stringent measures; this was
especially true with regard to the prohibition against a menstruating woman entering synagogue. 53

The laws of niddah, which were written first by the
(male) priestly writers of Leviticus and continually expanded
by the (male) rabbis, must have contributed in the extreme
to a sense of female inferiority and male superiority, at
least on the unconscious level but probably most often on the
conscious level. Rachel Adler makes the point clearly:

> The state of niddah became a monthly exile from
> the human race, a punitive shunning of the men-
> struant. Women were taught disgust and shame
> for their bodies and for the fluid which came out of
> them, that good, rich, red stuff which nourished

ungrateful men through nine fetal months. The
mikveh, instead of being the primal sea in which
all were made new, became the pool at which women were cleansed of their filth and thus became
acceptable sexual partners once more. Nor did it
help when rabbis informed offended women that
their filth was spiritual rather than physical. 54


3. MARRIED WOMEN

    The ancient rabbis urged in the strongest terms that
everyone, men and women, marry. Those men who did not
marry spent all their time "in sinful thoughts";55 "as soon
as a man takes a wife his sins are stopped up";56 in fact,
"any man who has no wife is no proper man."57 A girl who
was not married when she reached puberty ran the serious
risk that she would "become a whore."58 Indeed, it is said
that a woman will endure a bad marriage rather than be unmarried,59 but this was not meant only, perhaps not even
mainly, because of women's strong sexual drive, but rather
because they might well then be without a means of support.

    Of course, from the point of view of the race the
basic purpose of sex is the propagation of the race. This
is reflected in Judaism all the way back to the beginning of
the book of Genesis: "Male and female he created them.
God blessed them and said to them, 'Be fruitful and increase'" (Gen. 1:28). However, from around the last two
hundred years before the beginning of the Common Era onward there developed a tradition within Judaism of viewing
the proper purpose of sex to be not only exclusively restricted to within marriage, but even there to be restricted
to the procreation of children. In this tradition the exercising of sex for the sake of pleasure, to say nothing of
expressing affection, etc., was improper, indeed, sinful. 60
In the book of Tobit (ca. 200 B. C. E.) we read: "I take not
this my sister for lust, but in truth."61 This line was continued in the Testaments of the Twelve Patriarchs:62 "For
he knew that for the sake of children she wished to company
with Jacob, and not for lust of pleasure."63 The married
Essenes maintained the same idea: "They have no intercourse with them [their wives] during pregnancy, thus showing that their motive in marrying is not self-indulgence but
the procreation of children."64 In the same era we find
Philo continuing the tradition: in condemning infanticide he
stated that those who commit it are "pleasure-lovers when

they mate with their wives, not to procreate children and
perpetuate the race, but like pigs and goats in quest of the
enjoyment which such intercourse gives. "[65] The first century Palestinian Jew, Josephus, also insisted that the restriction of sexual intercourse was part of the Torah: "The
Law (nomos) recognizes no sexual connections, except the
natural union of man and wife, and that only for the procreation of children. "[66]

A similar idea seems imbedded in the statement of
the Mishnah forbidding a priest to marry a sterile woman:
"Rabbi Judah says: Although he already had a wife or children he may not marry a sterile woman, for such is the
harlot spoken of in the Law. "[67] It cannot be simply that
the priest had to fulfill the law about producing children that
he is forbidden to marry the sterile woman, for the negative
applies even if he has produced children; rather, sex for the
sake of pleasure was seen here as harlotry. The talmudic
commentary made this understanding emphatically clear when
it traced back a chain of approving rabbinic judgments which
were "'also of the same opinion as Rabbi Judah,' who holds
that a woman incapable of procreation is regarded as a harlot," and added: "Said Rabbi Huna ... any cohabitation
which results in no increase is nothing but meretricious intercourse. "[68]

The tradition among the rabbis of the obligation to
produce offspring (which was strictly binding only on men)[69]
was so strong that it was said: "A man shall not abstain
from the performance of the duty of the propagation of the
race,"[70] and "Rabbi Eliezer stated, He who does not engage
in propagation of the race is as though he sheds blood. "[71]
Indeed, if a man did not have any children by his wife within
ten years, he was obliged to divorce her: "Our Rabbis
taught: If a man took a wife and lived with her for ten years
and she bore no child, he shall divorce her. "[72] At the
same time there was a clear preference for male children
over female children: "It is well for those whose children
are male, but ill for those who are female. "[73] "At the
birth of a boy all are joyful ... at the birth of a girl all
are sorrowful. "[74] "When a boy comes into the world, peace
comes into the world.... When a girl comes, nothing
comes. "[75]

It was noted above that according to the Mishnah,
women were "acquired" in three ways, "by money, document
or sexual intercourse. "[76] As Raphael Loewe points out, "It

would be surprising if wives thought of themselves as the
'equals' of their husbands ... the nature of the relationship
of rabbinic spouses is fairly well illustrated by the circum-
stance that whereas the talmudic Aramaic corresponding to
'Mrs.' means literally '(she) of the house of,' in recorded
or contrived conversations the wife addresses her husband
as 'rabbi'--a form used by slaves, but also by disciples,
meaning 'my master'--whereas the husband addresses his
wife as 'my daughter.'"[77]  When it is recalled that in Hellenistic Greek and the Latin of first century Rome women
were addressed as "Lady," or "mistress" (kyria, domina),
the Judaic appelative appears even more reflective of male
superiority.[78]

   Bethrothals and marriages were normally arranged by
the parents, the girl having no voice in the matter unless she
had reached the age of 12 1/2, but it was customary to betroth a daughter between the ages of 12 and 12 1/2 (the girl
is a minor to age 12 years and 1 day, a maiden from 12 to
12 1/2, and a woman from 12 1/2 on).  As a maiden she
could express the wish to remain in the parental home until
she became a "woman," and from then on she had the right
to refuse a proposed husband, though from a psychological
point of view this could not have been very frequent.  It apparently even happened in mishnaic times that a man came
to the rabbis and said: "I gave my daughter in betrothal but
I do not know to whom I gave her."[79]  Agrippa I (first century C.E.) betrothed his two daughters at ages six and ten.[80]
It is even stated that "A girl aged three years and a day may
be acquired in marriage by coition, and if her deceased
husband's brother cohabited with her, she becomes his."[81]
"The husband (if it were his first marriage) would generally
be in his late teens or early twenties,"[82] though some would
suggest that for economic reasons the lower class man was
often in his thirties when he first married.

   Before marriage a daughter was pretty totally under
the control of her father, as is indicated by the following
mishnah: "The man may sell his daughter, but the woman
may not sell her daughter; the man may betroth his daughter,
but the woman may not betroth her daughter."[83]  There are
many statements throughout the rabbinic literature indicating
that at marriage the woman passed into the control of her
husband, or, as Blackman put it: "betrothal, making a woman the sacrosanct possession--the inviolable property--of
the husband."[84]  The following are samples of such statements taken only from writings from mishnaic times.  "The

husband can not annul (vows made by his wife) until she
passes under his control (at marriage)."[85]  "Since he has
acquired the woman (by marriage) should he not acquire also
her property?"[86]  "Since one has come into the possession
of the woman does it not follow that he should come into the
possession of her property too?"[87]  "If she has already entered into the control of the husband...."[88]  "She is under
the control of her husband."[89]  "She is under the control of
another (primarily her husband)."[90]  "She continues within
the control of the father until she enters into the control of
the husband at marriage."[91]  Indeed, as already indicated,
the father, and then the husband, can annul any vow the
daughter or wife may have taken without the approval of the
father or husband respectively.[92]  As noted above, Josephus
wrote: "The woman, says the Law, is in all things inferior
to the man.  Let her accordingly be submissive, not for her
humiliation, but that she may be directed; for the authority
has been given by God to the man."[93]  The portion of the
Torah referred to here of course is Gen. 3:16: "To the
woman he said ... You shall be eager for your husband, and
he shall be your master."

Both the unmarried and the married woman were expected to work, but if any profit resulted from her work it
went not to her but to her father or husband, in return for
her maintenance (an economic situation not unlike that of a
slave, and one that almost all women in Western civilization suffered until very recently).  The Mishnah was very
clear; a woman passed legally from one economic bondage
to another, the latter being even more stringent than the
former:

> A father has authority over his daughter in re-
> spect of her betrothal (whether it was effected) by
> money, deed or intercourse; he is entitled to any-
> thing she finds and to her handiwork; (he has the
> right) of annulling her vows and he receives her
> bill of divorce; but he has no usufruct during her
> lifetime.  When she marries, the husband sur-
> passes him (in his rights) in that he has usufruct
> during her lifetime, but he is also under the ob-
> ligation of maintaining and ransoming her and to
> provide for her burial.  Rabbi Judah ruled: even
> the poorest man in Israel must provide no less
> than two flutes and one lamenting woman.[94]

In one way, however, a woman's economic position legally

improved when she married, for "the father is not liable for his daughter's maintenance,"[95] whereas the husband is "under the obligation of maintaining and ransoming her."[96]

In another regard a woman's legal economic lot declined when she married, that is, in connection with things she found. The Mishnah stated: "What is found by a man's son or daughter that are minors, what is found by his Canaanitish bondman or bondwoman, and what is found by his wife, belong to him; but what is found by his son or daughter that are of age, what is found by his Hebrew bondman or bondwoman, and what is found by his wife whom he has divorced ... belong to them."[97] The minor daughter need only wait until she becomes 13, the Hebrew bondwoman need not wait at all, the Gentile bondwoman need wait until she was freed (which happened in a variety of ways), whereas the married woman could only await the death of her husband or a divorce by him before this restriction was lifted from her. A somewhat unessential matter is involved here, but it is perhaps indicative of the relative status of the married woman.

The husband was obliged by the Mishnah to provide his wife with food, shelter, clothing,[98] ransom if necessary,[99] medical care,[100] and burial;[101] he also had to provide a "kethubah," a sort of insurance policy against death and divorce.[102] In return, "These are works which the wife must perform for her husband: grinding flour and baking bread and washing clothes and cooking food and giving suck to her child[103] and making his bed and working in wool."[104] In commenting on this mishnah, the Talmud added: "fill his cup for him ... wash his face, hands and feet."[105]

One must also recall the sayings from Proverbs on through the rabbinic quotations[106] in praise of the good wife as the husband's crown, joy, etc., and the many stories from the beginning of the Bible onward about happy marriages and deep affection between men and women. These doubtless reflect historical reality in many individual instances. Doubtless also there were many instances when the wife was de facto the dominant personality in the family. Nevertheless, the structure of the institution of marriage placed the woman in a position that was clearly inferior and subordinate to her husband. As C. G. Montefiore was already noted as saying, many modern apologists feel compelled to claim that women in ancient Judaism were not

placed in a position inferior to men, that their function was
different, but not inferior. The ancient Jewish writers, not
having experienced the pressure of the feminist movement
of the 19th and 20th centuries, felt no such compulsion. The
rabbis stated clearly that the wife was "under the control of
the husband," and Josephus proclaimed bluntly that "the woman, says the Law, is in all things inferior to the man."
It would seem that the rabbis and their contemporaries not
only were closer to the facts (indeed they lived them) but
also stated them more accurately.


## 4.  POLYGYNY

       "That there is a tradition of polygamy among the
Jews no one can deny."[107]  Polyandry, one woman having
several husbands simultaneously, was forbidden: "A woman
is not eligible to two (men); but is not a man eligible to two
(women)?"[108]  Its opposite, polygyny, one man having several wives, was not: "If four brothers married four women
and then died, and the eldest (of the brothers that remained)
was minded to contract levirite marriage with all the widows,
it is his right."[109]  Even clearer is the following mishnah:
"If a man was married to four wives and he died ... If they
were all put away on the same day, whosoever preceded her
fellow even by an hour acquires (first) right.  Thus in Jerusalem they used to declare in writing the hour (of the divorce)."[110]

       Epstein noted that the Bible generally assumed a pat-
ronymic family organization among the  early Hebrews and
that consequently marriage represented acquisition, ownership
on the part of the husband.  Such a marriage was called
ba'al marriage, where the husband was the owner of his wife
in the same sense as he owned his slaves.  "Polygamy is
the logical corollary of ba'al marriage, for as one may own
many slaves so he may espouse many wives."[111]  He further
stated that though upon their return to the land of Canaan
from Egypt the Hebrews did not at first take up polygamy
(monogamy being the custom in Babylonia where Abraham and
Sarah came from, as well as in Egypt),

             with better times, however, even the masses in-
             dulged in polygamy, and it is so reported especial-
             ly of the tribe of Issachar.  In that formative
             period, it seems, bigamy became common among
             the Hebrews.  Noble and wealthy families had full

polygamy and larger or smaller harems, but the
common folk were satisfied with two wives....
We find the teachings of the Pharisees a continuation of the biblical attitude to polygamy, and the
teaching of the rabbis thereafter an extension of
the pharisaic tradition.  This tradition accepted
polygamy as legally permissible and did not even
imply a policy of monogamy as did the Church; for
while the Church shifted its center to the West,
where monogamy was the rule, the Synagogue continued in its oriental setting, where polygamy was
native.  Any resistance to polygamy in talmudic
times as in biblical days was created by life itself and was not formulated into law....  The Jewish family during that period was very like its
counterpart in the biblical period.  Rulers permitted themselves plural wives; bigamy was not
infrequent, but the people as a rule practiced
monogamy. [112]

Rabbinic writings frequently attest to the legality of
polygyny.  There is, of course, the entire tractate in the
Mishnah, Yebamoth (and a correspondingly long one in the
Talmud--two large volumes in the English Soncino edition of
the Babylonian Talmud), on levirite marriage, i.e., a
brother's marriage to the childless widow of his brother
(based on the obligations outlined in Deut. 25:9 ff.); polygyny
is very frequently presumed in its discussions. [113]  It is also
presumed in a number of other places in the Mishnah--and
their attendant commentaries in the Talmud. [114]  Nevertheless, in early rabbinic times polygamy must have been practiced only by a minority of the men since most of the literature of the period seems to refer to persons involved in
monogamous marriages.  The serious interpersonal difficulties likely to arise in a polygamous family were doubtless
one of the main reasons for its relatively infrequent practice. [115]

Still, polygyny was a clear, legal possibility that was
practiced by not a few.  Louis Finkelstein, in discussing
the disagreements between the plebeian and patrician elements in Palestinian Judaism, reflected among other places
in the patrician school of Shammai and the plebian school of
Hillel, wrote:  "The monogamous plebeians were less inclined to tolerate such abstinence in their wives than the
provincials and patricians, among whom plural marriage was
not unusual"[116] (emphasis added).  There are also a number

of documentary references to men around the beginning of
the Common Era who engaged in polygyny. Joseph the To-
biad (ca. 200 B. C. E.) took two wives,[117] and the Jewish
king Alexander Jannaeus (76 B. C. E.) "feasted with his concubines in a conspicuous place."[118]  King Herod the Great,
of course, had ten wives, many of them at the same time.[119]
In explaining this to a Hellenic and Roman world, where the
custom of monogamy was prevalent, Josephus stated: "His
wives were numerous, since polygamy was permitted by
Jewish custom and the king gladly availed himself of the
privilege,"[120] and "it is an ancestral custom of ours to
have several wives at the same time."[121]  Josephus also
told of Izates, a first century C. E. king of Adiabene, who
was a convert to Judaism and who had several wives.[122]
Archelaus and Herod Antipas were polygamous,[123] as was
also an epitropos to Agrippa.[124]  Josephus, himself from a
priestly family and who claimed he was a Pharisee, had
four wives, two of them and possibly three at the same
time.  Shortly after his capture by the Romans he "married
one of the women taken captive at Caesarea, a virgin and a
native of that place.  She did not, however, remain long
with me, for she left me on my obtaining my release and
accompanying Vespasian to Alexandria.  There I married
again."[125]  There is no evidence that his first wife, who
was in besieged Jerusalem, was dead at this time.  Later,
he noted, he "divorced my wife, being displeased at her behaviour.  She had borne me three children.... Afterwards
I married a woman of Jewish extraction who had settled in
Crete."[126]  Rabbi Joshua ben Hananyah (1st century C. E.)
recorded the polygyny of various specific high priestly families: "I may testify to you, however, concerning two great
families who flourished in Jerusalem, namely, the family of
Beth Mekoshesh, that they were descendants of rivals[127]
and yet some of them were High Priests who ministered
upon the altar."[128]

     In talmudic times there developed a certain opposi-
tion to the idea of the desirability of polygamy: "If the husband states that he intends taking another wife to test his
potency, Rabbi Ammi (a late 3rd century Amora) ruled:
'He must in this case also divorce (his present wife) and
pay her the amount of her kethubah; for I maintain that whosoever takes in addition to his present wife another one must
divorce the former and pay her the amount of her kethubah. '"[129]  However, juxtaposed with this statement is the
immediately following contradictory teaching by Raba (early
fourth century Babylonian Amora): "Raba said: A man may

marry wives in addition to his first wife; provided only that
he possesses the means to maintain them." The same
"Raba said: (If one has) a bad wife it is a meritorious act
to divorce her.... Raba further stated: A bad wife, the
amount of whose kethubah is large, (should be given) a rival
at her side."[130] Rab (early third century) said: "Do not
take two wives; if however you have taken two, then take a
third, for two could conspire together against you, but the
third will certainly break it up."[131]

It should be noted that apparently the rabbis themselves were almost always monogamists. Some exceptions
were Abba, son of Rabban Simeon ben Gamaliel I, who was
a member of the Sanhedron and who had two wives at
once,[132] and the unusual exception of Rabbi Tarfon, a Tanna who married 300 women during a period of famine so he
could use his right as a priest to distribute food to them
that they otherwise would not have received.[133] A further
and even stranger exception was apparently that of two
Babylonian rabbis who seem to have engaged in a series of
one-day marriages: "Rab, whenever he happened to visit
Dardeshir, used to announce, 'Who would be mine for the
day!' So also Rabbi Nahman, whenever he happened to visit
Shekunzib, used to announce, 'Who would be mine for the
day!'"[134]

Israel Slotki's explanation seems even stranger than
the quotation itself. In his footnote in the English Soncino
edition of Yebamoth, p. 235, he writes: "He was anxious
to establish a home in Shekunzib which he often visited on
business affairs and consequently wished to secure a wife to
bless his home whenever he would stay there." But does
one "establish a home," or "bless his home" by securing a
new wife for a day at each visit? Leo Jung's explanation in
the footnotes of the English Soncino edition of Yoma is at
least plausible, if not exactly documented. He suggested
that these women were taken as wives in appearance only,
so that the rabbis could avoid having a woman presented to
them for the night by the local Persian prince. Perhaps,
perhaps not. The strange thing is that the quotation is recorded in two places in the Talmud merely as an argument
against maintaining that the rabbis were opposed to marrying women in different countries. The procedure was surely
legal. Was it therefore concluded by all the Amoraim that
it was also moral? One would have thought with the prevalence of monogamy among the rabbis there would have been
some discussion of this procedure as a problem, but there

is none.    We are left with the fact of the quotations, and
their problematic pointing to the historical reality beyond
them. 135

        Referring to the statement by Rabbi Ammi opposing
polygamy, Moses David Herr notes: "Such statements possibly reflect the influence of Roman custom which prohibited
polygamy, especially since all the Jews of the empire became Roman citizens after 212 C. E.   The Roman emperor
Theodosius issued a prohibition against the practice of bigamy and polygamy among Jews, but it did not disappear
completely....   The Jews of Babylonia also practiced bigamy and polygamy, despite the Persian monogamistic background. "136   In another place the Talmud advised a maxi-
mum of four wives: "Sound advice was given:  Only four but
no more, so that each may receive one marital visit a
month. "137

        The public practice of polygyny and the forbidding of
polyandry is usually reflective of a severely inferior status
of women in a culture.   In turn, its practice, and even just
its legal possibility, is bound to reinforce the sense of inferiority in women and superiority in men.   This doubtless
was the case in ancient rabbinic Judaism, even though polygyny was apparently not practiced in the majority of cases.


5.   ADULTERY

        "The extramarital intercourse of a married man is
not per se a crime in biblical or later Jewish law.   This
distinction stems from the economic aspect of Israelite
marriage:   the wife was the husband's possession ... and
adultery constituted a violation of the husband's exclusive
right to her; the wife, as the husband's possession, had no
such right to him. "138   The decalogue reinforces this dual
moral standard, that is, it states "you shall not covet your
neighbor's wife,"139 but says nothing about not coveting a
neighbor's husband.   Apparently in patriarchal days it was
the husband's right, or at least the head of the family's
right, to punish the adulterous woman. 140   "It was only
when adultery was elevated to the rank of a grave offense
against God as well that the husband was required to resort
to the priests or to the courts. "141   Adultery was considered one of the three capital sins, 142 idolatry and murder
being the other two, and hence merited the most severe punishment, death--at least as far as the woman was concerned.

In a metaphorical description of wayward Jerusalem
as an adulterous woman by the prophet Ezekiel, which may
or may not have any historical referent, stripping and exposure is seen as one form of punishment:[143] "I will gather
all those lovers to whom you made advances.... I will put
you on trial for adultery.... Then I will hand you over to
them.... They will strip your clothes off, take away your
splendid ornaments, and leave you naked and exposed. They
will bring up the mob against you and stone you, they will
hack you to pieces with their swords ... and many women
shall see it."[144] Hosea said of his adulterous wife Gomer:
"I will strip her and expose her naked as the day she was
born; I will make her bare as the desert, and leave her to
die of thirst."[145]

Other means of execution were stoning, burning and
strangulation. The Mishnah lists these means of execution
in descending degrees of severity as follows: burning,
stoning, and strangling.[146] It also specifies the various
modes of execution thus:

> When he was four cubits from the place of stoning
> they stripped off his clothes. A man is kept cov-
> ered in front and a woman both in front and be-
> hind. So Rabbi Judah. But the Sages say: A
> man is stoned naked but a woman is not stoned
> naked. The place of stoning was twice the height
> of a man. One of the witnesses knocked him down
> on his loins; if he turned over on his heart the
> witness turned him over again on his loins. If
> he straightway died, that sufficed; but if not, the
> second (witness) took the stone and dropped it on
> his heart. If he straightway died, that sufficed;
> but if not, he was stoned by all Israel.[147]

> The ordinance of them that are to be burnt (is
> this): they set him in dung up to his knees and
> put a towel of coarse stuff within one of soft stuff
> and wrapt it around his neck; one (witness) pulled
> one end towards him and the other pulled one end
> towards him until he opened his mouth; a wick[148]
> was kindled and thrown into his mouth, and it went
> down to his stomach and burned his entrails.[149]

That women were burned for adultery, as was required in
the case of a priest's daughter (Lev. 21:9) in the early rabbinic period, is attested to in the same mishnah when it

states: "Rabbi Eliezer ben Zadok said:  It happened once
that a priest's daughter committed adultery and they encom-
passed her with bundles of branches and burnt her. "150   The
Talmud explicates that recollection thus:  "Rabbi Eleazar
ben Zadok said, 'I remember when I was a child riding on
my father's shoulder that a priest's adulterous daughter was
brought (to the place of execution) surrounded by faggots,
and burnt. '"151   H.  Freedman, in the English Soncino edition, notes that, based on J. Derenbourg, the event "took
place during the short interval between the death of Festus,
the Roman procurator (in 62 C. E. ), and the coming of Al-
binus (63 C. E. ). "152   Thus, apparently women were executed for adultery in the latter half of the first century. 153
Still later, in late third century Babylon, a similar execution was reported:  "Imarta the daughter of Tali, a priest,
committed adultery.   Therefore Rabbi Hama ben Tobiah had
her surrounded by faggots and burnt. "154

        The "lightest" mode of execution was as follows:
"The ordinance of them that are to be strangled (is this):
they set him in dung up to his knees and put a towel of
coarse stuff within one of soft stuff and wrapt it around his
neck; one (witness) pulled one end towards him and the other
pulled one end towards him, until his life departed. "155

        If the woman involved was married, then both the
adulterer and adulteress were to be executed.   The same
was also the case even with a girl who was simply betrothed,
if the intercourse took place in town, for it was presumed
that she could have screamed for help if she had been forced.
But if it took place in the country, only the man was executed, for it was presumed she could have screamed without
receiving any help. 156   However, "no such presumptive distinction is made in this passage regarding the married woman:  she and her lover must die in any case (Deut. 22:22;
unlike The Hittite Laws, 197, in:  Pritchard, Texts, 196,
which makes this very distinction for married women). "157
Togay also remarks that "other ancient Near Eastern law
collections also prescribe the death penalty for adulterers,
but, treating adultery as an offense against the husband
alone, permit the aggrieved husband to waive or mitigate the
punishment," although "biblical law allows no such mitiga-
tion. "158

        The book of Proverbs indicated that at least for the
adulterer it was possible to "compound" his offense, that is,
pay the wronged husband a sum of money in lieu of undergoing

the death penalty. [159]  Since this portion of the book of Proverbs was probably composed only in the third or fourth
century B. C. E. ,[160] this may be an indication of the lessening of the rigor of the earlier biblical injunctions. [161]  According to the available evidence, this lessening of the death
penalty was apparently applied only to the man; the woman,
who was often not likely to have any money available anyhow,
was presumably still put to death.   In addition, there were
doubtless situations where an adulterous relationship resulted in a pregnancy that betrayed the relationship.   Here
again, the woman alone would have been subject to punishment. [162]  There must also have been times when the physically more able male could make good his escape but the
woman could not, as is recorded in the gospel according to
John 8: 1 ff.

Another instance in the ancient biblical law concerning
sexual immorality where the woman was again the victim of
a double moral standard is found in Deut. 22:13-21.   There,
if a man claimed that his new wife was not a virgin the
father of the bride was expected to bring out a garment with
blood stains resulting from the breaking of the hymen during
the first marital intercourse and "spread the garment before
the elders of the town. "  If the elders were satisfied, they
fined the husband one hundred pieces of silver--payable to
the father!--and he would not be allowed to divorce the girl
ever.   However, if the elders were not satisfied with the
evidence--the obtaining of which must have presented no little
difficulty at times--"They shall bring her out of the door of
her father's house and the men of her town shall stone her
to death. "  The young bride, often less than a teenager, [163]
was in a no-win situation:  if she lost her case she was put
to death; if she won she had to live forever with--under--a
husband who was furious enough with her to try to have her
killed, but was frustrated and had to pay a huge fine on her
account.   On the other hand, no man suffered a penalty for
a lack of virginity.

All these punishments only took place if there was
hard evidence that adultery had occurred, usually including
the testimony of two witnesses.   However, even simply on
the basis of a suspicion, or only as the result of a fit of
jealousy, a husband could force his wife to submit to an
extremely humiliating and terrorizing trial by ordeal.   The
priestly portion of the book of Numbers (fifth century
B. C. E. ), i. e. , 5:11-31, is the only specific account in the
Bible of trial by ordeal.   The essential prescriptions there
are as follows:

When in such a case a fit of jealousy comes over
the husband which causes him to suspect his wife,
she being in fact defiled; or when, on the other
hand, a fit of jealousy comes over a husband which
causes him to suspect his wife, when she is not in
fact defiled; then in either case, the husband shall
bring his wife to the priest.... The priest shall
bring her forward and set her before the Lord.
He shall take clean water in an earthenware vessel, and shall take dust from the floor of the
Tabernacle and add it to the water.  He shall set
the woman before the Lord, uncover her head ...
[tell her in a formal manner that if she is innocent she will be unharmed, but if she is guilty]
... may the Lord make an example of you among
your people in adjurations and in swearing of oaths
by bringing upon you miscarriage and untimely
birth;165 and this water that brings out the truth
shall enter your body.... The priest shall write
these curses on a scroll and wash them off into
the water of contention; he shall make the woman
drink the water that brings out the truth, and the
water shall enter body.... If she has let herself
become defiled and has been unfaithful to her husband, then when the priest makes her drink the
water that brings out the truth and the water has
entered her body, she will suffer a miscarriage
or untimely birth, and her name will become an
example in adjuration among her kin.  But if the
woman has not let herself become defiled and is
pure, then her innocence is established and she
will bear her child.

Either way, the experience is horrible for the woman, but
"no guilt will attach to the husband, but the woman shall
bear the penalty of her guilt."

The variations on this teaching in the Mishnah are
several, some few protecting the woman somewhat with additional specifications, but many of them making the ordeal
even more severe.  On the positive side, the Mishnah made
it necessary that the wife be warned about her unbecoming
conduct in front of two witnesses; that is, for example, she
is told she should not speak with a particular man, and if
she disregarded this warning she could be made to undergo
the ordeal. 166  Rabbi Eliezer said that the husband's testimony that she disregarded his warning was sufficient, but

Rabbi Joshua, whose opinion was ultimately accepted, maintained that the testimony of two witnesses was necessary. She then was brought up to the Great Court in Jerusalem, where great pains were taken to get her to confess to adultery. If she did, she did not have to undergo the trial by ordeal, but apparently was also not subject to the death penalty; she was divorced by her husband with the forfeiture of her kethubah.[167] But if after forcing her to walk and climb a great deal and carry heavy things and after talking at her,[168] she still refused to confess to being guilty, the priests took her up to the Eastern Gate of the temple "and a priest takes hold of her garments--if they be torn they be torn, if they be rent to tatters they be rent to tatters--so that he bares her bosom, and he loosens her hair. Rabbi Judah says,[169] If her bosom were beautiful he did not uncover it;[170] if her hair were comely he did not dishevel it."[171] Blackman notes: "Lest, if she is proved blameless, the younger priests should lust for her." All her ornaments were then taken away from her and she was covered with a black, ugly garment, "and after that he brings a common rope and ties it above her breasts. And everyone who wishes to behold comes to behold ... and all women are permitted to behold her."[172]

Then the various adjurations, writings and the giving to drink the "bitter water," which has wormwood in it,[173] take place as described in Deuteronomy, with the following supplementary details: if she refuses to drink, "they must force her mouth open and oblige her to drink against her will. She has hardly finished to drink when her face turns yellow and her eyes protrude and she is covered with swollen veins. And they say, Take her out! Take her out! That she does not defile the temple court."[174]

Later in the Mishnah it was said that because of the prevalence of adultery, Rabbi Jochanan ben Zakkai, after the destruction of the Temple in 70 C. E. , abolished this trial by ordeal: "When adulterers increased in number, the application of the waters of jealousy ceased; and Rabbi Jochanan ben Zakkai abolished them, as it is said, 'I will not punish your daughters when they commit harlotry nor your daughters-in-law when they commit adultery; for they themselves. . . . '"[175] "Queen Helena of Adiabene--a proselyte to Judaism in the first century C. E. --sought to restore the practice (Yoma 3, 10; Tos. Yoma 2, 3)."[176] Later, when it was presumably a merely academic question, Rabbi Akiba (late 1st, early 2nd century C. E. ) stated that the bitter waters would also be ineffective if the husband "was not free of guilt."[177]

In sum, the severe penalties attached to adultery and the flagrant double standard applied to men and women, plus the extraordinarily humiliating and terrifying trial by ordeal for the merely suspected wife, made the whole issue of adultery an extreme expression of misogynism, which at times veered toward the sadistic. Fortunately mitigations did develop: the death penalty and the trial by ordeal were eventually eliminated,[178] but the double moral standard, because of the legal possibility of polygyny and general social mores, lingered on. However, in the days before the destruction of the Temple, misogynism in the matter of adultery was present in full force.

## 6.  DIVORCE

"The woman is acquired by three means and she regains her freedom by two methods. She is acquired by money, or by document, or by sexual connection.... And she recovers her freedom by a letter of divorce or on the death of the husband."[179] Ze'ev Falk notes that in ancient Israelite days divorce was "an arbitrary, unilateral, private act on the part of the husband and consisted of the wife's expulsion from the husband's house,"[180] the very term usually used to refer to a divorced wife being gerushah, "expelled."[181] "At a later stage (but before Deut. 24:1; Is. 50:1 and Jer. 3:8) the husband was required to deliver a bill of divorce to his wife at her expulsion."[182] The whole ceremony of the man handing the wife a writ of divorce was done privately, before two witnesses, down through the early rabbinic period.[183]

Already a number of decades before the beginning of the rabbinic period, and down through the time of the rabbinic writings, it was even considered obligatory to divorce a "bad wife," though of course the opposite, the divorce of a bad husband, was not possible. In the midst of vitriolic misogynism Ben Sira stated the obligation clearly and forcefully: "A bad wife brings humiliation, downcast looks, and a wounded heart. Slack of hand and weak of knee is the man whose wife fails to make him happy. Woman is the origin of sin, and it is through her that we all die. Do not leave a leaky cistern to drip or allow a bad wife to say what she likes. If she does not accept your control, divorce her and send her away."[184]

There was apparently some objection to the vigor of

this misogynism among some of the rabbis, but the talmudic
decision was in favor of making the misogynism of Ben
Sira its own: "Rabbi Joseph (late 3rd century Babylonian
Amora) said: It is also forbidden to read the book of Ben
Sira. Abaye (student of Rabbi Joseph) said to him: Why
so?... But if you take exception to the passage: 'A
daughter is a vain treasure to her father.... But the Rabbis have said the same: The world cannot exist without
males and females; happy is he whose children are males,
and woe to him whose children are females." Apparently
even Rabbi Joseph was convinced of the value of Ben Sira's
attitude toward women, for a few lines later he also referred to the misogynist passage quoted above as being especially suitable for teaching to the masses: "Rabbi Joseph
said: (Yet) we may expound to them185 the good things it
contains. E.g., 'a good woman is a precious gift, who
shall be given to the God-fearing man. An evil woman is
a plague to her husband: how shall he mend matters? Let
him divorce her: so shall he be healed of his plague.'"186
The same passage is quoted again in bYeb. 63b, and in the
same place one finds this clear statement about the obligation to divorce a "bad wife": "Raba said: it is a commandment to divorce a bad wife."

Elsewhere in the Talmud it is recorded that in the
first century or early second century C.E. several specific
kinds of actions by wives obliged their husbands to divorce
them. Of course there was adultery, proved either by witnesses, or by admission, or by the trial by ordeal, all discussed previously.187 Also: "If she ate in the street, if
she drank greedily in the street, if she suckled in the
street, in every case Rabbi Meir says that she must leave
her husband." But then Rabbi Akiba carried the matter
much farther: "Rabbi Akiba says she must do so as soon
as gossips who spin in the moon light begin to talk about
her." But an older contemporary felt he carried the matter too far: "Rabbi Johanan ben Nuri thereupon said to him:
If you go so far, you will not leave our father Abraham a
single daughter who can stay with her husband."188 And
again, "Rabbi Meir used to say ... a wife goes out with her
hair unfastened and spins cloth in the street with her arm-
pits uncovered and bathes with the men. Bathes with the
men, you say?--It should be, bathes in the same place as
the men. Such a one it is a religious duty to divorce."189
Even childlessness for a ten-year period was grounds for a
mandatory divorce, according to the Talmud, although according to the earlier Mishnah the barren wife need not be

divorced, but then another wife also had to be taken. "If a man took a wife and lived with her for ten years and she bore no child, he may not abstain (any longer from the duty of propagation),"[190] is the way the Mishnah stated the charge. However, the talmudic commentary makes the divorce of the unfruitful wife de rigeur: "Our Rabbis taught: If a man took a wife and lived with her for ten years and she bore no child, he shall divorce her and give her her kethubah."[191]

There is also listed in the Mishnah a rather strange long list of vows, on account of which, if a husband enforces them on the wife, she must automatically be divorced.[192] For example, that the wife should not eat a certain kind of fruit, or wear ornaments, or that she not go to a house of mourning or of feasting, or "that you shall fill and put out on the rubbish heap ... (because the meaning of his request is) that she shall allow herself to be filled and then scatter it."[193] Of this list Billerbeck remarks, probably with some justification: "The whole thing gives the general impression that the entire business is really only a shady excuse to provide the males with a convenient means for divorce."[194]

The same idea, that is, the duty to divorce a "bad wife," came to expression in another teaching, where it was also stated clearly that living with a "bad wife" is a hell on earth: "Three kinds of persons do not see the face of gehenna, namely, (one who suffers from) oppressive poverty, one who is afflicted with bowel diseases, and (one who is in the hands of) the (Roman) government; and some say: Also he who has a bad wife. And the other?[195] It is a duty to divorce a bad wife.[196] And the other?[197] It may sometimes happen that her kethubah amounts to a large sum."[198] No provision is made for the divorce of a "bad husband" by the wife.

There were, however, some limitations on the husband's power to divorce his wife. Two were biblical restrictions, both of them involving a considerable humiliation of the woman. One occurred when a man raped a virgin-- and was caught! "When a man comes upon a virgin who is not pledged in marriage and forces her to lie with him, and they are discovered, then the man who lies with her shall give the girl's father fifty pieces of silver, and she shall be his wife because he has dishonoured her. He is not free to divorce her all his life long."[200] (Because the girl was like

the father's property which was damaged, it was the father,
not the girl, who received the fifty pieces of silver.) The
second took effect when a husband wrongly accused his bride
of not being a virgin, with the necessary counter proof of
her nuptial defloration being given publicly. 201

The Mishnah added at least two further restrictions.
One was that, "if she became insane he must not divorce
her."202 The second restriction took effect when she was
taken captive, for according to Kethubah 4, 4, the husband
was liable for her ransom, as he was also liable for her
medical care if she was ill. 203 The same mishnah which
forbade the husband to divorce the unransomed wife also allowed the husband to renege on his obligation to provide
medical care for his sick wife by divorcing her: "If she
were taken captive, he must ransom her; and if he said,
'Here is her bill of divorce and her kethubah, 204 let her
redeem herself,' he has no such power. If she came to
harm, he must heal her. If he said 'Here is her bill of
divorce and her kethubah, let her cure herself,' he is entitled to do so."205

A further inhibition to divorce was the kethubah. One
of the constant concerns of the Hebrew prophets was the welfare of widows. In early rabbinic times this concern found
expression in the development of the "kethubah." This was
a written agreement entered into by the bridegroom whereby
he pledged a certain amount of money to go to the wife in
the event of his death or a divorce under certain conditions.
Its beginnings go back to the bride price which the prospec-
tive husband paid to the father of the bride, which developed
into a sum of money set aside in some fashion to care for
the wife if she were separated from her husband. The book
of Tobit (200 B. C. E.) speaks of a written marriage contract
(7:13), and Simeon ben Shetah (1st century B. C. E.) is referred to as the originator of the kethubah, 206 but it is more
likely that it already existed in his time and that he inaugur-
ated, rather, the custom of making the kethubah a lien on
the husband's property. 207 Thus the kethubah became not
only an insurance policy for the separated wife, but also an
obstacle to an arbitrary divorce by the husband; the husband
was more likely to think twice before giving his wife a bill
of divorce if it also entailed paying out a substantial sum.

Even a large kethubah, of course, did not prevent all
divorces, 208 as can be seen from the story about the Tan-
naite Rabbi Jose the Galilean, who had a contrary wife whom

he wished to divorce, but could not because "her dowry is
too great for me and I cannot divorce." Thereupon his students said "'We will apportion her dowry among ourselves,
so you can divorce her.' And they did so for him; they ap-
portioned her dowry and had her divorced from him, and
made him marry another and better wife."[209] The problem
of a dissatisfactory wife with a large kethubah was also
solved in another way: "Raba said: It is a commandment
to divorce a bad wife ... Raba further stated: A bad wife,
the amount of whose kethubah is large, (should be given) a
rival at her side."[210] In the same place there were several
other complaints by various rabbis about dissatisfactory
wives with large kethubahs: "'Behold I will bring evil upon
them, which they shall not be able to escape.' Rabbi Nahman said in the name of Rabbah ben Abbuha: This refers
to a bad wife, the amount of whose kethubah is large."
"'The Lord has delivered me into their hands against whom
I am not able to stand.' Rabbi Hisda said in the name of
Mar Ukba ben Hiyya: This refers to a bad wife the amount
of whose kethubah is large." "'I will provoke them with a
vile nation.' Rabbi Hanan ben Raba stated in the name of
Rab: This refers to a bad wife the amount of whose kethubah is large."

This dissatisfaction with having to pay a large kethubah for divorcing a wife was not limited to complaining, but
also took rather concrete form in mishnaic legislation which
provided a rather large number of circumstances under which
wives could be divorced without having to pay them their
kethubah. The first two were somewhat global categories,
which then, however, were specified:

> And these are they that are divorced without their
> kethubah: she who transgresses the Law of Moses
> and Jewish custom. And what is here meant by
> the Law of Moses? If she give him food that had
> not been tithed, or if she have sexual intercourse
> with him when she is a menstruant, or if she do
> not separate the priest's-share of the dough, or if
> she make a vow and does not fulfill it. And what
> is here meant by Jewish custom? If she go forth
> with her head uncovered, or if she spin in the
> street, or if she hold converse with all men.
> Abba Saul says, Also if she curse his parents[211]
> in his presence. Rabbi Tarfon says, Also if she
> be a loud-voiced woman. What is here meant by
> a loud-voiced woman? Such a one who speaks in
> her house so that her neighbours hear her voice.[212]

Here Blackman comments: "She unashamedly demands in
loud tones sexual intercourse with her husband or disputes
with him over intimate sexual matters so that others may
overhear their talk.  According to some authorities in all
such cases she must first have been admonished not to repeat such conduct before she can be made to forfeit her
kethubah. " (There is no similar sanction on a man's ribald-
ry.)  The talmudic commentary corroborates such an understanding partly by rejecting a second possible interpretation:
"Rabbi Tarfon said: Also one who screams.  What is meant
by a screamer?  Rab Judah replied in the name of Samuel:
One who speaks aloud on marital matters.  In a Baraitha it
was taught: (By screams was meant a wife) whose voice
[and here the English Soncino edition notes: "Her screams
of pain caused by the copulation"] during intercourse in one
court can be heard in another court.  But should not this,
then, have been taught in the Mishnah among defects?
Clearly we must revert to the original explanation," i. e. ,
that given in the name of Samuel. 213

    Two still further possibilities of the husband divorcing
a wife without paying her her kethubah were provided for.
One was that if the husband found out that his wife had taken
some vows he did not know about, "she is divorced without
her kethubah,"214 "because he could plead, 'I do not want a
wife that is in the habit of making vows. '"215  Examples of
such disqualifying vows include vows not to eat meat, or not
to drink wine, or not to wear bright colored clothes,216 or
"if she vowed that she shall neither borrow nor lend a win-
now, a sieve, a mill or an oven, or that she shall not weave
beautiful garments for his children, she may be divorced
without a kethubah, because (by acting on her wishes) she
gives him a bad name among his neighbours."217

    A second and even more far-reaching possibility was
if a man found bodily defects in the woman he had married
that he claimed must have been present before the betrothal.
These defects, which under those circumstances would incur
the forfeiture of the ketubah by the woman upon divorce, included all those which disqualified priests from serving in
the temple: "No man with a defect shall come, whether a
blind man, a lame man, a man stunted or overgrown, a man
deformed in foot or hand, or with mis-shapen brows or a
film over his eye or a discharge from it, a man who has a
scab or eruption."218  The talmudic commentary also specified several more: "A Tanna taught:  To these were added
perspiration, a mole and offensive breath....  If a dog bit

her and the spot of the bite turned into a scar (such a scar)
is considered a bodily defect.   Rabbi Hisda further stated:
A harsh voice in a woman is a bodily defect."[219]   Indeed,
even a deviation in the "normal" size or cleavage of a woman's breasts were grounds for divorce without kethubah:

> Rabbi Nathan of Bira learnt:  (The space) of one
> handbreadth between a woman's breasts.   Rabbi
> Aha the son of Raba intended to explain in the
> presence of Rabbi Ashi that this statement meant
> that '(the space of) a handbreadth' is to (a wo-
> man's) advantage, but Rabbi Ashi said to him:
> This was taught in connection with bodily defects.
> And what space (is deemed normal)?   Abaye re-
> plied:  (A space of) three fingers.   It was taught:
> Rabbi Nathan said, It is a bodily defect if a wo-
> man's breasts are bigger than those of others. [220]

Not every unwanted wife would have been divorcible
without her kethubah under these provisions, but very many
would have been.   The man suffered no such disabilities.

Except for the relatively infrequent exceptions mentioned above,[221] even if a man's wife did not fit into one of
the enumerated categories whereby she could be divorced
without her kethubah being paid, in mishnaic and talmudic
times the husband could always divorce his wife, regardless
of her wishes.   Early in mishnaic times there was a dispute
between those rabbis following Shammai and those following
Hillel.   Both lived in the first century B. C. E.   The Shammaites were of patrician background and tended to be more
conservative in their judgments, whereas the Hillelites tended
to be of plebian stock and more liberal.   In the dispute over
the grounds for divorce the former were more restrictive
and the latter quite unlimited in their interpretations of
those grounds.   The basic biblical text about which the dispute raged was:  "When a man has married a wife, but she
does not win his favour because he finds something shameful in her, and he writes her a note of divorce, gives it to
her and dismisses her...."[222]   The Mishnah comment on
this text is as follows:

> The School of Shammai say:  A man may not di-
> vorce his wife unless he has found something un-
> seemly in her, for it is written, Because he hath
> found in her indecency in anything.   And the School
> of Hillel say (He may divorce her) even if she

spoiled a dish for him, for it is written, Because
he hath found in her indecency in anything. Rabbi
Akiba says: Even if he found another more beautiful than she, for it is written, And it shall be if
she find no favour in his eyes. [223]

Akiba was very consistent in this matter for it was
also he who taught, against the earlier teachers who were
Shammaites, that a menstruous wife could continue to adorn
herself, so as not to give her husband a reason for finding
another woman more beautiful than her and hence divorce
her: "The early Sages ruled: That means that she must
not rouge nor paint nor adorn herself in dyed garments; until Rabbi Akiba came and taught: If so, you make her re-
pulsive to her husband, with the result that he will divorce
her!"[224]

That the more permissive view, the Hillelite view,
soon prevailed was borne out by remarks by at least two
first century C. E. Jews, who not only espoused the Hillelite
view, but also seemed to know of no other view. [225]   Josephus stated the Jewish law on divorce thus: "He who desired
to be divorced from the wife who is living with him for
whatsoever cause--and with mortals many such may arise--
must certify in writing."[226]   That he practiced this doctrine
was borne out by his remark about divorcing one of his four
wives: "At this period I divorced my wife, being displeased
at her behaviour."[227]   Philo also spoke of "parting from
her husband for any cause whatever."[228]   The triumph of
the permissive view was also attested to by the discussion
of the dispute in the Babylonian Talmud, where it is clear
that even a non-reason, a whim, is sufficient to make a
divorce valid: "Rabbi Papa asked Raba: If he has found in
her neither unseemliness nor any (lesser) thing, (and still
divorces her), what are we to do (according to Beth Hillel)?   He replied ... what is done is done."[229]

Thus, outside of the rare exceptions referred to, and
the possibility of the penalty of having to pay the kethubah,
a man could always divorce his wife for any reason whatsoever, or even on a whim.   The reverse was not possible.
The Mishnah itself stated this point quite clearly: "The man
who divorces is not like to the woman who is divorced, because the woman goes forth with her consent or against her
will, whereas the man divorces her only with his own free
will."[230]

Although it was impossible for a wife to divorce a
husband, there were circumstances when a wife could claim
the right to a divorce before a Jewish court--this was clearly an advance in the rights of the wife from earlier biblical
times to rabbinical times.   Abrahams described the power
of the court as follows:  "The Court could scourge, fine,
imprison, and excommunicate him, and had practically unlimited power to force him to deliver the necessary document freeing his wife. ...   But in case of his determined
contumely, there would be no redress, as the Court could
not of its own motion dissolve a marriage."[231]

The Mishnah provided very few grounds for a wife to
make a claim for a divorce:  "And these are they for which
they compel him to give divorce:  one afflicted with a skin-
disease, or one who has a polypus, or one that collects,[232]
or one who mines copper-ore, or a tanner."[233]   In later,
Amoraic, times, an additional ground was also granted by
some rabbis, namely, if the marriage was childless, it being demonstrable that the fault might be the husband's, and
the wife wanted to have children to support her in her old
age.[234]   At the same time it had to be made certain that
the divorce was not sought by the woman either because of
money or "because she set her eyes on another."[235]   Again,
no such limitations were set on the desires of the man.
Furthermore, "in all such cases where the wife was concerned as the moving party, she could only demand that her
husband should divorce her; the divorce was always from
first to last in Jewish law the husband's act."[236]

According to Josephus there were a number of instances in Herod's family when the wife divorced the husband.[237]   However, in the following passage Josephus makes
it clear that such actions were clearly against Jewish law--
they were possible only in the very strongly Hellenistic-in-
fluenced circles, for in Hellenistic custom the woman could
initiate divorce as well as the man:

> Some time afterwards Salome had occasion to quar-
> rel with Costobarus and soon sent him a document
> dissolving their marriage, which was not in ac-
> cordance with Jewish law.   For it is (only) the
> man who is permitted by us to do this, and not
> even a divorced woman may marry again on her
> own initiative unless her former husband consents.
> Salome, however, did not choose to follow her
> country's law.[238]

Because, as Rabbi Abrahams put it, "in case of his
determined contumely, there would be no redress, as the
Court could not of its own motion dissolve a marriage,"239
at least two very tragic problems would occasionally arise.
The Mishnah stated that if a husband "became a deaf-mute
or if he went out of his mind he may never set her free."240
The same Mishnah also stated that the husband may not divorce an insane wife, though he could divorce her if she
became a deaf-mute. The difference is that in the former
case the wife, though normal, could never again hope to
lead a normal married life and would be hard put to provide
for herself in a male dominated economic world. In the
latter case, when the husband is normal, the man could always take another wife, and so lead a normal married life.
The second problem perhaps occurred more often: "in case
of desertion, the wife could not obtain a divorce ... the
Court could not grant a divorce to the wife if the husband
had merely vanished and left no trace, unless they saw valid
grounds for presuming death."241 Both of these tragic cases
still plague Orthodox Judaism today.

There were of course a few who decried divorce, the
earliest of whom was probably the minor prophet Malachi
(fifth century B. C. E.), who said:

> You weep and moan, and you drown the altar of
> the Lord with tears, but he still refuses to look at
> the offering or receive an acceptable gift from
> you. You ask why. It is because the Lord has
> borne witness against you on behalf of the wife of
> your youth. You have been unfaithful to her,
> though she is your partner and your wife by solemn
> covenant. Did not the one God make her, both
> flesh and spirit? And what does the one God re-
> quire but godly children? Keep watch on your
> spirit, and do not be unfaithful to the wife of your
> youth. If a man divorces or puts away his
> spouse, he overwhelms her with cruelty, says the
> Lord of Hosts the God of Israel. Keep watch on
> your spirit, and do not be unfaithful. (Mal. 2:13-
> 16)

These are very moving and powerful words against
divorce. At the same time, at least three things ought to
be noticed about them. For one, the prophet repeatedly
decries divorcing the wife of one's youth, perhaps implying
that the taking of a second wife without divorcing the first

one would not be so objectionable.  Secondly, what might be
more important, these lines follow immediately upon several
others which condemn the marrying of foreign wives, who
might lead the men away from the worship of Yaweh.   If
these verses were not interpolated later, as some few
scholars believe, then the inveighing against the divorce of
the wife of one's youth, presumably Jewish (a body of Jews
had just returned from exile at about this time), was perhaps strongly motivated as a defense against an invasion of
idolatry by way of newly taken, Canaanite, etc., wives.
Shortly afterwards Ezra and Nehemiah even insisted on the
divorce and driving out of all foreign wives and children for
that very reason:  "Now, therefore, let us pledge ourselves
to our God to dismiss all these women and their brood, according to your advice, my lord" (Ez. 10:3).  In any case,
the words of Malachi were not understood in subsequent
Jewish law as forbidding either polygamy or divorce.   Indeed, one talmudic interpretation was as follows:  "In Israel
God has granted the possibility of divorce, but not among
the Gentiles; there he hates divorce!"242

     There was also the objection to polygamy in the
Damascus document which some scholars construe to be an
objection to divorce and remarriage as well. 243   There
were likewise a few rabbinic voices objecting to divorce,
the first one perhaps being Rabbi Eleazar (270 C. E.) who,
while he misquoted the above cited words of Malachi, nevertheless decried divorce:  "Rabbi Eleazar said:  If a man
divorces his first wife, even the altar sheds tears, as it
says, 'And this further ye do, ye cover the altar of the
Lord with tears....'"244   The next objector was Rabbi Johanan (279 C. E.):  "'For a hateful one put away:'  Rabbi
Judah (150 C. E.) said:  (This means that) if you hate her
you should put her away.  Rabbi Johanan says:  It means,
He that sends his wife away is hated."245   There was one
further talmudic objection:  "Rabbi Shaman ben Abba said:
Come and see with what great reluctance is divorce granted;
King David was permitted yihud (with Abishag), yet not di-
vorce (of one of his wives)."246

     It should be noted that the rabbinic objections to di-
vorce began only in the middle of the third century C. E.,
and were extremely rare.  Montefiore comments:  "There
are a few stock passages which Strack-Billerbeck are fair
enough to quote (p. 320) against divorce, especially against
divorcing a first wife, the wife of one's youth....  But it
would not appear that such passages are numerous, though it

is rather nice that Tractate Gittin (on Divorce) ends with
this saying of Rabbi Eleazar and the quotation from Malachi
2:13-14. "247

Perhaps this analysis of divorce as far as it reflected
the status of women in the formative period of Judaism, the
centuries just before and after the beginning of the Common
Era, can best be summed up in the words of one Orthodox
and one Liberal Jewish scholar.  Ze'ev Falk, an Orthodox
Jew, in the following passage evaluated in the first place the
status of women in the context of biblical divorce laws, but
his statement basically applies to the rabbinic period as
well, as the final sentence of the passage--and his following
pages--indicate:

> Two characteristics of the biblical law of divorce
> set it apart from present-day family law.  There
> was no consideration for the woman's wishes, as
> far as the future of the marriage was concerned,
> nor was there public supervision of divorce.  The
> husband alone had the power to decide whether the
> union should be severed, and if he disliked his
> wife there was nothing to prevent him from ex-
> pelling her from the home.  The wife, however,
> was unable to eject her husband, since she had
> been purchased by him, and not he by her; it was
> he who had taken her to wife, and he who put her
> out.  Such a restriction of the rights of woman
> was a feature characteristic of biblical law, and
> may perhaps not have existed to such an extent
> among other Semitic peoples.  The Jewish attitude
> did, however, change with the passage of time,
> so that in certain circumstances the wife was al-
> lowed to demand a divorce from her husband.
> Nevertheless, the original law still stood firm and
> unshaken, and laid down that the husband was free
> to divorce his wife arbitrarily without taking her
> opinion into consideration. "248

It is interesting to note the author's self-critical stance
toward his own tradition here, which also specifically included an unfavorable comparison of the Jewish divorce customs with those of the surrounding Semitic peoples.  The
same judgment would also have to be made in a comparison
with the divorce customs of the Egyptian, Hellenistic and
Roman neighbors.

The Liberal Jew, C. G. Montefiore, is similarly
critical in his evaluation:

> Rabbinic divorce, however, mitigated in practice
> and in theory, rested upon two fundamental im-
> proprieties.   (a) Divorce was the act of the man.
> Though the woman in certain circumstances could
> claim it, her claim, if the man was obstinately
> contumacious, could not be enforced.   In the last
> resort, the man could divorce his wife; the woman
> could not divorce her husband.   Thus Rabbinic di-
> vorce rests upon inequality.   The man has a power
> which the woman has not.   Whether Jesus felt and
> attacked this inequality, this inferiority of the wo-
> man to the man is not entirely certain.   (b) But
> what did obviously arouse the antagonism of Jesus
> was the second impropriety.   A man could divorce
> his wife, according to Rabbinic law, for many rea-
> sons over and above infidelity....   According to
> Jewish law, the woman could not divorce the man.
> It is this disparity which is the second great blot
> in the Jewish law of divorce.   The woman, in true
> accordance with Oriental conceptions, is the subor-
> dinate of the man.   The Jewish law--to its credit
> be it said--made some improvements in her inse-
> cure and unequal position; but she remained, and
> remains, religiously and legally, the inferior. [249]

# CHAPTER VII

## CONCLUSION

Although the two traditions on women--the prelapsarian, positive one, and the postlapsarian, negative one--continued throughout formative Judaism, the former grew weaker and the latter stronger during the period. Simply stated, the clear conclusion from the analysis of the foregoing evidence is that in the formative period of Judaism the status of women was not one of equality with men, but rather, severe inferiority, and that even intense misogynism was not infrequently present. Since the sacred and secular spheres of that society were so intertwined, this inferiority and subordination of women was consequently present in both the religious and civil areas of Jewish life.

In drawing this conclusion, it must also be recalled that Judaism was not simply following the pattern of the societies and cultures around it. On the contrary, it appeared to be running quite counter to the trends of at least the surrounding (Egyptian), Hellenistic, and Roman cultures. Not infrequently Jewish and Christian writers have attempted to argue that women's lot in Judaism or Christianity was not any worse, or indeed, was even better, than in Greek and/or Roman society. However, the "evidence" then presented is usually something dealing with ancient classical Greece or the early Roman republic, whereas the appropriate evidence to be looked at should have been from the Hellenistic and imperial Roman periods, i. e., 300 B. C. E. to 300 C. E. In those societies, for all of the disabilities many women suffered, the status of women not only was significantly higher than in the then contemporary Judaism, but it also generally improved throughout the period.

The question can be asked whether the inferior status of women in the formative period of Judaism was simply a continuation of feminine inferiority already present in

pre-exilic Hebrew religion and society, or whether it represented a decline from a higher status of women in antique
pre-exilic times through post-exilic to rabbinic times.
Though the status of the wives of the patriarchs and of a
judge like Deborah appears to be much higher than that of
the Jewish women of the time and society of Ben Sira and
Rabbi Eliezer, the scholarly answer to that question awaits
further thorough analysis of the ancient period. [1]

Whatever the facts are concerning the relationship between the status of women in ancient Hebraic society and in
the period here under analysis, on the basis of evidence at
least it can be stated that the inferior status of women, and
even misogynism, appear to have intensified and broadened
from the return from exile in the sixth century B. C. E.
through late biblical times and into rabbinic, talmudic times.
The developments that worked in women's favor, e. g. , the
gradual elimination of the execution of adulteresses, and the
doing away with the trial by ordeal of the suspected adulteress, were relatively few and were at least counter-balanced
by further negative developments, e. g. , the increasing restrictions of women in the temple and the synagogue, the introduction of harem-like customs in Alexandrian Judaism and
to a somewhat lesser extent in the cities of Palestine, the
misogynism of the Essenes, the teaching to the masses by
the rabbis of the violent misogynism of Ben Sira, and their
own.

This conclusion, of the dominance of a severely inferior status of women and even an intense misogynism in
the formative period of Judaism, is in no way weakened or
deflected by evidence that there existed at the same time
sincere human affection toward wives (and toward children
and others too, for that matter) or that there were some
domineering Jewish women. Human history on a one-by-one
basis defies any absolute categorization. But the evidence
still staggeringly indicates that formative Judaism's societal
and religious structures placed women in a position decidedly
inferior and subordinate to men.

Since the development of Judaism in this formative
period has had an overwhelmingly determinative influence on
the subsequent history of Jewish life, and since the subordinate position of women, and even misogynism, was so profoundly and intimately bound up with Judaism in this formative period, the inferiority of women and misogynism have
also tended to have an overwhelming influence in the

subsequent history of Judaism.   It would be necessary to re-
search carefully and unapologetically the history of the condition of women in Judaism following talmudic times to see
in detail the influence the inferior status and the misogynism
of the earlier period had, and the play of reinforcing and
countervailing forces, 2 plus the reforming efforts, particularly in modern times.

          These reforming efforts, of course, have a long his-
tory (e. g. , the Ashkenazic efforts to eliminate polygamy,
starting in the Middle Ages), but they became particularly
strong with the rise of Reform Judaism in the nineteenth
century.   Pretty well following the rising and falling of the
general feminist movement in modern Western civilization,
the movement for equality and justice for women within
Judaism also had limited success, and only in the 1970s is
it beginning to receive popular support.   Nor are these reform efforts limited to the Reform branch of Judaism; rather,
they spill over into Conservative Judaism, and even--though
to a much more limited extent--into Orthodox Judaism.

          Though the tendency of Orthodox Judaism in recent
centuries has been to resist changes in general, and concerning the status of women in particular, the Orthodox
tradition really goes beyond tolerating change and adaptation.
The whole point of rabbinism is to make the word of God,
the Torah, apply in a realistic, effective way to contemporary life; "change and adaptation" in that sense is its raison
d'être.   Hence, even though formative Judaism in the past
severely subordinated women, it is quite possible under new
circumstances that Orthodox Judaism could change its interpretation and application of Torah so as to eradicate all
practices and understandings that assume the inferiority of
women.

          Indeed, just this sort of thing happened in the criti-
cally important mishnaic period:   for example, Rabbi Joch-
hanan ben Zakkai eliminated the use of the trial by ordeal
of the suspected adulteress (Sotah), even though this practice was not simply a rabbinic extension or application of a
more general biblical command, but rather was a very explicit biblical command.   He felt circumstances had changed
sufficiently to warrant eliminating the practice; he merely
was careful, in good rabbinic fashion, to provide a corro-
borating biblical quotation to support his radical decision.

          If there were sufficient will, the same sort of

authentic rabbinic reinterpretation and adaptation--even very
radical reinterpretation and adaptation, judging from the
past--could eliminate all misogynism and subordination of
women even in Orthodox Judaism today.  This, in fact, is
exactly what the Orthodox rabbi Ze'ev Falk, Professor of
Matrimonial Law at the Hebrew University, Jerusalem,
calls for in his courageous, scholarly article on "The Position of Woman in the Halacha,"[3] in which he begins to out-
line how it should be accomplished within the authentic
tradition of Halacha.  The article itself must be read for
the development of the specific examples Falk uses to illus-
trate his point, but the statement of his basic principles,
usually cast in the form of questions, deserves to be quoted
here:

> Therefore it is to be asked whether agreement can
> be reached between the Halacha and the new frame-
> work of values, or whether the Halacha can exist
> only within the ancient societal norms.  Clearly
> the Halacha cannot maintain itself unchanged inde-
> finitely since many of its presuppositions have been
> overturned and loyalty to it hardly can be expected
> from a woman who claims personal happiness and
> equality before the law.  In my book on marriage
> and divorce I outlined the transition from the Ori-
> ental Jewish society to the European, as it took
> place at the time of Rabbenu Gershom (965-1028
> C. E.).  Now in our generation as well a similar
> transition has become apparent, from the tradi-
> tional to an urban-industrial order of society.  We
> must ask again whether those learned in Halacha
> will succeed in constructing the form demanded by
> the new structure and whether they possess the
> creative power and freshness to be signposts de-
> spite the vagaries of the times.

Falk focuses the question still more sharply:  "Does
the possibility exist today to correct the position of the woman in the Halacha so as to adapt it to her position in the
modern family, in contemporary society and in the state,
which have made the equality of women their goal?"  The
answer, he says, is clear:  "It is sufficient to point out that
the Halacha in the Mishnah is explained within the context of
the sociological givens; the conclusion is therefore near at
hand:  the Halacha would be different if and when these givens
in the meantime were to change."

Falk frames the question even more precisely in the "religious" sphere:

> To be sure, 'women have no pleasure' when they do not participate in the community prayer or when they have no opportunity to attend the prayer and the reading.... Where a woman has a knowledge of Torah that is superior to men's we must not forego her capabilities, but we must find a way to have her take part in the worship service. When we have gone so far as to have women as active participants in the various areas of life, it is particularly senseless to forego their contribution specifically in religious things.

Fortunately, Jewish women themselves who treasure much of the Jewish tradition have begun to become aware of their inferior status and have begun to work to change it.

> The 'Jewish Women's Movement'--if you can call those women who have been thinking, talking, and meeting together throughout the country over the past year or two a movement--is still young.... Ezrat Nashim, perhaps the first group publicly committed to equality for women within Judaism, began as a study group within the New York Havurah in September, 1971. Seeking to determine what position women have held in traditional Judaism, why, and what possibilities there were for change, a number of women began studying Talmud and other sources. Within a few months--after discovering that the concern for equality within a traditional Jewish framework was widespread--the group decided to 'go public,' and in March, 1972, appeared at the annual convention of the Rabbinical Assembly of America to confront the rabbis of the Conservative Movement. [4]

The call for equality for women was so well received that already in 1973 the Conservative Movement decided to allow women to be counted in a minyan in the United States.

In February, 1973, over 500 women from the United States and Canada met in New York for the first Jewish women's conference. "As a result of the conference, many new groups have been formed, a number of regional and local conferences have been held, a national newsletter has been

started, and Network is organizing a National Women's
Speakers Bureau. "[5]  At the conference Judith Plaskow Goldenberg spoke of the tension within the sensitized Jewish woman: "Can we--how can we--assure ourselves in advance
that if we are true to our own experiences we can remain
in continuity with tradition. "[6]

To begin to answer that question, and others, a special anthology on the Jewish woman was published in 1973.
A key portion dealt with the problem of retaining the Jewish
tradition in its best sense and eliminating its subordination
of women and its misogynism:

> The dynamic character of the halacha--the legal
> code--has made it not only possible, but manda-
> tory, for Jews in every age and culture to create
> an appropriate balance between the traditions of the
> past and Jewish ideals for the future.  One such
> ideal is tselem elohim--the image of God--in which
> human beings were created.  The Talmud (Sanhed-
> rin 37a) describes the image of God in terms of
> the absolute equality, absolute value, and unique-
> ness of every person.  The many laws and customs
> denying women independent legal status and equal
> participation in prayer, study, and ritual prevent
> the evolution of halacha toward its own ideals.
> The authors of the following articles, while pursu-
> ing different methods of change, nevertheless
> recognize the centrality of halacha and the need to
> couple the mechanisms of change with the sensiti-
> vities and values of Judaism in order to achieve
> equality of rights and obligations for women. [7]

This rising consciousness among Jewish women, and
some men, is even reflected on the political level in Israel.
On January 8, 1974, a headline in the New York Times read:
"Israel Feminist Wins Big Electoral Upset. "  The story was
about Shulamit Aloni, a lawyer and former member of the
Knesset, who was elected, along with another feminist, to
the Knesset.  Ms. Aloni had already exhibited a serious interest not only in the feminist cause,[8] but also in how to
deal with problems of marriage and divorce within the halacha. [9]

It is this author's hope that the attainment of full
equality for women within Judaism will proceed as rapidly
and creatively as possible and that this study will have

contributed a small bit toward that goal by presenting as carefully as possible one of the main sources of the contemporary status of women in Judaism, namely, the status of women as developed in the formative period of Judaism. There are many things of great value from the Jewish tradition, particularly from this formative period, which should be treasured, applied, adapted and expanded today. But the subordination of women and misogynism are not among them. These latter should be seen clearly in their starkness and be judged as something to be outgrown, as was slavery. Any attempt to gloss over these grim facts will produce revulsion in the sensitive, and hypocrisy in the not-so-sensitive. The sensitive will "drop out" of religious Judaism and the not-so-sensitive will become more and more like the Christian caricature of the Pharisee. The state of the second is even less human and less Jewish than the first; but both are serious losses to humanity and Judaism.

On the other hand, it is hoped that this study will not be the source of morbid breast-beating (though plenty of healthy self-criticism is surely in order) or become a sort of club with which to beat the "establishment," without at the same time taking appropriate positive and creative action to change that "establishment." One such positive, creative action already taken is the creation of "feminist seders" and other "feminist" communal worship services. 10 It is hoped that this study may be a true catharsis--and that the reader would then move on positively to change her or his own life and the surrounding societal patterns and structures.

The few bright spots from the past, e. g. , the extraordinary Beruria (surely she should be the heroine for the Jewish feminist, and indeed a model for all Jewish women-- and men too!), should be treasured--for the exceptions that they were. But it is to the broader principles of the value of the human person, justice, and love of one's neighbor that contemporary Judaism will have to return to develop most of its Jewish feminism, i. e. , justice and equality for women.

## CHAPTER I

### Rationale of the Study

1.  Apion, II, 201.

2.  I Tim. 2:11 ff.

### Status of Women in the Ancient Fertile Crescent and the Greco-Roman World

3.  Guillaume Cardascia, "Le Satut de la Femme dans les Droits cuneiformes," La Femme. Recueil de la Société Jean Bodin, XI, 1 (Brussels, 1959), pp. 81-94.

4.  Paper entitled "The Goddesses and the Theologians: Reflections on Women's Rights in Ancient Sumer," read by Samuel Noah Kramer at the XXII Recontre Assyriologique Internationale held in Rome, July, 1974. (Cf. also "Scholars Told Sexism is Divine," Philadelphia Inquirer, September 3, 1974, where the paper was reported on in some detail.)

5.  Ibid.

6.  Cf. Adam Falkenstein, Die Neusumerischen Gerichtsurkunden (Munich, 1956), esp. pp. 146-153.

7.  Cf. M. Schorr, Urkunden des altbabylonischen Zivil-und Prozessrechts (Leipzig, 1913), p. 15.

8.  Codex Hammurabi 142. See James Pritchard, Ancient Near Eastern Texts (Princeton, 1955), p. 172.

9.  Ibid., 143, p. 172.

10. Cf. Driver and Miles, The Assyrian Laws (Oxford, 1935), paragraphs 12-23, and Codex Hammurabi 143. See Pritchard, op. cit., pp. 172, 181 f.

11. Cf. Cardascia, op. cit., pp. 93 f.

12. Cf. Jacques Pirenne, "Le Statut de la Femme dans l'Ancienne Egypte," La Femme. op. cit., pp. 64 f.

13. Cf. ibid., p. 70.

14. Cf. ibid., p. 73.

15. Cf. ibid., p. 75.

16. Ibid., p. 76. He also goes on to say: "In Greece the status of women was far from being as developed as in Egypt. One knows how the Ptolemies attempted to restrict the Egyptian woman as were Greek women, i.e., placed under marital authority." However, as will be seen below, that attempt was largely unsuccessful. Rather, the reverse tended to happen.

17. Ibid., p. 77.

18. See, e.g., J. J. Bachofen, Myth, Religion and Mother Right, Selected Writings of Bachofen, tr. by Ralph Manheim (Princeton, 1967); Robert Briffault, The Mothers, 3 vols. (New York, 1927); Elizabeth Gould Davis, The First Sex (New York, 1971).

19. Vern L. Bullough, The Subordinate Sex (Baltimore, 1974), pp. 50ff.

20. Plutarch, Numa, 3, 5 f.

21. Plutarch, Moralia, p. 240d (Gorgo).

22. Aristotle, Politics II, 6, 9, 11.

23. Quoted in Johannes Leipoldt, Die Frau in der antiken Welt und im Urchristentum (Leipzig, 1954), p. 34.

24. Ibid., p. 29.

25. Ibid., p. 33.

26. The recent extensive article on "Frau" in the Reallexikon für Antike und Christentum by Klaus Thraede often takes a somewhat revisionist approach toward earlier scholarship which described the status of women in the ancient world as quite restricted. Thraede, for example, argues that Greek women were not nearly so restricted to household affairs as previously portrayed, partly by referring to counter-evidence and partly by stating that various instances of evidence put forward by his opponents were either over-valued (e.g., the quotation from the works of Demosthenes concerning hetaerae, concubines, and wives--col. 201) or were to be dismissed as not reflecting reality (e.g., four

references to late wisdom literature in the Bible and to the
Talmud that men ought not converse much with women--
col. 225).  However, Thraede himself offers no reason why
he finds such evidence overvalued or not reflective of reality; he simply states his claim flatly--a not very convincing
procedure.  Also, in his counter-claim that Greek women--
contrary to previous scholars, mostly unnamed by him--
did indeed participate significantly in Greek society, Thraede unfortunately largely fails to adhere carefully to the
all-important distinctions in place and time he usually does
in his otherwise excellent article, thereby making this aspect of his revisionist claim of ambiguous and confused
value.

27.  Leipoldt, op. cit. , pp. 62 ff.  It was Leipoldt who called my
     attention to this phenomenon of heightened sensitivity in the
     ancient world.

28.  How much more often do we find such expressions of joy in the
     Greek Luke's gospel than in the gospels of the other two,
     non-Greek, synoptics, Matthew and Mark.  Cf. John L.
     McKenzie, Dictionary of the Bible (Milwaukee, 1965), p.
     526: "The coming of salvation creates an atmosphere of
     joy, mentioned much more frequently in Lk than in Mt-Mk
     (1:4, 28, 58; 2:10; 10:17, 20f. ; 13:17; 19:6, 37; 24:41, 52).
     There is joy even in heaven at the repentance of sinners
     (15:7, 10, 32).  Joy breaks out in expressions of praise,
     again more frequent in Lk than in Mt-Mk (Benedictus; Mag-
     nificat)."  And it is only the New Testament writers who
     are strongly influenced by Hellenism who report that Jesus
     cried: "As he drew near and came in sight of the city he
     shed tears over it" (Luke 19:41); "At the sight of her
     tears, and those of the Jews who followed her, Jesus said
     in great distress, with a sigh that came straight from the
     heart.  'Where have you put him?'  They said, 'Lord,
     come and see. '  Jesus wept" (John 11:33-35); "During his
     life on earth, he offered up prayer and entreaty, aloud and
     in silent tears" (Letter to the Hebrews 5:7).

29.  Leipoldt, op. cit. , p. 64.

30.  The book of Tobit was written during the Hellenistic period,
     probably about 200 B. C. E. when all Palestine was under
     Greek rule: "The boy left with the angel, and the dog fol-
     lowed behind" (Tobit 6:1).  In Mark it was reported: "Now
     the woman was a pagan, by birth a Syrophoenician, and she
     begged him to cast the devil out of her daughter.  And he
     said to her, 'The children should be fed first, because it is
     not fair to take the children's food and throw it to house
     dogs. '  But she spoke up: 'Ah, yes, sir, ' she replied,
     'but the house dogs under the table can eat the children's
     scraps" (Mark 8:26-28).  But McKenzie, op. cit. , p. 202,
     comments: "In the ancient Near East the dog was not kept

as a pet and he was rarely employed in hunting of as a watch dog. Most dogs have no owners and are nuisances and scavengers which run about the streets. In ancient Hebrew law the dog was an unclean animal, to which unclean flesh might be thrown (Ex. 22:30). 'Dog,' 'dead dog,' 'dog's head' were terms of insult. "

31. Leipoldt, op. cit., pp. 64 f.

32. Gerhard Herrlinger, Totenklage um Tiere in der antiken Dictung, in Tübinger Beiträge zur Altertumwissenschaft, VIII (1930), pp. 30 f., 75 ff.

33. Theodor Birt, Aus dem Leben der Antike (Leipzig, 2nd ed., 1919), pp. 134 ff.

34. Klaus Thraede, "Frau," Reallexikon für Antike und Christentum, vol. VIII (Regensburg, 1970), col. 208, rejects the likelihood of I. Bruns' (Frauenemanzipation in Athen, Kiel, 1900) claim that there was a full-fledged women's movement led by Aspasia in Pericles' Athens.

35. Ibid., col. 198.

36. Cf. Claire Preaux, "Le statut de la femme à l'époque hellénistique, principalement en Egypte," La Femme. Op. cit., pp. 127-175.

37. See Grace Macurdy, Hellenistic Queens (Baltimore, 1932).

38. William Ferguson, Hellenistic Athens (London, 1911), p. 71.

39. Ibid., pp. 72, 85.

40. Ludwig Friedländer, Darstellungen aus der Sittengeschichte Roms, vol. I (8th, 1910), 449 ff. Already by 79 C. E., as one can see from the graffiti in Pompeii, the "domina" was shortened to "domna." In English we still have the honorary title "Dame," and its variant, Madam, but normally a Germanic equivalent is used, namely, Mrs. or Miss, or Ms. as abbreviations of "Mistress."

41. Cf. S. Liebermann, Greek in Jewish Palestine (New York, 1942), pp. 47-50.

42. Preaux, op. cit., p. 173.

43. Wilhelm Dittenberger, Sylloge inscriptionum graecorum (Leipzig, 1915-), vol. 2, p. 802.

44. M. Wegner, Das Musikleben der Griechen (Berlin, 1949), pp. 159 f.

45. Thraede, op. cit., col. 202.

46. Dittenberger, op. cit., vol. 1, p. 532.

47. Thraede, op. cit., cols. 204, 222 f.

48. Pliny, Natural History, referred to in Joan Morris, The Lady was a Bishop (New York, 1973), p. xi.

49. Dittenberger, op. cit., vol. 3, p. 1177.

50. Leipoldt, op. cit., pp. 37 ff.

51. O. Rubensohn, Elephantine-Papyri (Berlin, 1907), number 1.

52. E. g., see E. N. Adler, et al. The Adler Papyri (Oxford-London, 1939), Demotic Papyri no. 14, and Preaux, op. cit., p. 162.

53. Thraede, op. cit., col. 206. At this point Thraede adds the remark that "on the contrary in the orient the wife, on the basis of a legal contract, could be loaned out ... a procedure that would have been impossible in Greece and which glaringly illuminates the differences of the cultural levels."

54. See H. Kreller, Erbrechtliche Untersuchung auf Grund der gräko-ägyptischen Papyrusurkunden (Leipzig, 1919), pp. 142 ff., 174 ff., 307 ff., and R. Taubenschlag, The Law of Greco-Roman Egypt (Warsaw, 1955), pp. 184 f., 201.

55. Cf. C. Schneider, Kulturgeschichte des Hellenismus, I (Munich, 1967), p. 80. See also Pirenne, op. cit., pp. 164 f., 174 f.

56. Thraede, op. cit., col. 199.

57. Cf. L. Mitteis, Reichsrecht und Volksrecht (Leipzig, 1891), p. 66.

58. Cf. Taubenschlag, The Law of Greco-Roman Egypt, p. 177, and Preaux, op. cit., p. 142.

59. H. J. Wolff, "Hellenistic Private Law," in S. Safrai et al., The Jewish People in the First Century (Philadelphia, 1974), vol. I, pp. 538, 540, 542.

60. Cf. R. Taubenschlag, "La compétence du kyrios dans le droit gréco-égyptien," Archives d'histoire du droit oriental, II (1938), pp. 293-314.

61. Cf. Taubenschlag, "La compétence," pp. 293-314, and Claude Vatin, Recherches sur le mariage et la condition de la femme mariée à l'époque hellénistique (Paris, 1970), pp. 250 f. and Wolff, op. cit., p. 538.

62. Preaux, op. cit., p. 170.

63. See Chapter V, pp. 115-117.

64. Z. W. Falk, "Jewish Private Law," S. Safrai et al., op. cit., p. 513.

65. Cf. Wolff, op. cit., p. 538.

66. Ibid., pp. 540.

67. E. Ziebarth, Aus dem grieschischen Schulwesen (Leipzig, 1909), pp. 32, 50, 78; Th. Hopfner, Sexualleben der Griechen und Römer (Prague, 1938), pp. 380-382.

68. Cf. Ernst Majer-Leonard, Agrammatoi in Aeqypto qui litteras sciverint, qui nesciverint (Frankfurt, 1913).

69. Preaux, op. cit., p. 172.

70. Cf. Thraede, op. cit., col. 202, who lists a number of women poets whose work is extant; he describes them briefly --and the variety is quite broad, from the lyric and epigrammatic writing of Anyte of Tegea mentioned earlier (some of her writing was even done on paid commissions) to erotic verse--and gives references for further information.

71. Cf. Leipoldt, op. cit., p. 53, where he also refers to Deubner, who lists seventeen by name.

72. Athenaios, III, 95, pp. 122 f.; IV, 52, p. 161 cd. See also the Pythagorian prayer which reveals something of their attitude toward women: "Honor be to the woman on earth as in Heaven, and may she be sanctified, and help us to mount to the Great Soul of the world who gives birth, preserves, and renews--the divine Goddess who bears along all souls in her mantle of light." Quoted in Edouard Schure, The Great Initiates (New York, 1913), p. 92.

73. Quoted in Leipoldt, op. cit., p. 53. Cf. also Vatin, op. cit., p. 37: "A une date incertaine, mais probalement posterieure, ce probleme posé par l'existence de femmes dotées de pouvoirs politiques est évoqué dans les textes pythagoriciens: 'Ces qualités (réflexion et sagesse) rendent la femme capable de belles actions vis à vis d'elle-même, de son mari, de ses enfants, de sa famille; souvent aussi pour une cité, si une telle femme gouverne des cités ou des peuples, comme on le voit dans la monarchie.'" The reference is to Perictyonè, in Stobée, LXXXV, 19.

74. Cf. W. Nestle, Vom Mythos zum Logos (Stuttgart, 1942), pp. 473-96.

75.   The Republic, V, 451d ff.

76.   Laws, 805c.

77.   Dialogues, L, 3, 46.

78.   Politics, 1313b, 32; 1319b, 30 f.

79.   Ibid., 1269b, 12/1271b, 19.

80.   Ibid., 1254b, 17/9; 1259b, 1/17; 1260b, 16/8.   Aristotle's
      relatively low estimation of women had a profound influ-
      ence on later Christian theology through the work of
      Thomas Aquinas; for a detailed analysis of Aquinas' theol-
      ogy of woman see Gertrud Heinzelmann, Wir schweigen
      nicht länger! We Won't Keep Silence Any Longer! (Zurich,
      1964), pp. 20-44, 79-99.

81.   N. W. de Witt, Epicure and His Philosophy (Minneapolis,
      1954), pp. 95 f.

82.   See, e.g., Plutarch (46-120 C. E.).

83.   Leipoldt, op. cit., pp. 57.

84.   Ibid., p. 61.

85.   Cf. Leipoldt, ibid., pp. 56 f., states that the thought patterns
      of the rabbis were strongly influenced by the Stoics, as for
      example, the custom of making a teaching more vivid and
      attention-grabbing by casting it in the form of a conversa-
      tion; but the Stoics' attitude toward women are not similarly
      assimilated.

86.   Ibid., p. 57.

87.   Cf. Thraede, op. cit., col. 210.

88.   Leipoldt, op. cit., p. 43, and Thraede, op. cit., col. 207.

89.   Leipoldt, op. cit., p. 44.

90.   Mishnah, Abot 2, 2.

91.   A. D. Nock, "Eunuchs in Ancient Religion," Archiv für Reli-
      gionswissenschaft, vol. 23 (1925), p. 27; H. Bolkestein,
      Theophrastos' Charakter der Deisidaimonia (Giessen, 1929),
      pp. 68-70.

92.   Cyrillus Alex. in Is. 2, 2, in Patrologia Graeca, 70, col.
      441.

93. Cf. Günter Haufe, "Die Mysterien," in Johannes Leipoldt and Walter Grundmann, eds., Umwelt des Urchristentums (Berlin, 1965), pp. 101-126, for details.

94. Cf. Preaux, op. cit., p. 172.

95. Flavius Josephus, Jewish War, 2, 20.

96. Acts 16: 14 ff.

97. Cf. U. Türck, Zeitschrift für die alttestamentlichen wissenschaft, vol. 46 (1928), pp. 166 f. The influence of the Hellenistic women's liberation movement on Christianity can be seen in the writing of the gospels: "Cerfaux calls Luke's universalism as it stands the fruit of the union of the primitive traditions with the Hellenistic Christianity of Antioch and the preaching of Paul. Of a piece with Luke's universalism is the prominence given to women; more women appeark in Lk than in the other Gospels. In the Hellenistic world the social and legal position of woman was higher than it was in Judaism" (McKenzie, op. cit., p. 526).

98. Jacques Heurgon, Daily Life of the Etruscans (New York, 1964), p. 8.

99. Cf. ibid., p. 77.

100. Ibid., p. 89.

101. Ibid., p. 95.

102. Ibid., p. 96.

103. Ibid., p. 86.

104. Cf. J. P. V. Balsdon, Roman Women, Their History and Habits (London, 1962), pp. 2-6, and Robert Villers, "Le statut de la femme à Rome jusqu'à la fin de la République," Le Femme. Op. cit., p. 188.

105. Thraede, op. cit., col. 212; cf. also col. 207 where it is noted that women also bore witness within the widely popular mystery religions of Hellenism. This ability of a woman to bear witness at that time in at least significant portions of the Hellenistic and Roman worlds takes on a special importance in view of the radical inability of women to bear witness in the Judaism of the same time. See below, pp. 150-152.

106. H. Mattingly, Roman Coins (Chicago, 1962), p. 145.

107.    Quoted in Guglielmo Ferrero, Die Frauen der Cäsaren
        (Stuttgart, 1912), p. 7.

108.    Cf. Thraede, op. cit., cols. 213 f.   The evidence here ap-
        plies only to aristocratic women--for the rest there is
        silence.   Jean Gaudemet, "Le statut de la femme dans
        l'Empire romain," Le Femme.  Op. cit., pp. 191-222,
        did not seem to be aware of the positive evidence Thraede
        alluded to, for he wrote: "From the beginning of the em-
        pire the woman acquired an independence of action and a
        legal capacity which went way beyond ancient Roman cus-
        toms.   On the other hand, during the entire empire she
        had no more official part in political and administrative
        life than during the republic" (p. 191).

109.    Thraede, op. cit., col. 223.

110.    Gaudemet, op. cit., p. 198.

111.    Ibid., p. 201.

112.    Ibid., pp. 202, 204.

113.    Ibid., p. 208.

114.    "Gyne," in G. Kittel, Theological Dictionary of the New
        Testament (Grand Rapids, Mich., 1967), vol. 1, p. 777.


Ancient Hebrew Background

115.    Although many authors have alluded to the ambiguous attitude
        toward women expressed in the Bible, I am particularly
        indebted to George Tavard, Woman In Christian Tradition
        (Notre Dame, Indiana, 1973), for his insightful explana-
        tion.

116.    Cf. ibid., p. 5.   Cf. also Anne McGrew Bennett, "Overcom-
        ing the Biblical and Traditional Subordination of Women,"
        Radical Religion, vol. 1, no. 2 (Spring, 1974), p. 28,
        where when speaking of the Adam and Eve story she
        writes: "but it cannot be maintained that woman is in-
        ferior even if she was created after man without admitting
        that man is inferior to the creeping things because he was
        created after them.   Neither man nor woman in this story
        is said to be made 'in God's image.'  Furthermore, the
        word translated as 'help meet' or 'helper' is the Hebrew
        word used of divine, or superior, help.  The word never
        refers to inferior help in the Bible."

117.    Cf. Tavard, op. cit., pp. 7 f.   From a different perspec-
        tive, Phyllis Trible makes the same point: "The serpent
        speaks to the woman.   Why to the woman and not to the

man?  The simplest answer is that we do not know. . . .
But the silence of the text stimulates speculations, many
of which only confirm the patriarchal mentality that conceived them.  Let a female speculate.  If the serpent is
'more subtle' than its fellow creatures, the woman is
more appealing than her husband.  Throughout the myth
she is the more intelligent one, the more aggressive one
and the one with greater sensibilities. . . .  The initiative
and the decision are hers alone.  She seeks neither her
husband's advice nor his permission.  She acts indepen-
dently.  By contrast the man is a silent and bland recipi-
ent: 'She also gave some to her husband and he ate.'. . .
His one act is belly-oriented, and it is an act of quies-
cence, not of initiative.  The man is not dominant; he is
not aggressive; he is not a decision-maker. . . .  He follows his wife without question or comment, thereby deny-
ing his own individuality.  If the woman be intelligent,
sensitive and ingenious, the man is passive, brutish and
inept" ("Depatriarchalizing in Biblical Interpretation,"
Journal of the American Academy of Religion, vol. 41,
no. 1 (March, 1973), p. 40).

118.  Tavard, op. cit., p. 17.

119.  Ibid.


CHAPTER II

Wisdom Literature

1.    George Tavard, Woman in Christian Tradition (Notre Dame,
      Indiana, 1973), pp. 24 f.

2.    Cheryl Exum, "Images of Women in the Bible," Women's
      Caucus--Religious Studies Newsletter, vol. 2, no. 3
      (Fall, 1974), p. 5.

3.    Phyllis Trible, "Depatriarchalizing in Biblical Interpretation,"
      Journal of the American Academy of Religion, vol. 41,
      no. 1, pp. 46 f.

4.    Thierry Maertens, The Advancing Dignity of Woman in the
      Bible (DePere, Wis., 1969), p. 110.

5.    At this point the Jerusalem Bible suggests that this refers
      to another man's wife, but since this section is post-
      exilic, it could well refer to foreign women, for there
      was a fear of them as the corrupters of the people of
      Yahweh by the followers of Ezra and Nehemiah.  Indeed,
      their fear of alien women was almost pathological, for
      they saw the Jewish men as the fountains of Yahweh wor-
      ship and goodness, but the alien women as the sources of

idolatry and evil; despite human affection or years of marriage, the Jewish men were expected to drive away these
"evil" wives and children: "We have committed an offence
against our God in marrying foreign wives, daughters of
the foreign population. Now, therefore, let us pledge ourselves to our God to dismiss all these women and their
brood." (Ez. 10:3) Cf. also Nehemiah's action: "In those
days also I saw that some Jews had married women from
Ashdod, Ammon, and Moab.... I argued with them and
reviled them, I beat them and tore their hair out.... Are
we then to follow your example and commit this grave offense, breaking faith with our God by marrying foreign
women? Now one of the sons of Jehoiada, son of Eliashib
the high priest, had married a daughter of Sanballat the
Horonite; therefore I drove him out of my presence," (Neh.
13:23-28).

6.    The full text reads:
      "Preserving you from the woman subject to a husband,
      from the smooth tongue of the woman who is a stranger.
      Do not covet her beauty in your heart
      or let her captivate you with the play of her eyes;
      a harlot can be bought for a hunk of bread,
      but the adulteress is aiming to catch a precious life.
      Can a man hug fire to his breast
      without setting his clothes alight?
      Can a man walk on red-hot coals
      without burning his feet?
      So it is the man who consorts with his neighbour's wife:
      no one who touches her will go unpunished."

7.    The full text reads:
      "Call Perception your dearest friend,
      to preserve you from the alien woman,
      from the stranger, with her wheedling words.
      From the window of her house she looked out on the street,
      to see if among the men, young and callow,
      there was one young man who had no sense at all.
      And now he passes down the lane, and comes near her
            corner,
      reaching the path to her house
      at twilight when day is declining,
      at dead of night and in the dark.
      But look, the woman comes to meet him,
      dressed like a harlot, wrapped in a veil.
      She is loud and brazen;
      her feet cannot rest at home.
      Now in the street, now in the square,
      she is on the look-out at every corner.
      She cathces hold of him, she kisses him,
      the bold-faced creature says to him,
      'I had to offer sacrifices:
      I discharged my vows today,

that is why I came out to meet you,
to look for you, and now I have found you.
I have made my bed gay with quilts,
spread the best Egyptian sheets,
I have sprinkled my bed with myrrh,
with aloes and with cinnamon.
Come, let us drink deep of love until the morning,
and abandon ourselves to delight.
For my husband is not at home,
he has gone on a very long journey,
taking his moneybags with him;
he will not be back until the moon is full. '
With her persistent coaxing she entices him,
draws him on with her seductive patter.
Bemused, he follows her
like an ox being led to the slaughter,
like a stag caught in a noose,
til he is pierced to the liver by an arrow,
like a bird darting into a snare
not knowing its life is at stake.
And now, my son, listen to me,
pay attention to the words I have to say:
do not let your heart stray into her ways,
or wander into her paths;
she has done so many to death,
and the strongest have all been her victims.
Her house is the way to Sheol,
the descent to the courts of death. ''

8.    Cf. Jerusalem Bible, p. 977, note h.

9.    Roland Murphey, Seven Books of Wisdom (Milwaukee, 1960),
      p. 122, says: "But in almost every discussion of wifely
      virtue the primary consideration is the happiness that a
      good wife brings to the man.   The man of a different back-
      ground, such as that of today, might with reason say that
      little value is placed on woman as a person in the Old
      Testament; in short, this is a man's world. ''

10.   E. g. , Oepke's article on gyne in G. Kittel's Theologisches
      Wörterbuch zum Neuen Testament.   The Enclopaedia Judaica
      (Jerusalem, 1971), vol. 16, col. 626, notes: "The oft-
      quoted last section of Proverbs (31:10-31) in praise of the
      virtuous woman is somewhat ambiguous in that it still de-
      picts a situation in which the wife is definitely a subordi-
      nate. ''

11.   Cf. e. g. , bBer. 17a: "Rab asked Rabbi Hiyya (both late Tan-
      naitic rabbis):  Wherewith do women acquire merit?  By
      sending their children to learn (Torah) in the Synagogue,
      and husbands to study in the schools of the Rabbis, and by
      waiting for their husbands until they return from the school
      of the Rabbis. ''

12.   Somewhat later the rabbis stated clearly the custom of the
      husband appropriating the results of the wife's labor:  "The
      finds of a woman and the work of her hands belong to her
      husband, and he enjoys the usufruct of whatever she in-
      herits during her lifetime.   Compensation for indignity or
      damages for injury to her belongs to her.   Rabbi Judah ben
      Bathyra says, When in an unexposed part (in her body),
      two parts go to her and one part falls to him; but when in
      an exposed part, two parts are his and one part is hers.
      His must be given straightaway; but with hers land must be
      purchased and he enjoys the usufruct thereof' (Keth. 6, 1).

13.   The book was originally written in 175-200 B. C. E. by Ben
      Sira and translated into Greek by his grandson sometime
      after 132 B. C. E.; until the end of the 19th century only
      the latter text was known.   Since then about two-thirds of
      the book has been found in Hebrew mss.

14.   John L. McKenzie, Dictionary of the Bible (Milwaukee, 1965),
      article on "Ben Sira. "

15.   Cf. K. Thraede, "Frau," Reallexikon für Antike und Christen-
      tum (Stuttgart, 1972), vol. VIII, cols. 208 f. , and pp. 10-
      28 above.

16.   See chapter IV, pp. 94ff.

17.   This is the Jerusalem Bible translation; the RSV is similar.
      But the New American Bible, 1970, probably drawing on
      Syriac mss. , refers to an unruly wife rather than a head-
      strong daughter.

18.   Unlike the growing custom in Hellenistic and Roman society,
      Jewish women did not usually mix with male society or eat
      with men--see below for further discussion.

19.   Cf. the Syriac translation--quoted in Johannes Leipoldt, Die
      Frau in der antiken Welt und im Urchristentum (Leipzig,
      1954), p. 87.   The earliest rabbinical documentation takes
      off from here and sharpens the point even further by ap-
      plying the prohibition to one's own wife.   Rabbi Jose ben
      Jochanan, probably from the second century B. C. E. said:
      "Speak not much with the married woman"; later rabbis
      added: "this was said of one's own wife, therefore how
      much more is it true of the wife of one's neighbor" (Aboth
      1, 5).   This will be discussed in detail below.

20.   If such an understanding is accurate (see Jerusalem Bible, it
      would stand in contradistinction with earlier Hebrew tradi-
      tion which saw fornication only as an offense against the
      father of the unmarried girl (cf. Dt. 22:28 ff.).   Such a
      sexual asceticism might have been influenced positively in

that direction from the Stoic philosophy in the Hellenism
then spreading in Palestine--as was apparently the case
among the Jewish sect of the Therapeutae in first century
Alexandria--, or negatively as a reaction against the greater sexual freedom displayed in much of Hellenistic culture.
The dualisms of the East which saw matter as the principle of evil, and sex and woman as the most material of
material things, and hence to be rejected, may have played
a role in this development. Also, the traditional notions
of the defiling character of sex (including nocturnal emission) and women needed only to be further developed to ar-
rive at the idea of avoiding them both as much as possible.

21. See Chapter VI, "Adultery," for a discussion of the death penalty for adultery.

22. McKenzie, op. cit., p. 935, notes: "Both in Greece and in
the Near East there are numerous allusions to the popular
belief that woman is by instinct a nymphomaniac."

23. Cf. ibid., p. 929.

24. Cf. e.g., D. C. Simpson, "The Hebrew Book of Proverbs and
the Teaching of Amenophis," Journal of Egyptian Archeol-
ogy, vol. 12, (1926), pp. 232 ff.

25. James Pritchard (ed.), Ancient Near Eastern Texts (Princeton, 1955), pp. 413, 420 f.

26. Ibid., p. 427.

27. Ibid., p. 438.

28. E.g., see bSan. 100b, where the rabbis urge the use of Ben
Sira's misogynist teaching to instruct the multitudes.


## Pseudepigrapha

29. They are also referred to as apocalyptic literature; see below,
note. 51.

30. The following long passage from 1 Esdras 4:13-32 should also
be noted here. The setting of the story is at the court of
Darius, King of Persia, where the Jews were in exile (6th
century B.C.E.). Three pages dispute before the king as
to what is the strongest. The first argues for wine, the
great leveler; the second for the king; the third, Zerubbabel, the future leader of the Jews, for women:
"Then the third, that is Zerubbabel, who had spoken of
women and truth, began to speak: 'Gentlemen, is not the

king great, and are not men many, and is not wine strong?
Who then is their master, or who is their lord? Is it not
women? Women gave birth to the king and to every people that rules over sea and land. From women they came;
and women brought up the very men who plant the vine-
yards from which comes wine. Women make men's clothes;
they bring men glory; men cannot exist without women. If
men gather gold and silver or any other beautiful thing, and
then see a woman lovely in appearance and beauty, they let
all those things go, and gape at her, and with open mouths
stare at her, and all prefer her to gold or silver or any
other beautiful thing. A man leaves his own father, who
brought him up, and his own country, and cleaves to his
wife. With his wife he ends his days, with no thought of
his father or his mother or his country. Hence you must
realize that women rule over you!

"'Do you not labor and toil, and bring everything and
give it to women? A man takes his sword, and goes out
to travel and rob and steal and to sail the sea and rivers;
he faces lions, and he walks in darkness, and when he
steals and robs and plunders, he brings it back to the woman he loves. A man loves his wife more than his father
or his mother. Many men have lost their minds because
of women, and have become slaves because of them. Many
have perished, or stumbled, because of women. And now
do you not believe me?

"'Is not the king great in his power? Do not all lands
fear to touch him? Yet I have seen him with Apame, the
king's concubine, the daughter of the illustrious Bartacus;
she would sit at the king's right hand and take the crown
from the king's head and put it on her own, and slap the
king with her left hand. At this king would gaze at her
with mouth agape. If she smiles at him, he laughs; if she
loses her temper with him, he flatters her, that she may
be reconciled to him. Gentlemen, why are not women
strong, since they do such things?'" Zerubbabel then goes
on to argue that the truth is nevertheless the victor over
all.

This would seem to be an early version of the notion
that behind every great man is a great woman. It does not
indicate that women had a high status. On the contrary,
women seem to have been relegated to bearing men--who
then did all the important things in the world--and being the
object of men's sexual desires. Women's humanity and
their sexuality were co-extensive. Not so with men.

The book is part of the apochrypha, not the pseudepigrapha. It is found in the Septuagent Greek Bible, but not
in the Massoretic Hebrew text. Jerome included it in his
Latin Vulgate translation, but since the Council of Trent in
the 16th century the Catholic Church has not included it in ·
the regular part of the Bible.

First Esdras is largely the story of the return of the
Jews from exile and the subsequent events, mostly all found

in the canonical book Ezra-Nehemiah.  Hence, it is largely
either derived from Ezra-Nehemiah, or vice versa, or
both are from a common or parallel sources.   It is judged
to have been composed in the 2nd century B. C. E. (cf.
The Oxford Annotated Bible with the Apocrypha, New York,
1965, p. 1), and quite likely in Egypt (cf. John L. McKenzie, Dictionary of the Bible, Milwaukee, 1965, p. 42).
Since this story is missing from the Ezra-Nehemiah account, it probably was added from non-Jewish sources,
e. g., Egyptian: "The story probably originated outside the
Jewish community as a popular tale praising the relative
strength of wine, kings, and women (the original order was
perhaps kings, wine, and women).   The praise of the
strength of truth (4:33-41; compare 3:12) was added later
in the transmission of the story, perhaps by a Greek-
speaking editor (this part of the story has close parallels
to Greek thought and literature)" (Oxford Bible, pp. 5 f.).

The alternate theory is that this story was earlier in
the Ezra-Nehemiah account, but then excised: "Although
our O. T. has lost the story of Zerubbabel and the Praise
of Truth, there is no doubt that there is something 'un-
biblical' in the orations.   In the course of the growth of
the O. T., compilers and revisers have not unfrequently
obscured or omitted that to which they took exception, and
some light is thus often thrown upon other phases of contemporary Palestinian or Jewish thought" (R. H. Charles
(ed.), The Apocrypha and Pseudepigrapha of the Old Testament, Oxford, 1913, vol. I, p. 19).

In either case, if the story could be said to reflect a
high status for women, the reflected reality was not in
Palestinian Judaism, and in the second theory, even that
reflection was removed by the redactor of the canonical
Ezra-Nehemiah.

31.   Cf. also Charles, op. cit., vol. I, pp. 9-11.

32.   Charles, op. cit., vol. II, The Pseudepigrapha, pp. 123 ff.

33.   Testament of Simeon 5:3.   For this and the texts and com-
      mentary on the other pseudepigrapha see ibid.

34.   Ibid., p. 146.

35.   bYeb. 103b.

36.   bAZ. 22b.

37.   bShab. 146a.

38.   Note the title of address.   It is also interesting that the au-
      thor develops the Genesis quotation in this connection ("and
      your desire shall be for your husband and he shall be your
      master"--Gen. 3:16) even further in the direction of making

the woman still more inferior to the man: "and thy wife
shall tremble when she looketh upon thee.... I did not
create thy wife to command thee, but to obey" (Charles,
op. cit., p. 134).

39.    Ibid., p. 137.

40.    Ibid., pp. 142 f.

41.    Ibid., p. 142.

42.    Ibid., p. 145.

43.    Ibid.

44.    Could this partly be a psychological revenge for the obvious
       fact that women are the apparent source of new human
       life, a sort of uterus envy, in Freudian terms?

45.    Ibid., p. 141.

46.    30:17-18.   Text in ibid., p. 450.   Paul in II Cor. 11:3 and I
       Tim. 2:14 follows the same tradition.   IV Ezra, a pseude-
       pigraphal Jewish work composed around the end of the first
       century C.E., lays the blame simply at Adam's feet: "For
       the first Adam, clothing himself with the evil heart, trans-
       gressed and was overcome; and likewise also all who were
       born of him" (3:21, text in ibid., p. 563).   The rabbis re-
       peatedly said that Eve caused the death of Adam, that she
       brought death into the world, for which she was manifoldly
       punished, including the curse of menstruation.   See chapter
       IV, pp. 87ff.

47.    Ibid., p. 143.   The variant version is as follows: "And while
       they were walking, lo! suddenly there came a beast (a ser-
       pent) and attacked and bit Seth.   And as soon as Eve saw
       it, she wept and said: 'Alas, wretched woman that I am.
       I am accursed since I have not kept the commandment of
       God.'   And Eve said to the serpent in a loud voice: 'Ac-
       cursed beast! how (is it that) thou hast not feared to let
       thyself loose against the image of God, but hast dared to
       fight with it?'   The beast answered in the language of men:
       'Is it not against you, Eve, that our malice (is directed)?
       Are not ye the objects of our rage?   Tell me, Eve, how
       was thy mouth opened to eat of the fruit?'"

48.    Cf. ibid., p. 8.   Leonhard Rost, Einleitung in die altesta-
       mentlichen Apokryphen und Pseudepigraphen einschliesslich
       der grossen Qumran-Handschriften (Heidelberg, 1971), p.
       100, suggests the author was probably an Essene.   John L.
       McKenzie, op. cit., agrees with Charles that the author
       was a Pharisee.

49. Charles, op. cit. , p. 1.

50. Ibid. , p. 9.

51. For a detailed discussion of this influence see R. H. Charles,
    The Book of Jubilees (1902), pp. lxxiii-lxxxvii; also D. S.
    Russell, The Method and Message of Jewish Apocapyptic
    (London, 1964), pp. 28ff. : "The evidence points rather to
    the fact that apocapyptic was a fairly strong current in the
    mainstream of Judaism in the years immediately before and
    after the beginning of the Christian era. . . . Even though
    the writing of these books might have been confined to rela-
    tively restricted circles within Judaism and the initial read-
    ing and study of them to certain defined strata of Jewish
    society, their influence would make itself felt from an early
    time on in the life of the Jewish people as a whole. "

52. See above, note 31.

53. Later in the book in connection with the story of Tamar and
    Judah it was stated by the author that if a man had sexual
    intercourse with his mother-in-law or daughter-in-law, both
    the man and the woman should be burned (41:25-27), but
    nothing was said about punishing the man in other cases;
    there is merely a commendation of Judah for having at-
    tempted to follow the charge of Abraham by burning Tamar
    (41:28). Likewise, the severe condemnation and punish-
    ment, including the man, described in chapter 30--see
    above, chapter I, pp. 20ff. --was directed only at inter-
    marriage with non-Jews.

54. Cf. Charles, op. cit. , p. 282.

55. Testament of Benjamin, 9:2. See the note in Charles, ibid. ,
    p. 358, for further references to the salvation of the Gen-
    tiles as taught in the Testaments of the Twelve Patriarchs.

56. Testament of Reuben, 4:6.

57. Fragment of Testament of Levi (vss. 16, 17), found in
    Charles, op. cit. , p. 364.

58. Cf. Proverbs 31:3; Ben Sira 26:19-22.

59. Cf. also Jubilees 20:4; see above, p. 51.

60. Another ms. tradition has the following reading: "He that hath
    a pure mind in love, looketh not after a woman with a view
    to fornication; for he hath no defilement in his heart. "

61. See Charles, op. cit. , pp. 299, 192, for further references
    to where and how the use of these allurement techniques by
    women brought about the fall of angels--and men.

62. For a detailed discussion of the image of woman in pseudepi-
    graphal literature and its influence on early Christian
    writers see Bernard P. Prusak, "Woman: Seductive Siren
    and Source of Sin?" Rosemary Ruether (ed.), Religion and
    Sexism (New York, 1974), pp. 89-116.


CHAPTER III

Pharisees

1. Apion, II, 201.

2. "Queen Salome Alexandra," in The World History of the Jewish
   People--The Hellenistic Age, ed. by Abraham Schalit (Jerusalem, 1972), pp. 249-252.

3. Berlin, 1930, pp. 261 f.

4. See Charles, op. cit., vol. I, pp. 174 ff.

5. See Rost, op. cit., p. 46.

6. See chapter II, p. 36.

7. The highly respected Jewish scholar Solomon Zeitlin corrobor-
   ated this point when he paraphrased the Talmud (Ab. Zarah
   25b): "Judith had no army. She had charm and beauty and
   with this she was sure she could conquer the enemy by be-
   guiling Holofernes. The Talmud well said that woman had
   an army with her, that is sex. This is her main armor"
   (In an introduction to Morton S. Enslin, The Book of Judith.
   E. J. Brill, Leiden, 1972, p. 14).

8. Jerome's Vulgate version adds (15:11), in a rather mixed up
   metaphor, that in acting so continently Judith "behaved like
   a man" (quia fecisti viriliter).

9. Mary Gendler, "The Vindication of Vashti," The Jewish Woman. Response, 18 (Summer, 1973), pp. 156 f.

10. Aviva Cantor Zuckoff, "The Oppression of the Jewish Woman,"
    ibid., p. 49, made a similar point when she wrote of
    Esther: "In doing so she must act aggressively toward her
    own husband. She must engage in the same type of behav-
    ior that was condemned in Vashti--assertiveness, willing-
    ness to risk her life for her values, aggressiveness. But
    since she's doing this not for herself but for her people,
    and with Mordechai's approval and on his orders, it is con-
    doned. Esther's aggressiveness is praised and she becomes
    a role model for Jewish women.
        "Esther's aggressiveness is approved because it is al-
    truistic, as were the actions of Deborah, who judged the

people, and Judith, who cut off the head of the Syrian-Greek general besieging her city. What it all adds up to is that it's good for Jewish women to be strong and aggressive when the Jews are in danger and she's acting in the people's interest, in other words, when it's 'good for the Jews.' If we go through the Bible and legends carefully, we see that whenever Jewish survival is at stake, the Jewish woman is called upon to be strong and aggressive. When the crisis is over, it's back to patriarchy."

11. Esther is difficult to date, but probably was written in the second century B. C. E.

12. Gendler, op. cit., p. 158. She added an interesting proposal at the end of her articles: "I propose, then, that Vashti be reinstated on the throne along with her sister Esther, together to rule and guide the psyches and actions of women. Women, combining the attributes of these two remarkable females--beauty softened by grace; pride tempered by humility; independence checked by heartfelt loyalties; courage; dignity--such women will be much more whole and complete than are those who simply seek to emulate Esther. The Lillith, the Vashti in us is valuable. It is time that we recognize, cultivate and embrace her!"

13. See chapter VI, pp. 157ff. and note 153 for chapter VI. It was also the same Rabbi Simeon who had eighty women hanged for witchcraft.

14. Klausner, Jesus, p. 261.


Essenes--Qumran

15. Emil Schürer, Geschichte des jüdischen Volkes im Zeitalter Jesu Christi (Leipzig, 4th ed., 1907), vol. II, p. 673. After a full discussion of all the suggested and possible influences on the Essenes, Schürer stated: "Two things nevertheless can as a result of our investigation be affirmed: 1) Essenism is first and foremost a Jewish configuration, and 2) its non-Jewish characteristics are mostly from contact with the Pythagorian-oriented tradition of the Greeks" (p. 680). Apparently, however, Pythagorian feminism (see Thraede, op. cit., col. 208 f.) did not influence Essenism.

16. There have been some attempts to argue that the Essenes did not live a celibate life (e.g., Hans Hübner, "Zölibat in Qumran?" New Testament Studies, vol. 17, 1970-71, pp. 153-157), but the weight of scholarly opinion still agrees with the traditional evidence which stated clearly that the central group did lead a celibate life. Schürer suggests that one should not attempt to reject the evidence for the celibate life of the Essenes merely on the a priori grounds

that it was foreign to Judaism: "The rejection of marriage
is of course something heterogenous to genuine Judaism.
But even this can be explained on Jewish premises: Since
the marriage act as such makes man unclean and necessi-
tates a levitical purification bath, the effort to attain the
highest possible degree of purity and holiness could very
well lead to the complete rejection of marriage" (Schürer,
op. cit., p. 674). For a similar opinion see, William
Hugh Brownlee, The Meaning of the Qumran Scrolls for the
Bible (New York, 1964), p. 80.

17.  Natural History, quoted in Yigal Yadin, The Message of the
     Scrolls (London, 1957), p. 185.

18.  Life, 11.

19.  Antiquities, XVIII, 21.

20.  Theodor H. Gaster, The Scriptures of the Dead Sea Sect (Lon-
     don, 1957), p. 75. A little later Gaster continued: "The
     fact that two words (viz., 'pit' and 'trap') are used to de-
     scribe the net in which they will be caught alludes to the
     whorish practice of taking two wives at the same time, the
     true basis of nature being the pairing of one male with one
     female, even as it is said (of Adam and Eve), 'A male and
     a female created He them (Gen. 1:27), and of those that
     went into the ark, 'In pairs they entered' (Gen. 7:9).
     Similarly, too, it is said concerning a prince: 'He shall
     not take more than one wife' (Deut. 17:17)." Here we see
     that, apparently for all Jews, the normally permitted poly-
     gamy was to be rejected, perhaps even divorce and remar-
     riage while the first wife was still alive; cf. also Andre
     Dupont-Sommer, Die essenischen Schriften vom Toten Meer
     (Tübingen, 1960), and Brownlee, op. cit., p. 87. Gaster
     also added: "This principle is totally new in Judaism; it is
     found again in the gospel (Mt. 19:3-9; Mk. 10:2-12)."

21.  Jewish War, II, 120.

22.  Ibid., 121.

23.  Hypothetica, 11, 14-17.

24.  Philo with an English Translation, trans. and ed. by F. H.
     Colson (London, Cambridge, Mass., 1954), vol. IX, p. 442.

25.  See, e.g., Proverbs 7:5-27 (see above, pp. 33, 184
     note 7), Testament of Reuben 5:3ff. (p. 67).

26.  See pp. 65f.

27.  John Strugnell, "Flavius Josephus and the Essenes: Antiquities
     XVIII. 18-22," Journal of Biblical Literature, vol. LXXVII
     (1958), p. 110.

28.  John M. Allegro, Discoveries in the Judaean Desert of Jordan, vol. V. Qumran Cave 4 (Oxford, 1968), pp. 82-84. See also Brownlee, op. cit., pp. 77-80 for a detailed discussion of the Genesis Apocryphon scroll and the implications there of the subordination of the female sex.

29.  Jewish War, II, 160-161. The existence of this "third order" of married Essenes is confirmed by references in some of the Dead Sea documents, e.g., the "Manual of Discipline for the Future Congregation of Israel," (QSa), where it says: "All that present themselves are to be assembled together, women and children included. Then all the provisions of the Covenant are to be read out loud to them, and they are to be instructed about all its injunctions" (Gaster, op. cit., p. 285). At this point Lohse commented: "Here the married members of the community and their families are spoken of. According to Josephus there were married Essenes. Also in the Damascus Document several references to members who were married and had children are made" (Eduard Lohse, Die Texte aus Qumran, Darmstadt, 1971, p. 286). There were also remains of women and children found in what is presumed to be a somewhat outer graveyard of the Qumran community. Cf. Dupont-Sommer, op. cit., pp. 71 ff.

30.  See above, note 17.


Therapeutae

31.  Four and a half to over six feet.

32.  De Vita Contemplativa, vss. 32-33. Cf. James Hastings, A Dictionary of the Bible (New York, 1902), vol. IV, p. 935.

33.  See chapter IV, 2, "Segregation in Temple and Synagogue."

34.  See chapter IV, 4, "Women Studying Torah."

35.  See K. Thraede, "Frau," Reallexikon für Antike und Christentum (Stuttgart, 1972), vol. VIII, cols. 208 f.

36.  De Vita Contemplativa, vss. 85-87.

37.  They believed "the acquiring of slaves was contrary to nature, which indeed has brought all humans into the world as free men" (Leipoldt, Die Frau, p. 86). In this they were also similar to the Essenes who also rejected slavery.

38.  Ibid.

39.  See below, pp. 120f.

## Elephantine Women

40. Cf. pp. 42, 52, 53.

41. See below, pp. 161-163.


## The Rabbis

42. For detailed documentation see the chapter on "Die Schrift-
    gelehrten," in Joachim Jeremias, Jerusalem zur Zeit Jesu
    (Göttingen, 1958), pp. 101-114.

43. Tos. A. Z. 3, 10, 464, quoted in ibid. , p. 138.

44. Cf. ibid. , p. 122.

45. Ibid. , p. 138.

46. Antiquities, XVIII, 15.   Cf. also XVI, 41: "There was also a
    group of Jews ... called Pharisees by whom the women (of
    Herod's court) were ruled. "

47. Ibid. , XVIII, 17.


## Positive Evaluations of Women

48. This quotation is from Genesis Rabbah 18, 2; the text continues
    by giving proof-texts for each of the characteristics for a
    wife.   A somewhat parallel passage is found in the Baby-
    lonian Talmud, bYeb. 62b, where to the characteristics of
    goodness, joy and blessing are added Torah, a protecting
    wall, and peace; proof-texts are also provided.

49. bSan. 22a.   Except for the first two statements listed here,
    all these reflections refer to "first" wives, or the wife of
    one's youth, which would not only seem to show an appre-
    ciation of a first love, but would also seem to presuppose
    the possibility, or perhaps even the likelihood, of at least
    "successive" if not simultaneous polygyny.

50. See above, p. 36.

51. bSan. 22b.

52. See above, pp. 40f.

53. Samson Raphael Hirsch, Judaism Eternal (London:   Soncino
    Press, 1959), vol. II, pp. 57 f.

54. Ibid. , pp. 49-96.

55. Ibid., pp. 51, 55. Cf. George Foot Moore, Judaism, vol. II
    (New York, 1971), p. 126, where the famous Presbyterian
    scholar makes the following strikingly inaccurate statement
    in an overly apologetic spirit: "The legal status of woman
    under Jewish law compares to its advantage with that of
    contemporary civilizations, and represents a development
    of the biblical legislation consistently favorable to woman."

56. The latter by buying her more clothes and ornaments than he
    does for himself (cf. bShab. 62b and Rashi's comment on
    bSan. 76b; there is a possibility that here the motivation
    of vicarious conspicuous consumption as analyzed by Thor-
    sten Veblen may play a role).

57. All these quotations are from bYeb. 63a-b.

58. Ibid. If divorced, the kethubah, pledged by the man, would
    have to be repaid, and the husband could not manage it fi-
    nancially. See below, pp. 157ff.

59. Genesis Rabbah 17, 7.

60. Ibid., 17, 8.

61. bB. M. 59a.

62. Ibid.

63. bShab. 25b.

64. Louis Finkelstein, Akiba (New York-Philadelphia, 1962), p.
    80; see below, pp. 112ff.

65. Git. 9, 10. See below, pp. 161f.

66. bNid. 45b.

67. GenR. 18, 1.

68. Hirsch, op. cit., p. 95.

69. Cf. Jakob Winter (trans.), Sifra Halachischer Midrasch zu
    Leviticus (Breslau, 1938), p. 650.

70. bBer. 17a.

71. bSotah 47b.

72. Hirsch, op. cit., p. 94.

73. See below, pp. 150 ff. for a more thorough discussion of
    adultery.

74.    Hirsch, op. cit. , p. 93.

75.    Ibid. , p. 94.

76.    bGit. 89.

77.    Hirsch, op. cit. , p. 95.


Negative Evaluations of Women

78.    Aboth 2, 7.  It was doubtless true that there was a goodly
         amount of superstition and appeal to magic and the occult
         among women of ancient Judaism, but clearly the men
         were not exempt from such practices, quite common
         among uneducated peoples of all times and places.  How-
         ever, the additional restriction on women's education, par-
         ticularly religious education, in Judaism and their almost
         total exclusion from any significant active participation in
         the orthodox religious cult (both to be discussed in detail
         below, pp.  83ff.), enhanced the tendency of women to en-
         gage in such unorthodox religious practices.

79.    Sotah 3, 4.

80.    See above, pp.  42, 49f. , 53f. , 63f. , 187 note 22.

81.    bKeth. 65a.

82.    bShab. 152a.  This teaching is attributed to a "Tanna," i. e. ,
         a rabbi of the early period, the time before the Mishnah
         was finally edited in the second century C. E.

83.    Apparently the rabbinic tradition found this an impressive say-
         ing, for it is quoted in at least three different rabbinic col-
         lections:  Terum 15; and pKid. 4, 66b, 32; and Soferim
         41a, in The Minor Tractates of the Talmud, ed. by A.
         Cohen (London, 1971), p.  288.

84.    bShab. 33b.  It is interesting to note a contemporary Jewish
         scholar's use of this statement.  In commenting on women's
         not being allowed to bear witness in Judaism, Raphael
         Loewe stated:  "No reflection on their veracity is hereby
         intended, but merely (to cite an operative phrase) 'because
         they have light, i. e. , flighty minds'" (Raphael Loewe, The
         Position of Women in Judaism, London, 1966, p.  24).

85.    bKid. 80b.  Somewhat later, in the period of the amoraim,
         of the Talmud proper, i. e. , between 200 and 500 C. E. ,
         this thought was carried further in the direction of the
         thought, "every woman a gossip," the implication being
         that men are not (though in the Semitic world of the Near
         East it would seem that talking is a major male

preoccupation): "Rab [late second, early third century
C. E. ] said: Hence (it is proved) that women are fond of
talking" (bBer. 48b). "Ten measures of gossip descended
to the world: nine were taken by women and only one by
the rest of the world" (bKid. 49b).

86. bKid. 82b; cf. also bSan. 100b.

87. bNid. 31b.

88. Third century.

89. Last generation of Tannaim, i. e. , late second, early third
century.

90. Midrash Rabbah, Genesis, trans. by H. Freedman (London,
1951), p. 383--referred to from now on in the traditional
manner, i. e. , GnR. 45, 5. This ancient midrash material
was collected between the editing of the Palestinian and
the Babylonian Talmuds, i. e. , around 400 C. E. , by Amoraim rabbis, but the rabbis quoted in it are almost all
Tannaim, i. e. , 200 C. E. and earlier.

91. GnR. 18, 2. Cf. DtR. 6, 11 (the Midrash Rabbah on Deuteronomy) where the Tanna Rabbi Levi is said to have char-
acterized women as "greedy, inquisitive, envious, and in-
dolent" and other rabbis added that women were "querulous
and gossips. "

92. Tos. Ber. 7, 18.

93. pBer. 13b; bMen. 43b.

94. Seder Eliahu Rabba, edited by M. Friedmann (Jerusalem,
1960), chapter 10, p. 48.

95. The fact that the massively authoritative commentary on the
New Testament from talmudic and midrashic sources written by the Christian scholar Paul Billerbeck does not allude
to the relationship between the threefold prayer and Paul's
statement in Gal. 3:28 might suggest some doubt concerning
the validity of maintaining the relationship. But the evidence, internal and external, is so strongly in favor of a
clear connection that Billerbeck's omission can only be attributed to oversight. Both a Christian scholar and a Jewish scholar have made comments to this effect. The
Christian Hans Kosmala wrote: "Billerbeck unfortunately
did not recognize the connection between Gal. 3:28 and the
Jewish benediction formula and likewise did not refer to it
(Kommentar III, 557 ff. )" (Hans Kosmala, "Gedanken zur
Kontroverse Farbstein-Hoch," Judaica, IV, 3 (1948), p.
229). The Jewish scholar Raphael Loewe wrote: "All
three are controverted by St. Paul (Gal. 3:28) in his famous

'neither Jew nor Greek, bond nor free, male nor female...'
The formulations in the two talmudic passages are patient
of the interpretation that Rabbi Meir (or Judah) was insist-
ing on the authenticity of the liturgical use of an already
current benedictional formula.   Possibly something of the
sort was known to Paul, who controverted it; and the in-
sistence of Meir (Judah) may thus itself be apologetically
aimed at Christianity through recontroversion of St. Paul.
Strangely, (H. L. Strack and) P. Billerbeck, Kommentar
zum Neuen Testament aus Talmud und Midrasch, III (1926),
pp. 557 f., have nothing to say of this obvious parallel to
Gal. 3:28" (Loewe, op. cit., p. 43).

96.   In contemporary prayer books women are often also invited to
      recite the prayer, usually with the following substitute for
      the phrase about praising God for not having made the one
      praying a woman:  Praised be God who has created me ac-
      cording to his own good pleasure.  (Cf. S. Singer, Author-
      ised Daily Prayer Book, p. 5, and I. Abrahams, Companion
      to the Authorised Daily Prayer Book, 1922, p. xvi.)   Many
      Jewish communities (Reform and some Conservative) have,
      of course, done away with the prayer in modern times,
      i.e., since the Enlightenment.   The English Jewish scholar,
      C. G. Montefiore comments: "No amount of modern Jew-
      ish apologetic, endlessly poured forth, can alter the fact
      that the Rabbinic attitude towards women was very different
      from our own.   No amount of apologetics can get over the
      implications of the daily blessing, which orthodox Judaism
      has still lacked the courage to remove from its official
      Prayer Book.  'Blessed art thou, O Lord our God, who
      hast not made me a woman'" (A Rabbinic Anthology, Phila-
      delphia, 1938, p. 507).

97.   E.g., see bSan. 100b where the Talmud defends vigorously
      the use of Ben Sira's misogynist passages in teaching the
      masses.

98.   Montefiore, Rabbinic Anthology, p. xviii.


CHAPTER IV

Women Fulfilling Torah

1.   Sotah 3, 8.

2.   Kid. 1, 7.

3.   Sukka 2, 8:  "Women and slaves and children are exempt from
     Succoth"--a revealing grouping of persons, which will be
     discussed below, pp. 117 ff.

4.   Tassels and prayer straps specified for the recitation of certain
     daily prayers.

5.  Tos. Kid. 2, 7, 224, 1, which one would have thought would
    be the one thing women should read.

6.  bKid. 33b and Ber. 3, 3.  In the latter reference, from the
    Mishnah, it states: "Women, slaves, and children are
    exempt...."

7.  Jalq Shim on Sm 78.  It might be noted that this teaching is
    extraordinarily similar to Paul's in I Cor. 7:32-34: "An
    unmarried man can devote himself to the Lord's affairs,
    all he need worry about is pleasing the Lord; but a mar-
    ried man has to bother about the world's affairs and devote
    himself to pleasing his wife:  he is torn two ways.  In the
    same way an unmarried woman, like a young girl, can de-
    vote herself to the Lord's affairs; all she need worry
    about is being holy in body and spirit.  The married wo-
    man, on the other hand, has to worry about the world's
    affairs and devote herself to pleasing her husband."  One
    main difference, of course, is that here Paul makes no
    distinction between the husband and the wife.

8.  For just one example cf. R. Loewe, op. cit., pp. 41 ff.  It
    is, however, not clear why, especially in light of the
    significantly better work attendance record women often
    have, men were not also thought to be liable to occasional
    prohibitive physical disabilities, or why they would not also
    have similarly onerous householder's or worker's obliga-
    tions--unless the wife was expected to work so the husband
    could have the leisure to study, as apparently was the case
    with the "perfect wife" of the Book of Proverbs (31:10-31),
    or the "model" wife of Rabbi Akiba, or hundreds of thou-
    sands of Orthodox wives over the centuries and at present
    at Mea Shearim--see above, pp. 36 f.

9.  Kid. 1, 7.

10. Cf. bKid. 29a.

11. bKid. 34a.

12. Zuckoff, "The oppression of the Jewish Woman," op. cit., pp.
    49 f.

13. Ber. 3, 3.

14. Tos. Ber. 5, 17; cf. bBer. 20b.

15. bBer. 20b.

16. bSuk. 38a.  The reference is to the recitation of the Hallel
    psalms during the feast of Succoth.  On the same page of
    the English translation (p. 172) the editor explains the ref-
    erence to women or children as making "use in divine ser-
    vice of inferior or second rate deputies."

17. Ber. 7, 2. This is similar to the principle that women, and children and slaves, are not counted toward a minyan; see below, p. 92.

18. bBer. 45a-47b. If a group of women are at meal they may invite each other; the same with a group of slaves; but slaves may not invite women or vice versa "because it might lead to immorality."

19. bBer. 47b; cf. also below, pp. 118 f.

20. Women were ritually unclean during and after menstruation, etc.

21. Shab. 2, 6.

22. Tos. Shab. 2, 10 (112); pShab. 2, 5b, 34; bShab. 31b, 32a; GnR. 17, 8.

23. pShab. 2, 5b, 34. See above, pp. 47 ff. for other traditions, some earlier, also maintaining that Eve caused the death of Adam.

24. In the Genesis Rabbah citation the English translation (Midrash Rabbah, trans. and ed. by Rabbi H. Friedman, London, 1951, vol. I, p. 139) ends, "Because she extinguished the soul of Adam, therefore was the precept of the Sabbath lights given to her." The editor then footnotes that portion --perhaps more profoundly than he realized--as follows: "The attitude of Judaism toward woman is shown in these replies."

25. A not dissimilar discussion was held by Christians for a long time about whether non-Christians can merit by their good acts--some still maintain the negative!

26. bA. Z. 3a.

27. Loewe, op. cit., p. 44.

28. Ibid., p. 45. Actually Regina Jonas was ordained a Reform rabbi in Germany in the 1930s; she was killed by the Nazis. In 1972 and 1974 Sally Preisand and Sandy Eisenberg Sasso were ordained, respectively, in the U.S. This pattern of logic, the non-obligation of women vis a vis certain prescriptions of the Law equals the non-allowance of the same, would, if applied elsewhere, have drastic results, for example: Americans are not, as in many communist countries, obliged to vote; therefore, they are not allowed to vote.

Segregation in Temple and Synagogue

29.  Josephus, Antiquities, XV, 418 f.

30.  Middoth 2, 5.

31.  Josephus, Jewish War, V, 5, par. 198 f.

32.  Josephus, Apion, II, 103; cf. Lv. 12: 2 ff.

33.  Irene Brennan, "Women in the Gospels," New Blackfriars
     (1971), p. 293.

34.  Josephus, Antiquities, XVI, 164.

35.  Loewe, op. cit., p. 44, notes that "separate seating arrange-
     ments in the synagogue probably go back to the origins of
     that institution in antiquity."

36.  Cf. Jeremias, op. cit., p. 248.

37.  Ancient Synagogues in Palestine and Greece (London, 1934),
     pp. 47 ff.

38.  pSuk. 55b.

39.  In the French translation Le Talmud de Jérusalem by Moise
     Schwab (Paris, 1883), vol. VI, pp. 43 f.

40.  Cf. Mekh. Shirah 10, 44a, Midrash Lekah Tov to Ex. 15:30,
     quoted in article on "Song of the Sea," Encyclopaedia
     Judaica (Jerusalem, 1971), vol. 14, col. 1072.

41.  Isaiah Sonne, "Synagogue," The Interpreter's Dictionary of the
     Bible (4 vols.), (New York, 1962), vol. IV, pp. 486-87.
     To today this separation is maintained in all Orthodox
     synagogues, and many Conservative ones.  The custom was
     also taken over into Christianity and persists in many
     Orthodox Christian churches and in some more conservative
     Protestant and Catholic communities--indeed the current
     Code of Canon Law in the Catholic Church, issued in 1918,
     states in canon 1262:  "In keeping with ancient discipline,
     women in the church should be separated from the men."
     Islam has a similar custom of separation in the mosque.


No Men, No Minyan

42.  Loewe, op. cit., p. 45.

43.  Cf. Aboth 3, 6.

44.  bBer. 47b.  Cf. also below, pp. 117 ff.

## Women Reading Torah

45. The order used, i. e. , first a child and second a woman,
    and the word "even" are by themselves revelatory of the
    relative status of women in the synagogue.

46. Tos. Meg. 4, 11, 226, 4.

47. bMeg. 23a.

48. Der jüdischen Gottesdienst in seiner geschichtlichen Entwick-
    lung (Frankfurt a. M. , 1924), p. 170.

49. Op. cit. , vol. III, p. 467.

50. Cf. Leipoldt, Die Frau in der Antiken Welt, pp. 96, 252;
    Jeremias, op. cit. , p. 248; Schürer, op. cit. , vol. III,
    pp. 88 f.


## Women Studying Torah

51. The ancient Mishnah put it this way: "He who is not versed
    in Scripture and in Mishnah and in good conduct is of no
    benefit to the public weal" (Kid. 1, 10).

52. The Encyclopaedia Judaica article on "Woman" states: "There
    was general agreement that a woman was not obliged to
    study Torah.  As a result few women were learned."

53. Sotah 3, 4.  Shalom Ben-Chorin, Mutter Mirjam (Munich,
    1971), p. 98, explains Rabbi Eliezer's angry statement as
    follows: "He speaks from sad experience with his famous
    wife Ima-Shalom. ...  This Ima-Shalom appeared to have
    been what elsewhere is called a bluestocking."  It is diffi-
    cult to see how on the basis of what is known about Imma
    Shalom she can be either called a bluestocking or that she
    could therefore have caused the outburst.  See below, pp.
    104 ff.

54. bSotah 21b.

55. pSotah 3, 4.   Cf. also bYoma 66b.

56. "Gedanken zur Kontroverse Farbstein-Hoch," Judaica (1948),
    pp. 225-27.

57. Here the English Soncino edition comments: "The duty of
    Torah study is not obligatory upon a woman; therefore she
    cannot acquire so much merit even if she does so" that is,
    to warrant a three year postponement.  See above, p. 119.

58. bSotah 21a.

59.  bKid. 29a.

60.  bKid. 29b. "How do we know that she (the mother) has no
     duty (to teach her children)?  Because it is written we-
     limaddetem (and ye shall teach), (which also reads) u-
     lemadetem (and ye shall study): (hence) whoever is com-
     manded to study, is commanded to teach; whoever is not
     commanded to study, is not commanded to teach.  And
     how do we know that she is not bound to teach herself?
     Because it is written, we-limaddetem (and ye shall teach)--
     u-lemadetem (and ye shall learn):  the one whom others
     are commanded to teach is commanded to teach oneself;
     and the one whom others are not commanded to teach, is
     not commanded to teach oneself.  How then do we know that
     others are not commanded to teach her?  Because it is
     written, 'And ye shall teach them your sons'--but not your
     daughters. "
        It should also be noted that in the Mishnah's discussion
     about what a man who has taken a vow not "to derive any
     benefit from his fellow" (Ned. 4, 2), may nevertheless do
     for his fellow it is stated that the vow-maker may teach
     the sons and daughters of his fellow Scripture (Ned. 4, 3).
     However, the word daughter is missing in many editions;
     secondly, it is Scripture, not the full Torah that is men-
     tioned; thirdly, and most importantly, it is merely said that
     he may teach Scripture--again the lack of obligation.

61.  Kallah 50b.  The Minor Tractates of the Talmud, vol. II, p.
     402.

62.  bShab. 147b.

63.  Loewe, op. cit. , p. 30.

64.  Sefer ha-mizwoth (Ausgabe Zolkiew, 1855), fol. 45c.  Quoted
     in Kosmala, op. cit. , pp. 226 f.  The assumption that the
     study of Torah was not a matter for women is stated, im-
     plied or assumed time and again throughout rabbinic writ-
     ing.  Let two brief examples suffice here.  In giving rea-
     sons why croup comes into the world the Talmud states:
     "Let women prove it!"  The English edition notes here:
     "Who are not bidden to study (bKid 129b), and yet suffer
     from croup (cf. Sot. 3, 4)" (bShab. 33b).  Again, "Torah
     and kingship ... apply neither to women nor to slaves. "
     In fact, according to the same teaching even "Covenant ...
     does not apply to women!" (bBer. 49a).

65.  C. G. Montefiore and H. Loewe, A Rabbinic Anthology (Phila-
     delphia, 1960), pp. xviii-xix.

Beruria: The Exception That Proves the Rule

66. Cf., e.g., Hans Bietenhard, Die Mishnah (Berlin, 1965), vol.
    III, p. 71.

67. bYeb. 46a. Valeria the proselyte is also mentioned in bR. H.
    17b and Gerim 60b, Minor Tractates of the Talmud, vol.
    II, p. 606. In the latter place she is referred to as Queen
    Valeria, but the story is the same as in the other refer-
    ences. There are basically seven references to Beruria
    in the Babylonian Talmud, none in the Palestinian Talmud,
    and one reference in the Tosephta.

68. bPes. 62b and bA. Z. 18a.

69. In keeping with his suggestion that Beruria is a proselyte Lei-
    poldt stated that, "this woman would be more readily un-
    derstandable if she were a Greek." Jesu Verhältnis zu
    Griechen und Juden, p. 21.

70. bPes. 62b.

71. Tos. Kelim B. K. 4, 17.

72. Tos. Kelim B. M. 1, 6.

73. bEr. 53b.

74. Anne Goldfeld, "Women as Sources of Torah in the Rabbinic
    Tradition," Judaism (Spring, 1975), pp. 245-256.

75. bBer. 10a.

76. Ibid.

77. B. M. Lerner, The Babylonian and Jerusalem Talmud Trans-
    lated Into English With Commentary, A. Ehrman, ed.
    (Jerusalem, 1965 ff.), Ber. 10a, p. 189.

78. Midrash Prov. 30, 10.

79. bA. Z. 17b-18a.

80. bEr. 53b.

81. bA. Z. 18a.

82. Ad loc. Translated into German in Kosmala, op. cit., pp.
    231 f. In giving the translation of the Rashi recorded
    legend Kosmala notes: "Beruria is in every way an extra-
    ordinary woman; but she has not become the rabbis' ideal
    of a Jewish wife. Specifically because of her self-aware-
    ness and her superiority she was for them unbearable. It

is therefore not at all surprising that a scandalous story
was told about her so as finally to morally annihilate her.
She is supposed to have ended her life in an ignominious
fashion.   We find the legend about her handed on exactly a
thousand years later by Rashi (in his commentary on A. Z.
18b.   The Talmud itself of course deftly refers to an 'incident about Beruria,' from which probably we can conclude that already at that time a dark story was told about
her.).   The story is to my knowledge nowhere translated,
and in more recent Jewish writing is only infrequently referred to."   In a footnote to the English Soncino translation
of the Babylonian Talmud (Abodah Zarah, London, 1935, p.
94) the editor gives the jist of the scandalous legend and
says, "the incident as related in Kid. 80b is to the effect ...," but Kid. 80b makes no reference to it all, nor
does any of the rest of the Talmud.

83.  bSan 74a; idol worship, sexual immorality and murder.

84.  For a similar opinion, see the modern Jewish scholar Henry
Zirndorf, Some Jewish Women (Philadelphia, 1892), p. 173:
"Now, in the light of all that we positively know to be true
concerning Rabbi Meir and his distinguished wife, the im-
probability of this occurrence is too obvious for demonstra-
tion.   Without attempting any critical elucidation, therefore, I shall conclude by simply recording my conviction
that this calumny ought no longer to be permitted to tarnish
the memory of the pure and noble-minded Beruria."

## Imma Shalom: No Exception

85.  The Universal Jewish Encyclopedia article on "Woman"; see
below, p. 140.   See also Raphael Loewe, op. cit. , p. 30,
who along with Beruria mentioned Imma Shalom, "who if
they were not exactly rabbinical scholars knew enough of
the academic aspect of Jewish scholarship for their sayings
to have been recorded in the talmudic literature."

86.  See above, p. 94.

87.  Cf. bShab 116a.

88.  Cf. The Jewish Encyclopedia (New York, 1904), vol. VI, p.
562.   Italics added.

89.  The other references to Imma Shalom in the Talmud are
bB. M. 59b; bEr. 63a; bNed. 20b.

## Other Non-Exceptions

90.  New York, 1943, vol. 10, p. 565.

91. Op. cit., p. 99.

92. See note 53.

93. Cf. Zirndorf, op. cit., pp. 243-252, where she is referred
    to as Homa, apparently from later sources.

94. Cf. bBaba batra 12b and bYeb. 34b.

95. bBer. 62a.

96. bKet. 85a.

97. bKeth. 65a; cf. also bYeb. 64b.

98. bBer. 51b. See below, pp. 124 f.

99. bHul. 109b.

100. See above, p. 106.

101. Ben-Chorin, op. cit., p. 99.

102. Zirndorf, op. cit., p. 200.

103. bEr. 53b.

104. bMeg. 18a. Parts of these reports are also recorded in
     bNazir 3a (concerning "curling hair") and bRosh Hashanah
     26b (concerning "at intervals"). Cf. also pShebiit 9, 1 and
     pMeg. 2, 2.

105. Susan Wall, "Forgotten Jewish Women in Jewish History,"
     The Jewish Digest (November, 1974), p. 9.

106. Zirndorf, op. cit., p. 198.

107. See above, note 104.

108. bMoed katan 17a.

109. bKeth. 104a. Henry Zirndorf, op. cit., pp. 203 f., explained
     the passage thusly: "According to a prevailing belief of
     the times, so long as the sick man heard these impas-
     sioned prayers--and as he lay in the upper chamber he could
     scarcely help hearing them--it was impossible for him to
     draw his last breath. This belief is no conclusive proof
     of faith in miracles; the prolongation of life through intense
     momentary excitement is readily explained on psychological,
     and perhaps also on physiological grounds. But, however
     this may be, on the roof stood the maid-servant ... trying
     in vain to make her voice heard below. Then, seizing a
     jug all of a sudden, she threw it in the midst of the earnest

crowd of suppliants.  A dreadful pause ensued and, in the
inimitable language of the Talmud, 'the soul of Rabbi Judah
the Patriarch reposed. '"

110.  Ben-Chorin, op. cit. , p. 99.

111.  Blackman, op. cit. , vol. III, p. 348.  Herbert Danby, The
Mishnah (Oxford, 1964), 296, translates the word perushah, "a woman who is a hypocrite. "  Louis Finkelstein,
The Pharisees (Philadelphia, 1962), vol. II, p. 837 confirms this understanding when he says:  "Rabbi Joshua
ben Hananya, one of the leading plebian scholars of his
day (i. e. , from about 80-118 C. E.), used to say, 'A
pious fool, a clever knave, an ascetic woman, and the
sufferings of the Pharisees destroy the world' (Mishnah
Sotah 3, 4).  It is interesting to notice that in this statement the Hebrew word rendered by 'sanctimonious' is
perushah, meaning literally a 'Pharisaic woman. '  Since
Rabbi Joshua himself was a leading Pharisee, however,
it is clear that what he was objecting to was, in reality,
the wife whose piety expressed itself in a reluctance to
normal marital life as degrading or impure.  The monogamous plebians were less inclined to tolerate such abstinence in their wives than the provincials and patricians,
among whom plural marriage was not unusual (cf. further
the views of the Hillelites in Mishnah Ketubot 5, 6; Niddah
10, 1; and see also ibid. 2, 4).  The word perushim occurs in passages where it cannot possibly have any other
meaning than 'ascetics'; see, e. g. , Baba Batra 60b. "
Following Finkelstein, the quotation in question would have
a misogynist rather than pro-feminist meaning.

112.  It is interesting to note that just before the remark about the
pharisaical woman Ben-Chorin writes:  "Christian theologians have gladly seen here a turning-point and have
spoken of a religious liberation of the woman by Christianity.  This interpretation however is not tenable, for
we are moving here entirely on Jewish ground in a pre-
Christian time. "  (He is referring to the various women
mentioned in the gospels and their relationship to Jesus. )
There is surely a strong element of truth in this charge
as far as Christianity is concerned; as far as Jesus, the
Jew, is concerned another Jewish scholar, C. G. Montefiore, has the following pertinent remarks:  "It would
seem indubitable that in his relations with, and in his effect upon, women Jesus was highly original" (The Synoptic
Gospels, New York, 1968, vol. II, p. 438).  "The implied
attack upon the inferiority of women in Oriental society,
and upon the unjust power of divorce given to men, was
of the highest importance and value.  Thus, upon the
whole, we have to recognize that his (Jesus') words have
been of service towards a higher conception of womanhood" (ibid. , p. 67).  "Was not Jesus the champion of

woman?" (ibid. , vol. I. , p. 281). "There can be little
doubt that in Jesus's attitude towards women we have a
highly original and significant feature of his life and
teaching" (ibid. , p. 389). "The relation of Jesus to women seems unlike what would have been usual for a Rabbi.   He seems to have definitely broken with orientalism
in this particular....   But certainly the relations of Jesus
towards women, and of theirs towards him, seem to
strike a new note, and a higher note, and to be off the
line of Rabbinic tradition" (Rabbinic Literature and Gospel
Teachings, London, 1930, pp. 217 f. ).   In commenting on
the gospel according to Matthew 5:31 f. , on the theme of
divorce: "In these verses the originality of Jesus is made
manifest.   So far, in the Sermon on the Mount, we have
found nothing which goes beyond Rabbinic religion and Rabbinic morality, or which greatly differs from them.   Here
we do.   The attitude of Jesus towards women is very striking.   He breaks through oriental limitations in more direc-
tions than one.   For (1) he associates with, and is much
looked after by, women in a manner which was unusual;
(2) he is more strict about divorce; (3) he is also more
merciful and compassionate.   He is a great champion of
womanhood.   And in this combination of freedom and pity,
as well as in his strict attitude to divorce, he makes a
new departure of enormous significance and importance.
If he had done no more than this, he might justly be regarded as one of the great teachers of the world.   Mr.
H. Loewe, generously anxious to champion the Rabbis,
and to weaken any difference between their teaching and
that of Jesus, if the teaching of Jesus appears superior
to theirs,..." (ibid. , pp. 46 f. ).   The accuracy of Montefiore's judgment will be the task of further study.

113.   Op. cit. , p. 99.

114.   Ibid. , pp. 98 f.


## Women Distract From Torah Study

115.   8:8.

116.   Keth. 5, 6.

117.   bKeth. 62b.

118.   Ibid.

119.   bKeth. 61b.

120.   bKeth. 63a.   Parallel in bNed. 50a.

121.   Akiba (New York-Philadelphia, 1962), p. 135.

122.  Ibid. , p. 80.

123.  bEr. 22a.  For that matter, in bMeg. 16b it says: "The
      study of the Torah is superior to the honoring of father
      and mother," and even: "The study of the Torah is
      superior to the saving of life!"

124.  Cf. Ferdinand Weber, Jüdische Theologie (Leipzig, 1897),
      pp. 30 f.

125.  Or as was apparently also exhibited by the story about Rabbi
      Eliezer ben Hyrcanus:  Imma Shalom,  his wife, said:
      "He (my husband) 'converses' with me neither at the be-
      ginning nor at the end of the night, but (only) at mid-
      night, and when he 'converses,' he uncovers a handbreath
      and covers a handbreath, and is as though he were com-
      pelled by a demon.   And when I asked him, what is the
      reason for this (for choosing midnight), he replied, So
      that I may not think of another woman, lest my children
      be as bastards" (bNed. 20b).

126.  bBer. 17a.  In bSotah 21a it says: "they have their sons
      taught Scripture. "  See above, p. 96.

127.  See above, pp. 94 ff.   There is also a legend that Ben
      Azzai married one of the daughters of Rabbi Akiba, but
      shortly afterward divorced her and remained unmarried
      thereafter.

128.  bYeb. 63b.

129.  For example, Marcus Lehman, Akiba (New York, 1956), and
      Finkelstein, op. cit. , e.g. , p. 23: "She must be recog-
      nized as one of the most remarkable women in the whole
      of Jewish tradition. "


CHAPTER V

Women's Education

1.    "Education," in Encyclopaedia Judaica, vol. 6, col. 397.

2.    Loewe, op. cit. , pp. 22 f.

3.    pPea 1, 1, 15c.  In a later period (fourth century C. E. ) in
      Babylonia there was a reference to the foster mother of
      Rabbi Abaye who had a knowledge of medical remedies.
      ("Abaye," in Encyclopaedia Judaica, vol. 2, col. 45).

4.    Kid. 4, 13:  "A woman may not be a teacher of children. "

5.    bKid. 82a.

6.    See the footnote on p. 422 of the Soncino English translation.


## Bearing Witness

7.    Shab. 4, 1; see also Sifre Dt. 190 on 19:17 (46d 52).

8.    Yeb. 16, 7.   See also R. H. 1, 8, where it states: "These
      are they that are ineligible (to bear witness concerning the
      new moon):  a diceplayer, a usurer, pigeon-flyers, traf-
      fickers in Seventh Year produce, and slaves.   This is the
      general rule:  any evidence that a woman is not eligible to
      bring, these are not eligible to bring."   In the medieval
      period Maimonides also provided a list of types of persons
      who could not testify:  women, slaves, minors, lunatics,
      deaf, blind, wicked, contemptible, relatives and interested
      parties.   (Yad, Edut 9:1).

9.    bB. K. 88a.

10.   Josephus, Antiquities, IV, 219.

11.   I, 82 (ed. Wilna 1898, 49a).

12.   Cf. bEr. 100b where ten curses are listed, differing some-
      what from the above, including not listing the curse on
      bearing witness.   The midrash NuR 10 (157c) refers to
      there being seven curses, but does not list them.

13.   Loewe, op. cit., p. 24.

14.   Cf. also bB,K. 14b where it states: "... on the evidence of
      witnesses who are free and persons under the jurisdiction
      of the Law (bnai brith) ... 'Free man' excludes slaves;
      'persons under the jurisdiction of the Law,' excludes
      heathens."

15.   Boaz Cohen, Jewish and Roman Law (New York, 1966), pp.
      128 f.   In his small volume, Hebrew Law in Biblical
      Times (Jerusalem, 1964), p. 112, Ze'ev W. Falk merely
      says that women "did not act as witnesses."

16.   Cohen, op. cit., pp. 128 f.   See above, pp. 6 f., 17, 22.


## Women, Children and Slaves

17.   Ber, 3, 3.   See bBer. 20a for a development on this Mishnah
      teaching.

18.   Suk. 2, 7.

19.   See above, pp. 87 ff.

20.  B. M.  1,  5.

21.  Hag.  1,  1.

22.  R. H.  1,  8.

23.  See above, p.  84.

24.  Kid.  1,  1.  Danby, in his English translation of the Mishnah notes here that according to the twelfth century commentary of Maimonides and the fifteenth century commentary of Bertinoro, the sexual intercourse must be "in the presence of witnesses" but that according to the nineteenth century commentary, Tiferet Yisrael, by Israel Lipschutz, "not literally, but that there must be witnesses to their being alone together, and to his saying, Thou art betrothed to me by this intercourse."

25.  Kid.  1,  2.

26.  Kid.  1,  3.

27.  Kid.  1,  4.

28.  Kid.  1,  5.

29.  Ber.  7,  2.

30.  See above, pp.  145.

31.  Minyan.  See above, p.  92.

32.  bBer.  47a.

33.  A Rabbinic Anthology, p.  xviii.


## Women Appearing in Public

34.  Keth.  1,  10.

35.  B. M.  1,  6.

36.  bBer.  3b.

37.  bB. Q.  119a.

38.  Keth.  9,  4.

39.  Tos.  Suk.  4,  1 (198,6); see above, pp.  89 ff.

40.  The example of Queen Alexandra (76-67 B. C. E. ) does not seem to have had much effect on the pious upper class or

the rest of the population.   Perhaps that was because being ruled by a queen was thought of as not Jewish but Hellenistic, since there were Seleucid and Ptolomaic queens;
it was ironic, of course, that Queen Alexandra was supportive of the Pharisees.

41.   Ecclesiasticus 42:11-12; cf. also 26:10.

42.   IV Maccabees 8:6-8.   The commentary in Charles op. cit.,
      vol II, p. 684, notes: "No seducer of the desert.   This is
      a curious instance of the Jewish belief that evil spirits
      haunted the waste, to which we have the references in the
      New Testament.   It seems hardly credible to us, but the
      Jews did actually believe that out in the desert there were
      demons who would lie in wait for women and lead them
      astray.   The Australian Arunta similarly hold that certain
      rocky places in their deserts are the habitation of wanton
      spirits, and that women venturing near them may become
      mothers, apparently without knowing it."

43.   Flaccus, 89.   This of course matches with the evidence given
      above, especially the advice offered by Ben Sira, and also
      with the rabbinical story about Juda not recognizing his
      daughter-in-law Tamar; see below, note 62.

44.   De specialibus legibus, III, 169.   At this point Philo added
      another indication of the lower estimate of women's abil-
      ities: "Organized communities are of two sorts, the greater
      which we call cities and the smaller which we call house-
      holds.   Both of these have their governors; the government
      of the greater is assigned to men under the name of states-
      manship, that of the lesser, known as household manage-
      ment, to women" (ibid., 170).

45.   Ibid., 171.

46.   Keth. 6, 6.

47.   A contemporary of Akiba, hence, latter first century C. E.

48.   bGit. 90a.   Parallel passages in: Tos. Sotah 5, 9 (302);
      pSotah 1, 17a, 32; NuR 9 (152b).   The concern about spin-
      ning in the street is that the woman may have to bare her
      arm to do the work.

49.   GnR 8, 12.   The Genesis Rabbah is an early collection of
      midrashic materials produced by Amoraic rabbis in Pales-
      tine, i. e., the generations immediately following the editing
      of the Mishnah, hence, in the third and fourth centuries
      C. E.

50.   It might be added that in the Talmud (bYeb. 76b-77a) it is
      stated: "It is customary for a man to meet (wayfarers); it

is not customary for a woman to meet (them)." In a footnote on the following page (519) the editor of the English
Soncino edition remarked: "Respectable women remain at
home and do not go into the open road even to meet members of their sex."

51. Leipoldt, Frau in der antiken Welt, p. 90, remarks on this
    situation: "Such a development must lead to the strict
    closing off of the women's quarters from the outside world,
    and thus a harem arises. That does not happen in a day,
    nor everywhere, and where it does happen it is not always
    equally so. But this line of development by and large suc-
    ceeds. Probably first in the city of Jerusalem, less so in
    the smaller localities, and hardly anywhere in the villages.
    The freedom and responsible position of an Abigail would
    have been impossible in earlier Judaism. But a harem in
    a farmer's house is nonsense (Unding) and hardly feasible."

## Women's Head and Face Covering

52. By woman here is meant a married woman; it is possible that
    a woman did not cover her head before she was married.
    But since the usual marriage age for a girl was 13, and
    marriagable virgins were usually restricted to their homes,
    this distinction is not terribly significant here.

53. For an extremely thorough discussion of the whole question of
    the head covering of Jewish women, complete with very
    detailed references and documentation from various rabbinic
    sources see Billerbeck, op. cit., vol. III, pp. 427-436.

54. In commenting on the words of the Mishnah (Shab. 8, 3) con-
    cerning the painting of one eye, Rab Huna (d. 297 C.E.)
    said: "Because modest women paint (only) one eye" (bShab.
    80a). The editor of the English translation of the Soncino
    Press notes here: "They go veiled, leaving only one eye
    visible." The Talmud then proceeds to speak of the
    "adornment of two eyes" and how this "was taught in refer-
    ence to small towners." Again the editor of the English
    translation notes here: "Or, villagers. Temptation not
    being so great there, it is safe even for modest women to
    paint both eyes." This comment is probably based on the
    medieval commentator Rashi, who said: "Modest women
    who enter covered, uncover only one eye so they can see,
    and they adorn it.... The women living in the villages do
    not need to be so withdrawn, for there is not so much
    banter and levity there ... and they do not cover their
    faces and adorn both their eyes" (quoted in Billerbeck, op.
    cit., vol. III, p. 430).

55. pSotah 1, 16b, 28. Indeed, the Babylonian Talmud says, "A
    woman's hair is an immoral thing" (bBer. 24a).

56.  Keth. 7, 6.

57.  Tos. Sotah 5, 9 (302); cf. bGit. 90a-b (see above, pp. 120
     f.).

58.  B. K. 8, 6.

59.  See Keth. 72a.  Since, however, this Babylonian talmudic dis-
     cussion stems from the early fourth century C. E. in Baby-
     lon it is quite possible that a certain laxness in this re-
     gard developed since the time of more stringent custom in
     Palestine during the period before the destruction of the
     Temple in 70 C. E.

60.  bYoma 47a.  Cf. Billerbeck, op. cit. , vol. III, p. 430, for
     the many parallel passages.

61.  Billerbeck, op. cit. , vol. III, pp. 428 ff.

62.  For example, the Talmud tells a story about Tamar that
     would indicate it was quite believable in rabbinic times that
     a woman would live at home with her face so constantly
     covered that it would not even be seen by her own relatives
     living there: "Every bride who is modest in the house of
     her father-in-law is rewarded by having kings and prophets
     among her descendants.  How do we prove this?  From
     Tamar, as it is written. . . .  What it means is that because
     she had covered her face in the house of her father-in-law
     and he did not know her, she was rewarded. . ." (bMeg. 10b).
     See Billerbeck, ibid. , p. 431 for further examples.

63.  PesiqR 26 (129b).

64.  Billerbeck, op. cit. , vol. III, p. 434.


Conversation with Women

65.  Aboth 1, 5.

66.  Ibid.

67.  See pp. 94 ff.

68.  See above, pp. 112 ff.

69.  bEr. 53b.  See above, p. 72.

70.  bNed. 20a.  At this point the editor of the English Soncino
     edition adds a note that, in view of the evidence gathered
     above, is rather ironic, though it was not intended to be,
     but was probably written out of embarrassment: "The pre-
     sent statement is not meant to be derogatory to women,
     who were held in high esteem" (p. 57).

71.  bBer. 43b.

72.  bKid. 70a-b.

73.  bHag. 5b.

74.  At this point the editor of the English Soncino edition notes: "I. e., he was ravenous in his desires like a newly-wed."

75.  See above, p. 94.

76.  bNed. 20b.  However, apparently the conversation was to be somewhat limited on the side of the wife since in the Mishnah, when listing women who may be divorced without their kethubah, it is stated: "Rabbi Tarfon (a first century C. E. rabbi) says:  Also if she be a loud-voiced woman.  What is here meant by a loud-voiced woman?  Such a one who speaks in her house so that her neighbors hear her voice" (Keth. 7, 6).  In commenting on that passage the Talmud asks what is meant by a loud-voiced woman and responds:  "In a Baraitha it was taught:  one whose voice during her intercourse in one court can be heard in another court" (bKeth. 72b).

## Women's Absence from Meals

77.  bKid. 70a.   See p. 124.

78.  bBer. 51b.

79.  Billerbeck, op. cit., vol. I, p. 882.

80.  bKid. 70a.

### CHAPTER VI

## Woman as Sex Object

1.  Keth. 7, 7.

2.  bBer. 61a.

3.  bMeg. 15a.

4.  bNed. 20a.

5.  bA. Z. 20a-b.

6.  All these statements are from bBer. 24a.  The latter has a parallel in bShab. 64b:  "Whoever looks upon a woman's little finger is as though he gazed upon the pudenda."

7.   A woman during her period of menstruation and seven days
     following.

8.   bNed. 20a.

9.   Lazarus Goldschmidt, Der Babylonische Talmud (Haag, 1933),
     vol. IV, p. 877.

10.  Robert Graves and Raphael Patai (eds.), Hebrew Myths (Lon-
     don, 1965), p. 65.

11.  Ibid. , p. 68 f.

12.  bNed. 20a.

13.  Ibid.

14.  bYeb. 54a.

15.  Montefiore, Rabbinic Anthology, p. xix.


Impure Menstruous Woman

16.  Article on "Purity" in vol. 13, col. 1405.   In Leviticus 11:43-
     44 purity and holiness are clearly linked together: "You
     shall not contaminate yourselves through any teeming crea-
     ture.   You shall not defile yourselves with them and make
     yourselves unclean by them. For I am the Lord your God;
     you shall make yourselves holy and keep yourselves holy,
     because I am holy. "

17.  Cf. bA. Z. 20b.

18.  Mary Douglas, Purity and Danger, quoted in Rachel Adler,
     "Tum'ah and Toharah," The Jewish Woman.   Response, 18
     (Summer, 1973), p. 118.

19.  Tos. Yoma 1, 12.

20.  San. 9, 6.

21.  "Purity," op. cit. , col. 1411.

22.  Cf. "Niddah," Encyclopaedia Judaica, vol. 12, cols. 1146 f.

23.  Ibid. , col. 1141.

24.  Aboth 3, 19.

25.  Liz Koltum, ed. , The Jewish Woman, op. cit. , p. 125.

26.  Cf. bShab. 13a.

27. bNid. 66a.

28. P. xxii.

29. "Niddah," Encyclopedia Judaica, vol. 12, cols. 1141 f. In the same place it is also noted that, "the halakhah as at present is that sexual intercourse (and any other intimacies which may lead to it) is forbidden from the time the woman expects her menses until seven clean days ... have elapsed.... Thus the minimum period of separation is 12 days."

30. Ibid., col. 1144.

31. Shab. 2, 6. See above, pp. 76, 87 f., and below, note 51.

32. "Niddah," op. cit., col. 1147.

33. Shab. 9, 1. The same teaching is repeated elsewhere in the Mishnah: A. Z. 3, 6.

34. "Niddah," op. cit., col. 1147.

35. Adler, op. cit., p. 126.

36. The bShab. 13b version says simply: "in the days of thy menstruation."

37. When she was not menstruating, but was going through the seven "unclean" days afterwards. See bShab. 13b.

38. ARN 1, 5. This translation is taken from Judah Goldin, trans., The Fathers According to Rabbi Nathan (New Haven, 1955), pp. 16 f. Almost the identical story is repeated in the Babylonian Talmud, bShab. 13b; the former work reports only tannaitic teachings and is earlier than the Talmud.

39. After her period of menstruation.

40. bPes. 111a.

41. See Pliny, Natural History, XXVIII, 23; VII, 65. Cf. also J. G. Frazer, The Golden Bough. Balder the Beautiful (London, 3rd. ed., 1923). vol. I. pp. 22 ff. for examples of the putative effects of menstruous blood and customs concerning menstruants among the primitive peoples of the world.

42. Cf. "Niddah," op. cit., col. 1146. Perhaps a contemporary echo of this is the current slang reference by women to menstruation as "the curse."

43.  bShab. 13a.  Cf. also Tos. Shab. 1, 14.

44.  Nid. 7, 4.

45.  On "conversing" with one's wife for the sake of cajoling her
     into sexual intercourse see above, p. 124.

46.  Emphasis added.

47.  ARN 1, 4.  It should be noticed that this text is probably
     quite early since it does not yet allow the woman to adorn
     herself during her menstrual period, whereas she was al-
     lowed to do so by Rabbi Akiba in the first century C.E.
     (Sifra, Mezora 9, 12).

48.  Segregated.

49.  bR. H. 26a.

50.  Edited in 1890 by C. M. Horowitz.

51.  It is perhaps ironic that a menstruating woman should here
     be forbidden to light the Sabbath light since the one rabbin-
     ical explanation given (in several ancient sources) for the
     woman's obligation to enkindle the light is that she "put
     out" the light of the world, i.e., caused the death of Adam;
     but in the same rabbinic passage the menstruation regula-
     tions are said to be the woman's punishment for having
     caused the death of Adam, the blood of the world.  See
     above, pp. 76, 87 f.

52.  Cf. Baraita-de-Niddah, pp. 3 ff. and 17 ff.

53.  Cf. "Niddah," op. cit., col. 1146

54.  Adler, op. cit., p. 126.


Married Women

55.  bKid. 29b.

56.  bYeb. 63b.

57.  bYeb. 63a.

58.  bSan. 76a.

59.  bKid. 7a.

60.  Many Christian Fathers and broad strands of Christian theol-
     ogy also carried the same notion forward to the present.

61. The Greek text reads: "ep alētheias", in truth; the Vulgate reads: "sola posteritatis dilectione," only for the love of posterity (8:7).

62. Probably the first century before or after the beginning of the Common Era. See above, pp. 51 f.

63. Testament of Issachar 2:3.

64. Josephus, Jewish War, II, 161.

65. Philo, De Specialibus Legibus, III, 113.

66. Josephus, Against Apion, vol. II, 199. The Loeb Classical Library edition of the English translation by H. St. J. Thackeray (London & Cambridge, Mass., 1961), p. 373, notes at this point: "Restriction not specified in the Pentateuch, but implied by the Talmud (passages cited by Reinach)," the reference being to Oeuvres complètes de Flav. Josèphe traduites en Français sous la direction de Théodore Reinach, tome vii, fasc. 1 (Paris, 1902). Unfortunately this volume was not available to me to check the references.

67. Yeb. 6, 5.

68. bYeb. 61b.

69. bYeb. 65b.

70. Yeb. 6, 6.

71. bYeb. 63b.

72. bYeb. 64a. This is a commentary on the earlier Mishnah: "If a man took a wife and lived with her for ten years and she bore no child, he may not abstain (any longer from the duty of propagation)" (Yeb 6, 6). See also bYeb. 65a: "Our Rabbis taught: A woman who had been married to one husband and had no children and to a second husband and again had no children, may marry a third man only if he has children. If she married one who has had no children she must be divorced without receiving her kethubah."

73. bKid. 82b.

74. bNid. 31b.

75. Ibid. Cf. also Ber. 93; bBer. 31b; bB. M. 84b. Also, bNid. 71a, where it is implied that boys are desired: "Twelve questions did the Alexandrians address to Rabbi Joshua ben Hananiah (first century C. E.).... What must a man do that he may have male children? He replied: He shall marry

a wife that is worthy of him and conduct himself in modesty
at the time of marital intercourse.   Did not many they
said to him, act in this manner but it did not avail them?
Rather let him pray for mercy from Him to whom are the
children, for it is said, 'Lo, children are a heritage of the
Lord; the fruit of the womb is a reward. '   What then does
he teach us?   That one without the other does not suffice. "

76.  See the discussion above on pp. 118 ff.   In this connection it
     is interesting to note what Raphael Posner has to say:
     "Although the act of marriage can be effected in different
     ways (see below, Legal Aspects) it has become the univer-
     sal Jewish practice to use a ring, except in a very few
     oriental communities where a coin is used. ...   In some
     Reform and Conservative congregations in the U. S. the
     'double ring' ceremony is practiced in which the bride also
     gives a ring to the groom and recites a marriage formula.
     Since, according to the halakhah, it is the groom who is
     acquiring the bride, this innovation raises serious halakhic
     doubts which, according to some authorities, even affect
     the validity of the marriage" ("Marriage," Encyclopaedia
     Judaica, vol. 11, cols. 1041 f. ).

77.  Loewe, op. cit. , p. 23.   Leipoldt noted that in the Hebrew
     Bible and among the rabbis the husband was referred to as
     the "lord of the woman (ba'al)," and that in Jewish-Greek
     the married woman was called "the one under the man
     (hypandros)"--giving the Testament of Reuben as a refer-
     ence.   Cf. Leipoldt, Jesus und die Frauen, p. 43.

78.  See Leipoldt, Die Frau in der antiken Welt, pp. 65 f. , where
     he comments, "This polite phraseology found it more diffi-
     cult to gain entrance into the Semitic Orient. "

79.  Kid. 3, 7.

80.  Josephus, Antiquities, XIX, 354.

81.  bSan 69a.

82.  Loewe, op. cit. , p. 23.

83.  Sotah 3, 8.

84.  Philip Blackman, Mishnayoth (London, 1953), vol. III, p. 449.

85.  Ned. 10, 5.

86.  Keth. 8, 1.

87.  Ibid.

88.  Keth. 7, 8.

89.  Tos. Kid. 1, 11 (336).

90.  Sifre Lev. 19, 343.

91.  Keth. 4, 5.

92.  Ned. 10, 1 ff.

93.  Josephus, Apion, II, 201.

94.  Keth. 4, 4.

95.  Keth. 4, 6. The Talmud nuanced this rather bald mishnaic teaching by stating: "Since he is only exempt from legal obligation he is, obviously, still subject to a moral duty" (bKeth. 49a). It is interesting to note that the same Gemara teaches that "(since it has been said that) he is under no obligation to maintain his daughter only, it follows that he is under an obligation to maintain his son.... For it was taught: It is a moral duty to feed one's daughters, and much more so one's sons, since the latter are engaged in the study of Torah; so taught Rabbi Meir." However, the reverse was also argued: "Rabbi Judah ruled: It is a moral duty to feed one's sons, and much more so one's daughter, in order to (prevent their) degradation."

96.  Keth. 4, 4.

97.  B. M. 1, 5. Women, slaves and minors are here again treated jointly; see above, pp. 117 ff.

98.  Keth. 5, 8.

99.  Keth. 4, 4.

100.  Keth. 4, 9. However, Keth. 4, 9, also states: "If she received injury he is liable for her healing; but if he said, 'Lo, here is her bill of divorce and her Kethubah: let her heal herself,' he has the right (to do so)."

101.  Keth. 4, 4.

102.  See below, pp. 157 ff.

103.  It is interesting that this is seen as a work the wife must do for the husband.

104.  Keth. 5, 5.

105.  bKeth. 61a.

106.  See above, pp. 34-36, 40f., 73 ff.

Polygyny

107.  Louis Epstein, Marriage Laws in the Bible and the Talmud
      (Cambridge, Mass. , 1942), p. 4.

108.  bKid. 7a.

109.  Yeb. 4, 11.

110.  Keth. 10, 5.  The reference in this quotation would seem to
      indicate at least a sufficient incidence of multiple divorce
      on the same day some time during the early rabbinic
      period in Jerusalem to warrant the instituting of the pro-
      cedure of putting the hour of the divorce in the written
      document.  In commenting in another place on the number
      of wives a king should be allowed (18) the mishnaic Rabbi
      Judah limited the number, but in an open-ended way:
      "'Nor shall he multiply wives to himself'--eighteen only.
      Rabbi Judah says:  He may multiply them to himself pro-
      vided that they do not turn away his heart. "   Rabbi Simeon
      adds:  "If there was but one and she would turn away his
      heart he may not marry her" (San. 2, 4).   Cf. also Kid.
      2, 7, where a man betroths himself to three women at
      once.

111.  Epstein, op. cit. , p. 7.

112.  Ibid. , pp. 12-17.

113.  The school of Shammai was in favor of the fulfillment of
      levirite marriage, whereas the school of Hillel was op-
      posed to it.

114.  E. g. , Keth. 10, 1-6; Git. 2, 7; Git. 3, 1; Kid. 2, 6-7;
      Sotah 6, 2; Ber. 8, 4.

115.  In 1927 in the small village, Artas, near Bethlehem, of the
      112 men in the village, twelve, i. e. , about 10%, had
      more than one wife--eleven had two and one had three.
      (H. Granqvist, Marriage Conditions in a Palestinian Vil-
      lage, Helsinki, 1935, vol. II, p. 205. )  When visiting
      Israel in October, 1972, I was in the village of Deir
      Samit, a Muslim Arab village of about 1000 inhabitants
      west of Hebron.   I met and had dinner with seven mar-
      ried men of the village, two of whom had several wives--
      one had three and the other was about to marry his sixth,
      though he had divorced two of them so as to stay within
      the Muslim restriction of four wives at once (which tradi-
      tion probably stems from an amoraic rabbinic recommenda-
      tion).   These last figures, of course, cannot be extrapol-
      ated to yield a percentage for the entire village, nor can
      either of the references be automatically transferred back
      to the Palestine of 1900 years ago.   However, it is

somewhat amazing how much of that 1972 village life was
like what it must have been two millenia ago; many of
the customs, costumes, techniques (e. g. , a very primitive pottery technique), instruments (e. g. , a stone age-
like wooden plow), etc. go back that far and even much
farther. Hence, because the situation is somewhat similar
to, but at the same time different from, anthropologists
working with contemporary primitive tribes, these modern
observations of primitive Palestine can at least suggest
possibilities for what it must have been like in Palestine
before the Roman destruction 1900 years ago.

116.  The Pharisees (Philadelphia, 1962), vol. II, p. 837.

117.  Josephus, Antiquities, vol. XII, 186.

118.  Ibid. , XIII, 380.

119.  Cf. ibid. , XIV, 300; XV, 319.

120.  Josephus, Jewish War, XVI, 477.

121.  Josephus, Antiquities, XVII, 14.   Cf. also Jewish War, I,
      511, where it is related how Herod presented to Arche-
      laus, the father of his daughter-in-law, "a concubine,
      named Pannychis. "

122.  Cf. Josephus, Antiquities, XX, 85, where a reference is
      made to his wives.   In ibid. , XX, 89, reference is made
      to his wife or wives; the manuscript tradition is mixed.

123.  Ibid. , XVII, 341.

124.  bSuk. 27a.

125.  Josephus, Life of Josephus, 414.

126.  Ibid. , 426.

127.  Term referring to the two or more simultaneous wives of the
      same husband.

128.  bYeb. 15b.   The names in the parallel passages, Tos. Yeb.
      1, 10 and pYeb. 1, 3a, 48, differ in part.   The Pales-
      tinian Talmud also records a story about Rabbi Judah I
      (late second, early third centuries) who advised a brother
      to take all twelve childless widows of his dead brothers
      in levirite marriages, which he did, and fathered 36 chil-
      dren, who Rabbi Judah then helped support (pYeb. 4, 6b,
      35).

129.  bYeb. 65a.   There was, of course, also the earlier opposition
      of the Essenes, discussed above, p. 194 note 20.

130.   bYeb. 63b.

131.   bPes. 113a.

132.   bYeb. 15a.

133.   Cf. Tos. Keth. 5, 1; pYeb. 6b; and Wilhelm Bacher, Die
       Agada der Tannaiten (Strassburg, 1903), vol. I, p. 343.

134.   bYeb. 37b, and bYoma 18b.

135.   See C. G. Montefiore, Rabbinic Literature and Gospel Teach-
       ings (London, 1930), pp. 44-46, for a discussion of the
       passage that is favorable to the rabbis.

136.   "Monogamy," Encyclopaedia Judaica, vol. 12, col. 259.

137.   bYeb. 44a.   Herr also notes that "this would appear to be the
       source of the Muslim law which permits only four wives."
       ("Monogamy," op. cit., col. 259).   He likewise adds:
       "In Germany and northern France polygamy was rare,
       mainly due to the economic conditions and to the influence
       of the Christian environment.   It seems that at the be-
       ginning of the 12th century, the Jewish communities issued
       a regulation which forbade polygyny (among Ashkenasic,
       but not Sephardic, Jews).   Later this regulation became a
       herem (ban), attributed to R. Gershom b. Judah (of the
       10th century) ... in the State of Israel it (polygamy) is
       prohibited by law (the 1951 law on equal rights for wo-
       men)."   Raphael Loewe, op. cit., p. 22, notes: "Jewry
       has never formally repudiated polygamy, and indeed
       amongst polygamous non-Jewish environments it has some-
       times been maintained (or readopted)."

Adultery

138.   Jeffry Howard Togay, "Adultery," Encyclopaedia Judaica, vol.
       II, col. 313.

139.   Ex. 20:13; Dt. 5:17.

140.   See Gen. 38:24, where Judah ordered Tamar burnt.

141.   Chaim Hermann Cohn, "Adultery," Encyclopaedia Judaica,
       vol. II, col. 315.

142.   Cf. bSan. 74a.

143.   The book was probably composed in the late sixth century
       B. C. E.

144.   Ezk. 16:37-41.

145.  Hos. 2:3.  The book dates from the eighth century B. C. E.

146.  San. 7, 1.  Beheading was listed as a fourth, but it was not used in cases of adultery.

147.  San. 6, 3-4.  Although during the Roman procuratorship the death penalty was legally reserved to the Romans, stoning by an official Jewish body apparently did occur at least once; the Acts of the Apostles relates how Stephen was brought before the Council, "then they made one rush at him, and flinging him out of the city, set about stoning him" (Acts 7:57 f. ).

148.  According to the Gemara bSan. 52a molten lead was used.

149.  San. 7, 2.

150.  San. 7, 3.

151.  bSan. 52b.

152.  P. 353.  Parallel passages are pSan. 8, 24b and Tos. San. 9.

153.  Unless this Eliezer ben Zadok lived earlier; cf. "Eleasar Be-r. Zadok," Encyclopaedia Judaica (Berlin, 1930), vol. 6, col. 445.  The Mishnah also states that Simeon ben Shetah (first century B. C. E. "initiator" of the kethubah-- see above, pp. 157 f. ) "hanged eighty women" in Ashkelon (San. 6, 4).

154.  bSan. 52b.

155.  San. 7, 3.

156.  Dt. 22:23-27.

157.  Togay, op. cit. , col. 314.

158.  Ibid. , col. 313.

159.  Prov. 6:35.  Cf. Cohn, op. cit. , col. 315, and "Compounding Offenses," ibid. , vol. V, col. 856; "Ehebruch," Encyclopaedia Judaica (Berlin, 1930), vol. VI, col. 254.

160.  Cf. John L. McKenzie, Dictionary of the Bible (Milwaukee, 1965), p. 701, under "Proverbs. "

161.  Compounding offenses in general, except homicide, became possible in rabbinic times.  Cf. "Compounding," op. cit.

162.  It is interesting to note that according to the gospel of Matthew Joseph, the betrothed spouse of Mary, mother of

Jesus, wished to avoid this: "Being a man of principle, and at the same time wanting to save her from exposure, Joseph desired to have the marriage contract set aside quietly" (1:19).

163.   In general an adulteress was subject to the death penalty from age 12 years and 1 day old, and adulterers at age 13 plus 1 day.

164.   Cf. "Ordeal," Encyclopaedia Judaica, vol. XIII, col. 1448.

165.   This is the translation of the New English Bible. Literally the Hebrew means something like, "make your belly swell and thigh waste away."

166.   Sotah 1, 1.

167.   One German Jewish scholar argued that she need not be divorced, since it was feared she might have planned this as a device to obtain a divorce so as to marry another-- something that of course was allowed to a man but not to a woman. Cf. "Ehebruch," op. cit., col. 256.

168.   Cf. Sotah 1, 4-5.

169.   Blackman says: "His opinion is rejected."

170.   How he would know it was beautiful if he did not see it is not explained.

171.   Sotah 1, 5. See above, p. 123 for a description of the dishevelling of the hair and how one priest administered this ordeal to his own mother!

172.   Sotah 1, 6. Blackman comments here that, "this is really obligatory upon women, whereas it is only voluntary for men."

173.   Cf. Blackman, op. cit., vol. III, p. 342.

174.   Sotah 3, 3-4. For a description of the ensuing discussion at this point in the Mishnah about whether a woman should receive enough instruction in Torah to learn that earlier meritorious living might postpone the effect of the bitter waters--decided in the negative--see above, pp. 94 ff.

175.   Sotah 9, 9.

176.   I. Abrahams, Studies in Phariseeism and the Gospels (Cambridge, 1917), p. 74.

177.   bSotah 47b.

178. The extent to which the death penalty was actually inflicted is difficult to determine, as is also the determination of exactly when it ceased being imposed under Jewish law, for the Roman reservation of capital punishment etc. did not prevent the two executions described above.

## Divorce

179. Kid. 1, 1.

180. Falk, op. cit. , p. 154.

181. Cf. Lev. 21:7, 14; Num. 30:10; Ez. 44:22.

182. Falk, op. cit. , p. 154.

183. Cf. Abrahams, op. cit. , p. 70.

184. Ecclesiasticus 25:25.

185. The English Soncino edition notes here: "I. e. , to the masses, in the public lectures. "

186. bSan 100b.

187. See above, pp. 149 ff.

188. bGit. 89a.

189. bGit. 90a-b. Parallel passages in Tos. Sotah 5, 9 (302) and pSotah 1, 17a, 32.

190. Yeb. 6, 6.

191. bYeb. 64a. Parallel passages in Tos. Yeb. 8, 4 (249) and GnR 45 (28b).

192. Cf. Keth. 7, 1-5.

193. English Soncino edition note: "Euphemism for vigorous exercise after intercourse in order to prevent conception" (bKeth. 72a).

194. Falls out.

195. Billerbeck, op. cit. , vol. I, p. 318.

196. The English Soncino edition comments: "Sc. who has not a bad wife mentioned in the first version. "

197. Note ibid. : "Consequently one would not be suffering very long from such a woman. "

198. Note ibid. : "The second version."

199. Note ibid. : "Which the man cannot afford to pay. He cannot
divorce her unless he is in a position to meet his obligation" (bEr. 41b).

200. Dt. 22:28-29.

201. Dt. 22:13-19. See above, pp. 151 f.

202. Yeb. 14, 1.

203. Keth. 4, 9.

204. See below for explanation of term.

205. Keth. 4, 9.

206. bShab. 14b.

207. Keth. 8, 8; bKeth. 82b. Falk, op. cit. , p. 156, notes that,
"Biblical law, moreover, did not include any provision
for the payment of a sum to the divorcee.... Only in the
post-exilic Aramaic (Elephantine colony) papyri was a
provision for payment of 'divorce money' included."
Yaron, op. cit. , p. 53, states that this was due to
Egyptian influence; it should be recalled that this distant
Jewish military outpost on the upper reaches of the Nile
in the fifth century B. C. E. remained isolated and without
apparent influence on mainstream Judaism.

208. Cf. e. g. , bGit. 58a.

209. GnR 17, 3.

210. bYeb. 63b.

211. Blackman notes here: "His father or grandfather, but not his
mother because a woman and her daughter-in-law are often
enemies."

212. Keth. 7, 6. See also the partly parallel Tos. Keth. 7, 6 f.

213. bKeth. 72b.

214. Keth. 7, 7.

215. bKeth. 73b.

216. Tos. Keth. 7, 8 f. (269).

217. bKeth. 72a.

218. Lev. 21:18-20.  See also bBek. 43b.

219. bKeth. 75a.

220. Ibid.  Blackman, in his commentary on Keth. 7, 7, also
     mentions unbearable odour and ugly unusual hair.  See
     also Tos. Keth. 7, 8 f. (269) and pKid. 26, 62d, 18.
     If the matter came to a legal dispute, the wife and father
     of the wife were not without legal defenses, as provided
     in Keth. 7, 8, and the talmudic gemara on it; however,
     the weight of the law leaned heavily on the side of the
     husband--see bKeth. 75b-76a and the notes on p. 475 of
     the English Soncino edition.

221. See pp. 157 f.

222. Dt. 24:1.

223. Git. 9, 10.

224. bShab. 64b.  See also Sifra on Lev. 15:33.

225. However, the dispute between the two schools was reflected
     in the gospel according to Matthew 19:3, where Jesus
     was asked, "is it lawful to put away one's wife for every
     cause?"

226. Josephus, Antiquities, vol. IV, 253.

227. Josephus, Life, 426.  See above, pp. 146 f.

228. Philo, De Specialibus Legibus, III, 30.

229. bGit. 90b.

230. Yeb. 14, 1.  This eventually was changed in Western Europe
     during the Middle Ages when the wife's consent to the
     divorce was required when legally acceptable grounds for
     the divorce were missing, although "if a man chose to
     ignore the law and divorce according to his lights his act
     was irreversible.  The wife could not demand that her
     husband reinstate her, merely because he had divorced in
     contravention of the ban." Ze'ev Falk, Jewish Matri-
     monial Law in the Middle Ages (Oxford, 1966), p. 142.

231. Abrahams, op. cit., p. 75.

232. Excrement of dogs.

233. Keth. 7, 10.

234. bYeb. 65b.

235.  bYeb. 117a.

236.  Abrahams, op. cit., p. 72.

237.  See, e.g., Antiquities, XVIII, 136; XX, 142, 146, 147.

238.  Ibid., XV, 259 f.

239.  Abrahams, op. cit., p. 75.

240.  Yeb. 14, 1.

241.  Abrahams, op. cit., p. 77.

242.  pKid. 1, 58c, 16, as paraphrased in Heinrich Baltensweiler,
      Die Ehe im Neuen Testament (Zurich, 1967), p. 37.  See
      Billerbeck, op. cit., vol. I, p. 312.

243.  See p. 194 note 20.

244.  bGit. 90b.  Parallel in bSan. 22a.

245.  bGit. 90b.

246.  bSan. 22a.

247.  C. G. Montefiore, Rabbinic Literature and Gospel Teachings
      (London, 1930), pp. 47 f.

248.  Falk, Law in Middle Ages, p. 113.

249.  C. G. Montefiore, The Synoptic Gospels (New York, 1968--
      reprint of the 2nd ed., 1927), pp. 226, 234.

CHAPTER VII

1.    For an initial probing of the related question on the level of
      world religions see:  Leonard Swidler, "Is Sexism a Sign
      of Decadence in Religion," Women and Religion:  1972,
      ed. by Judith Plaskow Goddenberg (American Academy of
      Religion, 1973), pp. 53-62.

2.    Already scholars like Ze'ev Falk, Jewish Matrimonial Law
      in the Middle Ages (London, 1966), have begun to do this
      sort of thing.  Of course a great deal of Jewish history
      still awaits careful, unapologetic research.

3.    Originally appearing in Hebrew, the article is translated into
      German:  "Die Stellung der Frau in der Halacha," Frei-
      burger Rundbrief, XXV (1973).

4.    Martha Ackelsberg, "Introduction," in:  Liz Koltum, et al.,
      The Jewish Woman.  Response, 18 (Summer, 1973), p. 7.

5.   Ibid., p. 8. The national newsletter is Lilith's Rib, P.O.
     Box 60142, 1723 W. Devon, Chicago, Ill. 60660. The
     First number appeared in May, 1973.

6.   Judith Plaskow Goldenberg, "The Jewish Feminist: Conflict
     in Identities," in ibid., pp. 14 f.

7.   Editorial comment in ibid., p. 67.

8.   Shulamit Aloni, "Israeli Women Need Women's Lib!" Israel
     Magazine (April, 1971), pp. 58-68.

9.   Shulamit Aloni, "Comment on Marriage Law in Israel,"
     (1965), mimeo.

10.  See, e.g., Arlene Swidler, Sistercelebrations (Philadelphia,
     1974), where both a feminist seder and a ceremony for
     the naming of a girl are printed along with an explanation
     by their authors.

# INDEX